The Extension of Life

The Extension of Life

Fiction and History
in the American Novel

R. A. York

Madison • Teaneck
Fairleigh Dickinson University Press
London: Associated University Presses

© 2003 by Rosemont Publishing & Printing Corp.

All rights reserved. Authorization to photocopy items for internal or personal use, or the internal or personal use of specific clients, is granted by the copyright owner, provided that a base fee of $10.00, plus eight cents per page, per copy is paid directly to the Copyright Clearance Center, 222 Rosewood Drive, Danvers, Massachusetts 01923. [0-8386-3989-5/03 $10.00 + 8¢ pp, pc.]

Associated University Presses
2010 Eastpark Boulevard
Cranbury, NJ 08512

Associated University Presses
Unit 304
The Chandlery
50 Westminster Bridge Road
London SE1 7QY, England

Associated University Presses
P.O. Box 338, Port Credit
Mississauga, Ontario
Canada L5G 4L8

The paper used in this publication meets the requirements of the American National Standard for Permanence of Paper for Printed Library Materials Z39.48-1984.

Library of Congress Cataloging-in-Publication Data

York, R. A., 1941–
  The extension of life : fiction and history in the American novel / R. A. York.
    p. cm.
  Includes bibliographical references (p.) and index.
  ISBN 0-8386-3989-5 (alk. paper)
  1. American fiction—20th century—History and criticism—Theory, etc. 2. Literature and history—United States—History—20th century. 3. Mimesis in literature. 4. Narration (Rhetoric) I. Title.
PS379.Y675 2003
813'.509358—dc21   2003005049

PRINTED IN THE UNITED STATES OF AMERICA

For Rosemary

... the extension of life, which is the novel's best gift.
Henry James, *Letters*

Contents

	Acknowledgments	9
	Introduction	13
1.	Malamud: *The Natural*	26
2.	Bellow: *Mr. Sammler's Planet*	38
3.	Capote: *In Cold Blood*	50
4.	Barth: *Giles Goat-Boy*	63
5.	Doctorow: *The Book of Daniel*	76
6.	Morrison: *Beloved*	89
7.	Oates: *Blonde*	101
8.	Ford: *The Sportswriter*	114
9.	Smiley: *A Thousand Acres*	126
10.	Kingsolver: *The Poisonwood Bible*	138
	Conclusion	150
	Notes	157
	Bibliography	168
	Index	176

Acknowledgments

I SHOULD LIKE TO THANK:
—the British Academy, for a grant to assist research for this book;
—the Research Sub-committee of the Faculty of Arts of the University of Ulster, for granting study leave for the first semester of the year 1999–2000;
—my wife, Rosemary, for reading and commenting on parts of the text.

The Extension of Life

Introduction

W HY DO WE ENJOY FICTION? WHY ARE THINGS THAT HAVEN'T HAP-
pened more interesting than things which have? Not everyone thinks they are. Quite a lot of people read only or chiefly nonfiction, because they think the real has an authenticity that mere invention doesn't; the bestseller lists are full of biographies. This book is not meant for those people. It is meant to help those who enjoy fiction think about why they like it and to try to say something about the way invention contributes to our understanding of the real world outside the pages of the book or the head of the writer.

It will be a cautious book. There are lots of sorts of fiction and lots of reasons for reading it: people can read to be amused, to be thrilled, to imagine they are living in a more glamorous world, to enlarge their vocabulary, to familiarize themselves with a foreign language, to prepare for academic tests, to be fashionable. They can read to find things out: what life was like in nineteenth-century Kansas, what the effects of misguided use of insecticides might be, how we should judge Henry Kissinger. And they can read to feel different: to be amused, thrilled, excited, curious, saddened, angered, admiring, or to feel many more sorts of emotion. One cannot claim that any of these sorts of readings are wrong. The last two points are paradoxical: people read fiction to discover facts or grounds for judging facts; and they have feelings about people who don't exist. This book will discuss these issues especially in the context of recent American literature, because it has been so eager to record and judge the real. War, political and social conflict, the assertion of identity by women and by ethnic groups, changing conceptions of education and culture, new understandings of the relationship of humanity to the environment, differing senses of what the past means: the issues debated in novels are the same ones debated in the newspapers. But people read newspapers (or large parts of them) with a sense of sober concern; they can read novels that way too, but their sobriety is mixed with enjoyment, with, at the least, a sense of the author's skill.

The question of why readers enjoy fiction will be approached through this other question: what can fiction do that factual narrative (or other factual writing) can't do? And here reference will be made to a huge amount of scholarly writing on the topic that has been published over the last forty years or so. In particular this study will be indebted to the discipline known as *narratology*.[1]

Narratology could trace its origins most aptly to the writings of Henry James. One of the greatest of all critics of the novel, as well as one of the greatest of all novelists, James was concerned to articulate in his critical writings the lessons he had learned in the practice of writing: lessons not only about the events or characters of novels, or about the view of life expressed through them, but especially about how these events and characters and views are expressed in the process of writing. What James stresses most strongly is the need for the novelist to find a perspective—often by adopting the point of view of a character—which will most richly illuminate the themes of the work; he tends to be hostile to any form of writing that indicates to the reader that his responses are being deliberately manipulated, and also to any explicit commentary on the action by the author, of the kind common in nineteenth-century fiction. James, in other words, aspires to a sort of artistic impersonality and discipline, of the kind he found in such authors as Flaubert, but which he thought lacking in the "fluid puddings" of the Victorian novel, or of Dostoyevsky and Tolstoy. His stress on the choice of point of view as the key to the achievement of artistic fiction is significant ideologically as well as aesthetically; it implies that what matters in the complex psychological relationships that form the matter of novels such as his own is the varying perspectives of the characters, and their attempt to understand as fully as possible the uncertainties and shades of emotion in which they are involved. There is in his novels no unambiguous truth and no straightforward moral code external to the characters (such as might be formulated by an intrusive author); there are only varied, conflicting, and developing perspectives.

James, then, had developed a form of criticism which laid stress primarily on the composition of the novel rather than the content. His approach was the basis of a kind of criticism most clearly exemplified by Percy Lubbock's *The Craft of Fiction* (first published 1921), a book often criticized for seeming to make James's patient explorations of literary form into hard dogma.[2] The title of Lubbock's work is characteristic: he seeks to treat fiction as a matter of craft, and to expect from the novelist a mastery of the skill of conveying emotion and understanding of life through "the various forms of narrative, the forms in which a story may be told" (20). Even if it is true that his approach fails to do justice to those forms of narrative that differ from the Jamesian model, it is certainly also true that his work contains much subtle analysis of the relation of dramatized scene to narrative summary, of point of view, of the effect of first-person narrative, and of the explicit presence of the author, and it undoubtedly did much to increase readers' awareness of the choices made by authors in the way their stories are told and of the way these choices affect the total import of the novels.

The origin of narratology proper, in the English-speaking world, lies with a response to the Lubbock tradition. Wayne Booth's important volume *The Rhetoric of Fiction* stresses that the novel is an act of communication, in which an author offers a message to a reader, and in doing so seeks to "control his reader," to "impose his fictional world upon the reader," and to "help the reader grasp the work." He stresses that there is a great variety of ways in which the techniques of fiction contribute to this communication, and that they need not be limited to the ones favored by Lubbock. There actually is an author behind the text, and Booth analyzes perceptively and systematically the ways in which the author can establish a rapport—direct or indirect—with the reader. There are fictive narrators—personalized or impersonal—within the text, and these should not be confused with the author. They may furthermore be reliable or unreliable, they may comment or present events dramatically, and they may enter into the inner consciousness of the characters or view the characters from the outside, reporting only their words and actions. There is also an implied author, whose character and attitudes may be deduced from the text, and who should not be confused either with the narrator or with the real historical author as he or she appears in documents outside the novel itself. Booth thus provides the basis for a rigorous reading of the text of novels, focused strongly on the way information is provided to the reader and on the ideological slant that may be inherent in this ordering of information. Since the publication of the first edition of *The Rhetoric of Fiction* in 1961, this concern with close and systematic reading of the novel as communication has been very much developed by many authors who have added refinements, such as the study of what is implied in a text about the reader's knowledge and attitudes; some of the key concepts of this body of thought will be discussed later in this introduction. One should specifically mention the contribution of continental European scholars such as Gérard Genette, who were inspired by the desire of the French structuralist movement to create a science of literature, an objective and meticulous description of the form (or structure) of literature and the experience of reading, a contribution that has added valuably to the ongoing discussions among English-language scholars.

Narratology has been applied especially to fictitious narrative (although in principle no doubt some of the issues it raises are pertinent to nonfictional narrative, such as history). A work of special importance to the questions that will be discussed in this book is Dorrit Cohn's *The Distinction of Fiction* (1999), which provides a lucid and sensitive account of those aspects of narrative technique that can *only* be used in fiction, and therefore of what is special about fiction. There has been another tradition of thought about fiction that will also be considered in this study, a tradition which is much less concerned with the detail of the text: the philosophical and aesthetic concern with what fiction, as such, means to readers and how their understanding of a fictional story differs from their understanding of a nonfictional story. The philosophical importance of the issue is obvious: since philosophers have always been concerned with the nature of truth, and of the way that reality is represented in language, and since they have increasingly emphasized the ways in which language does not only concern itself with providing true information about the world, it is apt that they should seek to define the nature of a much-respected cultural institution which consists precisely of providing untrue information. The major work in this debate is no doubt Kendall Walton's *Mimesis as Make-Believe* (1990), the essential conception of which is indicated in the title: reading fiction is an experience akin to play; the reader has an active part in agreeing to make-believe that the events of the story are real. There are aspects of this view that are debatable, and there has in fact been much debate about them; the debate itself indicates something of the fruitfulness of the concept. A final body of thought that must be recognized in analyzing the nature of fiction arises within the discipline of history and is especially associated with the name of Hayden White: it is a questioning of the hard dividing line normally drawn between fiction and history. The writing of history is itself a sort of rhetoric, as is the writing of novels; the historian needs to use the resources of literary language and presentation to communicate his view of the shape of events. In a sense then the historian creates the events he writes about, as does the writer of fiction. The view of course is extremely controversial (since everyone agrees that history relies to some extent on objective evidence about the past); what it suggests, at least, is that the desire for events to form a coherent sequence, in which one state of affairs arises from another in a way that readers feel they can understand, or follow as being natural, and the desire for this sequence to correspond to some sense of human destiny, some movement of progress or decline, is very deeply instilled in human beings and manifests itself both in the stories told by historians about the real world and in the stories invented by novelists about a possible world.

These are, in broad terms, the conceptions of narrative that have been formulated and debated in recent years. What, more specifically, do they indicate about the forms narrative may take, and about the differences between fictional storytelling and historical storytelling? There are certainly analogies between them. So much so, in fact, that scholars are obliged to discuss whether it is possible for the same series of words to form either a novel or a nonfictional text, such as a diary, a collection of letters, or an autobiography.[3] It seems that it is possible, at least in principle; what we need to remember, though, is that we almost always can tell the difference—if only from external factors such as the appearance of the book's cover—and that our reading of the text will differ depending on whether we think it is fictional. This book will be exploring just how it differs.

What then are the advantages of fiction? First, it simply multiplies the number of stories. A lot more things haven't happened than have. People love stories. They love to be carried on from one event to the next. Novelists sometimes rhapsodize over the delight of stories; so do critics.[4] Possible stories add to the variety and surprisingness of the real stories that surround us.

But, second, fiction allows a kind of story that isn't possible in nonfiction. In reality, we have to be able to stand over the truth of any story we tell;[5] we need evidence. And we never have absolutely satisfactory evidence for the precise feelings and thoughts of other people. But novelists can imagine what anyone may be thinking, and there are fictional techniques for showing what they imagine. There are two crucial factors. First, the narrator of a work of fiction does not have to be impersonal (as the instructing voice in a chemistry textbook, for instance, normally is). The narrator may be a distinctive personality who establishes a clear relationship with the reader; he or she may be a character of greater or lesser importance in the story. He or she may also get things wrong (the narrator, in the standard term, may be *unreliable*); facts may be inaccurately presented and judgments may be objectionable. This of course is more likely if the narrator is also a character, but in principle this could happen with external narrators. Second, the external narrator may be omniscient; in other words, he may tell us the unexpressed thoughts of the characters and provide a range of information that is not accessible to any one of these characters. Alternatively, he may choose to restrict what he tells his reader to what is known or thought by a single character and can choose to do this either consistently throughout the novel or for limited periods; this technique, known as *focalization*, is especially characteristic of fiction (though not unknown in certain kinds of historical writing—which we may then feel "read like a novel"). A particularly important and common technique is *free indirect style*, in which a character's thoughts or words are presented in the third person but with no explicit statement that they are what X said or thought, so that the reader may be tempted to think that the narrator has disappeared and been replaced by the sensibility of a character. Yet again, the narrator may choose to give only an external view of the acts of the characters, with no direct indication of their thoughts or feelings, thus restricting the information available beyond what is normal in everyday real speech.[6] In short, the novel presents events not as objective fact but as they are perceived subjectively, and novelists and readers often delight in the contradictions and uncertainties that arise from the multiplicity of subjective viewpoints.[7] They also delight in the kinds of knowledge or feeling that can hardly be defined objectively: the sense of atmosphere or imprecise apprehension, of pleasure, menace or enlightenment, a sense that sometimes rises to the level of symbol.[8]

Third, and most obviously, novels, unlike history and other kinds of non-fictional writing, don't have to tell the truth;[9] the events of the novel depend not on documentary evidence but on the author's decisions. It is not possible to check on the accuracy of novels, as it is with newspapers or works of history. If a novelist says that the Confederate states won the civil war, then they did win—within that novel—and no amount of checking on documents, war memorials, or family traditions is going to alter the fact.[10] "Real writing" is *efferent*, in the technical term;[11] it invites the reader to assess it in terms of the known outside world. Fiction doesn't; it is self-contained, and the only disproof of which it is capable is if it is inconsistent (though it may not be very interesting if it is too unlike the world we know). That, at least, is the position in theory. In practice, readers expect the world of the novel to be the world they are accustomed to, unless they are told the opposite. Faulkner's novels would be unintelligible if the South had won the Civil War. There is, in other words, a principle of "minimal departure" from the real, or a "Reality Principle."[12] Readers assume the novel to be, in some way, about the world they live in, at the same time that they know that it isn't. Critics at different times have stressed either the autonomy of the literary work, its freedom from depiction of the real world, or its responsibility to show an image of that real world based on full understanding and sound judgment. This book will claim that neither emphasis is satisfactory in itself. Readers do enter into the world of novels and understand each episode by reference to other episodes. But they also understand by reference to the way they think things happen in reality. This is one aspect of the contract they establish with an author. As they read, they have expectations, they make interpretations, they judge and assess. They can only do these things on the basis of the knowledge they have in their real lives. If they assume that the suspect cannot have committed a murder in New York because he was in San Francisco at the time, they will feel cheated if they discover that the author has adopted a fictional geography in which San Francisco is only thirty miles from New York—although there might conceivably be works of science fiction where such a fictional geography was acceptable. Crucial here is not scholarly truth but what people believe. There is a mutual belief principle: reader and writer share the beliefs of a (perhaps hypothetical) society.[13] Such beliefs contribute to the reader's encyclopedia—the package of information which people take for granted and acquire through education, mass media, everyday conversation, and the like;[14] the encyclopedia varies somewhat from person to person and is inevitably very incomplete for everyone. A detective story set among Polish Americans refers to a photograph of a character in front of a building marked in Cyrillic script. The acute reader will suspect that the character is not in Poland, where Roman script is used, but in Russia. The less acute reader will be as vague as the author, and so actually be better equipped to follow the story without the distraction of accurate knowledge about the exterior world.

Novels, then, can only be read—like most other texts, but perhaps more crucially—in the light of the author's intentions. What novels mean is what the author intends them to mean—or rather what the reader can reasonably suppose the author to want them to mean.[15] To understand a novel it is not necessary to have studied what the author has said in diaries, critical essays, interviews, or the like. What is significant is not an intention outside the work. What matters is the intention implied throughout the work itself, which readers are all, to a greater or lesser extent, skilled in recognizing. Philosophers have paid much attention to "utterance meaning" in practical communication;[16] they show that in the light of context, manner of speech, norms of behavior, and communication in our culture, and in the light of their own relationship with the speaker, participants in conversation can generally perceive what that speaker wants them to get out of the speech—even if an analysis of it out of context could produce other meanings. What must be stressed in fiction is that the utterer's meaning extends not just to opinions expressed, but also to the events narrated and to the choice of point of view through which they are narrated. One doesn't choose a point of view when one tells one's friends about a holiday, since one only has one point of view; but a novelist can choose to narrate a crime from the point of view of a criminal, a victim, a witness—and the novelist has some reason for this choice, and the reason is part of the total meaning of the book.

The reader's contact with a novel is then a sort of dialogue. The reader recognizes a personality in the book; he or she recognizes that making fictions is one way of being a self, and enjoyment of the novel is to a considerable extent a matter of how much one likes or respects the personality that makes it.[17] It is also a matter of how far one likes or respects the personality of the reader that the novelist expects the reader to be. The novel (and this too applies to other sorts of text) contains many implications about how much the reader knows, what the reader's ideology is, and what his or her attitude to the novel is. There is a sense in which the author creates a fictional reader, and the real reader has to decide whether to play the part of this fictional being (just as the personality of the author implied in the book is a fictional creation that may not be identical with the real author).[18]

The term *contract*, which is widely used to describe the relationship of author and reader, is of course metaphorical;[19] readers don't sign a paper agreeing to read on the author's terms or negotiate with the author what they are to put into and get out of the reading. What it means is that there is mutual trust. The author trusts the reader to accept that the work is not literally true, and that it needn't be literally true, and yet to read it with a level of attention and sympathy that he or she might give to some sorts of literally true writing. The author invites participation in his work; he says, as it were, in the powerful formulation of one critic, "I imagine myself in and invite you to conceive a world in which . . ."[20] The reader trusts the author to provide a level of insight, thoughtfulness, and emotional awareness that deserves the attention the reader gives.

The term often used to describe what the author requires of the reader is *make-believe*.[21] Some formulations of this insight may be too crude; the view that people use novels as theatrical props for their own imagination, in the same way that they can use a tree stump as a make-believe bear in playing at forest adventures, surely much underestimates how far readers allow their imagination to be controlled by the author—at least while they are still reading.[22] People read *as if* they read an account of true things, even though they know that no account of true things could contain the specific features of fictional writing.[23] They *entertain* the sense of a novel;[24] they don't commit themselves to it. But even in entertaining ideas, one normally reads from within the text; one accepts the novel itself as the context of each sentence, each event, and each response by a character. To this extent readers are within the world of the novel. It is possible to refuse such immersion in the world of the book; one can read the events primarily in the context of real-life knowledge. Some novels invite readers to do so, as with the works of Robbe-Grillet, sometimes aptly called antinovels, and many other works of *metafiction*, that is, works which conspicuously display their fictional status and invite the reader to respond not so much to the situations and events within the world of the novel as to the activity of the novelist in creating that world.[25] But if the novelist doesn't encourage such distancing from the world of the novel, and if a reader refuses to enter it because it is trivial, inconsistent, tasteless, and inadequate to his or her sense of the quality of life, that is likely to be a sign of partial or total failure on the part of the author.

An important problem here is that of what have been called "immigrant characters and objects," that is, real people or events or places which are referred to in the fictional works.[26] It is argued, with some plausibility, that make-believe is an attitude that can apply to the real, so that we can make believe that Napoleon was the emperor of France or that the United States fought in the Second World War.[27] If this seems unduly paradoxical, it might be useful to modify it by saying that we make-believe that the real Napoleon affects the life of the imaginary Pierre Bezukhov and that the real war is judged by the imaginary Yossarian.

The author, then, demands of the reader make-believe (or in traditional terms a suspension of disbelief). The reader demands of the author plausibility and interest.

Plausibility (or *verisimilitude*) means that we have to be able to believe in the world depicted.[28] This doesn't exclude the literature of fantasy or science fiction, ghosts or monsters; it means that we have to feel that the actions of the characters fit into some recognizable pattern of behavior, in terms of physical possibility and social or psychological normality; and the patterns that can be recognized are partly those of other literature and largely those of daily experience. Authors can deviate, as long as they say so; if a character can run a mile in three minutes, has a detailed knowledge of medieval paleography despite having left school at fifteen, and is indifferent when her house is burned down, the reader wants to know why. The novel accordingly is often thought to be a genre which is intimately dependent on realism;[29] and it undoubtedly is true that one of the great epochs of the novel was the realistic period of the nineteenth century, and that many later novels, while they may very much vary the practice of the great realists, continue to rely to a very large extent on accurate representation of the circumstances, physical and social, of everyday life of ordinary people.

The novel, one may say, tends to imitate the real. A much discussed issue is this: does the writing of a novel imitate the activity of a nonfictional author? Do novelists *pretend* to tell real stories, with all the different speech acts that entails?[30] The view is often criticized, essentially because it makes literary writing parasitic on nonliterary language.[31] If it is tempting, it is because it does stress that the novel has to be read as the utterance of a narrator, and that the reader is very likely to take that utterance as guided by principles of coherence, clarity, and interest—of *followability*, in the term used by some historians[32]—not so very different from the principles that are taken for granted in real narrators.

But the interest is not quite the same. One does get from fiction some of the interest that arises from one's attitude to the characters—whether of sympathy or of judgment: excitement, humor, noble gravity, charm, indignation—and this would certainly seem to be basically the same sort of interest that might be found in stories about real people (so much so that there has been substantial philosophical debate as to whether readers *ought* to get so emotional about nonexistent people).[33] But there is another sort of interest as well, at least in literature of a certain level of intellectual ambition, and this is not so readily perceived in real-life narratives. That is the interest that arises from a shaping of experience, which gives some overall significance to the events and perspectives of a story and makes it an image of some important aspect of life. Fiction, it has been well said, is "not a falsification of reality, but a necessary ordering of it."[34] Fiction, according to W. H. Auden, forms a "felicitous pattern," and this pattern, crucially, is the *necessary cause* of the events in the novel, not their *accidental effect*;[35] in fiction the acts of the characters relate to some overall destiny in a way they may not perceive but which the reader can grasp.[36] Their lives becomes an illustration of some more or less complex conception; they become a thought experiment. More formally put, the story is organized not just as cause and effect, event and response, but by *themes*: events, sensations, thoughts, comments can be read as consistently illustrating an underlying set of concepts.[37] The novel, that is, is not just a matter of sequence, of one thing happening after another; it is also a matter of repetition, of a series of events that are variants of the same material.

This thematic organization is sometimes thought to be an essential aspect of literature. Recently historians have recognized that history too is subject to such organization and so to some extent a work of literary skill, and of imagination. This emphasis on the creative activity of the historian has aroused much debate and is sometimes represented as a belief in the fictionality of history.[38] What it means is that the historian shares with the novelist the possibility of finding—or imposing—a shape in events (that may imply an ideology of progress or decline) but is subject to a constraint the novelist does not normally have, the constraint of dealing only with documented events. This in turn means that the historian speaks in good faith. He cannot invent an irresponsible or misguided narrator. The novel allows irony and play in a way that history doesn't.[39] "The novel," a major contemporary novelist has said, "is, by definition, the ironic art."[40]

Here then is the distinctiveness of the novel. The image readers form of the novelist is not exactly that of a well-informed and thoughtful person, as it is with the historian. There may be thoughtfulness, but there may be nothing to be informed about, only things to be invented. Of course all novelists do know something about real life and count on this knowledge in producing the interest of their work, but that interest comes from what the novelist adds to the real, as much as from how well he knows the real. The reader, in his or her contract with the author, assesses the salient shifts the author introduces into his or her expectations, the author's transfigurations of the known world.[41] He or she admires the activity of the author, the rhetoric of the author, the ability to persuade readers of a perception different from that they started with.

This perception, it is often felt, is concerned with the general (whereas the historian, even though he may generalize and seek for laws, has to be judged in the first instance by his accuracy on the specific).[42] In reading a successful novel, one may feel that this is the *sort* of thing that happens; it may appear that the novel reveals a *system* that fits our experience and perhaps illuminates it.[43] The novel has a logic, which in one way is a sign of its autonomy;[44] its logic is not necessarily the logic of cause and effect that is operative in the outside world, but this logic is also an *analogy* with the real world.[45] This degree of abstraction contributes to three crucial effects of fiction: the claim of typicality, the exploration of the possible, and the sense of the strange. The novelist may suggest that his or her characters are representative of some group of people (such as "modern man"); or show what life might be like, what the potential of human beings might be if things were different;[46] or that the world we live in is odd, alien, that it does not correspond to what we *think* human life is like or should be like. (It has been convincingly argued that what makes the nonfiction novel a novel is precisely this sense of the strangeness of the life depicted.)[47] These structures allow, of course, many ideologies. The world may seem strange because it is overdisciplined or because it is anarchic, because power is arbitrarily restricted or because it is insufficiently focused. What they have in common is the sense that the world as a whole—or some large part of it—can be judged, and that reader and author together can participate in a process of judging. Readers do not meekly submit to the author's rhetoric; people hate any "palpable design" on them.[48] They do not want literature to be simply didactic or authoritarian;[49] readers can be critical rather than credulous.[50] One learns from reading fiction. One learns to be attentive, one extends and enriches one's sense of how one can think about the ways people live, of the experiences that merit interest and judgment.[51]

This then is the critical framework that will be used in the chapters that follow. It no doubt fits any works of fiction equally well or equally imperfectly. So why is this book about American fiction? For one thing, because since 1945, at a time when British and Continental fiction have been comparatively modest in their achievements, American fiction has shown extraordinary strength and variety. There are many American novelists who merit consideration in a book of this sort, and I hope readers will accept that the selection made here is a reasonable one. Crucially, this remarkable vitality seems to arise from an eagerness on the part of Americans to come to terms with the vicissitudes of their history, a sense that the guiding values of American society are still open to debate, and that this debate is aptly carried out through imagination, through fiction, through the force of creative personality, as well as through social and political theory. There is a great precision about many of the novels that will be studied here, an intense sense of the character of real places and the atmosphere of specific historic moments. And there is an intimate relationship between the imagined lives of the characters and the actual events of history. Bellow's Mr. Sammler, for instance, is an invented character—as readers instantly recognize. His concerns in the novel are largely private ones: his scholarly activity, his relationship to his daughter, to his benefactor, to the young man who invites him to lecture. But these fictitious private concerns are set, insistently, in the real public world: the world of the Holocaust, of the Arab-Israeli conflict, of the intellectual culture of Europe and America—many representatives of which are mentioned by name—of

1960s America, a place of sexual liberation, student discontent, racial tension, and crime in the streets. And Sammler's contacts with his relatives and acquaintances are determined by his judgment of historical change, by his sense of having lost a civilized past and his revulsion against what he sees as a crude and antagonistic present. Sammler is a historical being, located in a recognizable real world. The degree of sympathy the reader feels for him (and so the reader's perception of the novel as a whole) must depend on how far he or she can endorse Sammler's judgment of history; in other words it must depend on the reader's own knowledge of history and response to it. Other novels of the period, of course, show much less direct fidelity to the depiction of the real world; Malamud's *The Natural,* for instance, is in many respects fantastic. But it is not wholly so; it depends on a recognition that the modern world does demand success, and that the drive to success can lead to corruption—and it reminds the reader of specific cases where sport has been exposed to corruption. It provides evidence (if not the sort of evidence required by historians) for the validity of the world it depicts.

All of this means that the novels display a special dialectic: on the one hand a passionate loyalty to the facts of history, politics, society, to the sensations of life in the city, to controversies about race, gender, criminality, to the frustrations and ambitions of dynamic individuals and self-conscious groups; on the other there is an intense inventiveness, whether in the form of ingenious sophistication or of gothic excess and fantasy. The novels bear witness to the authors' commitment to understanding and shaping the multiplicity and extremity of American life; it is a heroic view of the task of literature.

1
Malamud: *The Natural*

> He wanted to know where stories came from.
> Cohn said from other stories.
> "Where did they come from?"
> "Someone spoke a metaphor and that broke into a story. Man began to tell them to keep his life from washing away."
> —Malamud, *God's Grace*

IN OFFERING STORIES TO HIS CHIMPANZEE PUPIL, THE LAST MAN IN MAlamud's last novel, the former rabbinical student who preserves the wisdom of a Judaic humanism dear to the author, imparts three points: stories are intertextual; stories come from metaphor; stories preserve. The points merit reflection, not least for what they don't say; they don't say that stories are about actions in time, about bits of history, about people desiring and succeeding or failing, about novelty; they say that stories preserve the past and that the Ur-story is not a sequence but a comparison. In fact, Malamud's novels seem to be about the way time does erode, or wash away, some part of the human reality, how the dynamic young criminal becomes the guilty stoic, how the bold secularist becomes the voice of the religion he has rejected; perhaps telling the story of failure and restriction protects against further diminution in the reader's and author's present (as perhaps Dubin's *Lives* give him a sense of how life can remain —within reasonable bounds—vital). And yet story is defined not in terms of change but in terms of sameness.

In fact Malamud's novels do tell stories, as novels must. What is unusual about them is that the author's rhetoric is one that foregrounds not so much the processes of change, which one might take to be the essence of narrative, but the consistency of experience and the many possible interpretations of it. He uses, to this end, a narrative structure involving repetition and coincidence, one moreover in which the events of the modern-day story repeat elements of myth from various segments of Western cultural traditions, and he presents it through a skillful control of focalization and through a very explicit presence of the author's voice within the text.

The Natural is a sporting story. It is a story of excitement, tension, and achievement or possible achievement. Malamud's hero, Roy Hobbs, is an incarnation of precisely this spirit of ambition, achievement, and competition; consistently he asserts his wish to be the best ever, to beat all the records. The novel very skillfully (and not too subtly) builds up the tension. Roy seems to be the young hero coming from the boondocks to conquer Chicago; he is halted by the astounding misfortune of an apparently unmotivated shooting. He tries again. The odds are against him because he is now thirty-four years old. He joins a team which is in the doldrums, makes an immediate impact, and lifts the team from the bottom of the league; he wavers, slumps, and the promise of the pennant becomes remote; he recovers. His desire for sporting success is paralleled by his desire for success in love, and here too his hopes fluctuate. He regains his form, the woman he desires seems more favorable, and the season approaches the final playoff. He is tempted by a bribe to throw the game; in the bottom of the ninth of the final game he recovers his will to win—and he fails.

The reader, in all this, is eager for a conclusion, for a demonstration that Roy is extraordinary, that he is capable of more than most mortals (or that he isn't). This the author in fact does; it is easy to admire the skilful pacing of such scenes as the challenge of Roy to the reigning champion, the Whammer, at his first meeting. In this scene, the dismissive attitude of the older man gradually comes under threat, while Roy remains rather timid and stolid and the journalist Max and Roy's mentor Sam provocatively tease the players. Harriet's excitement raises the stakes by the suggestion of sexual reward for the winner. Finally there is the slow crescendo of the three strikes and the sudden climax of the Whammer's admission of defeat. The reader wants this sort of contest to be intelligible and so plausible, and (although one critic considers that the novel lacks "a density of realistic motivation") Malamud does provide a clear and realistic motivation of Roy's successes and failures.[1] It is one that has the special value of linking success with morality. (Here one needs to be just a bit more sophisticated to question the plausibility of the structure; are great sportsmen in real life good people? Some of them may seem to be. Anyway, the reader can forget sophistication for a while and accept that success and goodness go together.) The key is in the concept of confidence. Roy's team, the New York Knights, has a hypnotist whose job is to "pacify" the players and so eliminate their lack of self-confidence: "If you think you are winners, you will be. If you don't, you won't. That's psychology," he tells them (74).[2] Roy, hubristically, refuses this "outside assistance." But he later comes to discover something even more important: that self-confidence depends on the confidence of others, and that this depends on one's service to them. He learns this first through the admiration of the almost saintly Iris, who stands up in the bleachers during one of the games, "to show her confidence in him" (149); the achievement is all the greater because he has, reluctantly, promised to hit a homer for a dying boy and in doing so, inspired by Iris's gesture, saves the boy's life. Iris tells him that "I felt that if you knew people believed in you, you'd regain your power," that "I hoped you might become yourself again," and Roy replies that she has broken his jinx (155–56). Ball players, the novel insists, are superstitious; the point suggests that great batting is a matter of entering a kind of community of faith. The issue becomes crucial in the great climactic game; estranged from her by his desire for the evil Memo, Roy accidentally strikes Iris with a foul in his final game. Deeply repentant, he tends to her; she tells him that she is pregnant by him and asks him: "Win for us, you were meant to" (226). And he tries to. Fate, love, the continuity of the generations, selflessness, success: for once they all go together. Roy, cleansed of his corruption, is a "different man." He fails. Conversion is not enough, and he fails for a very practical reason, which has been well established throughout: he has the habit of hitting at bad balls. With two strikes against him in his very last inning, facing a new young pitcher, growing ever more nervous, conscious of opportunities previously lost, he again leaped for a bad ball and "struck out with a roar" (234).

So far, then, a clear and exciting story, with clear and unsurprising morals: love good women and not bad ones and don't take bribes. But there is more to the novel than this; Malamud has enriched this framework with a general psychological reflectiveness. Roy himself is no friend of psychology. In his crucial conversation with Iris he is tempted to tell her about his past, but "on the other hand, talk about his inner self was always like plowing up a graveyard" (156). He rejects the inner self because the self is the past and the (recent) past means failure. Action, for him, is an escape from self-revelation: "he hated the pill, which represented more of himself than he was willing to give away for nothing to whoever found it one dull day in a dirty lot" (169). Against Roy, then, the story questions what the self is. It asks two kinds of question. First, if the self is attunement to the future, what kind of attunement is acceptable? Second, is the self something other than attunement to the future? The self that Roy admits to is composed of ambition; this ambition turns to greed in the later part of the novel, crude greed for food that incapacitates him at one time through a monstrous bellyache. Greed isolates. Like his predecessor and rival Bump he is "for [himself] and not for the team" (62); granted a lavish benefit, he resolves this argument by failing in modesty and in recognition of his comrades, simply promising his fans "to be the greatest there ever was in the game" (116)—a promise that many think has jinxed him (116). He recovers; one reason he rejects the bribe is his loyalty to his team. But the offer of the bribe finally also forces him to choose (like Fidelman, and equally unsuccessfully) between perfection of the life and perfection of the work, between being a great player and dishonestly getting enough money to marry the mercenary Memo. (He "betrays his true capacities as one of nature's noblemen" and "chooses fidelity to his genius too late, after he has already betrayed it for cash," as one critic puts it.)[3] He is indecisive; he repents too late; he doesn't make the existential choice of a self. If he rejects the offer, he reflects, echoing Iris's words, "maybe he'd be himself—his real self" (206). But he isn't.

You can't turn away from the past to build a self out of ambition; the self is in the past too. The novel starts, aptly, with Roy uneasy, surprised, inhibited by the sight of himself—reflected in a train window— peering in at himself. In dream and memory through the novel he recreates his past self, not the failed self of the years after his shooting, but the innocent self of childhood, in the deepest, stillest woods with his dog (54; cf. 124, 130, 208). This peace he has destroyed; driving with Memo, he has a vision of running down a boy and dog, of killing his younger self (126). His years of ambition are characterized by dissatisfaction, by the sense of endless motion (that original train journey repeating itself again and again, most notably as he approaches Memo's bed, 191), of frustrating circular movement. His most usual feeling, despite his external success, is of frustration; the point is made very explicit when he dreams, implausibly, of a cozy domestic life with Memo and reflects, "that would end the dissatisfactions that ate him, no matter how great were his triumphs, and made his life still wanting and not having" (181). "Dissatisfaction" is the key word; it is ironically echoed later when the team manager Pop tells him that if they win the pennant, "I will be satisfied, and win or lose in the Series, I will quit baseball for ever" (217). Pop can envisage departing in peace. The novel ends with Roy departing without peace.

So far, then, *The Natural* seems to be a realistic and moralistic novel, of none too original or subtle a type. Literature and film have shown often enough that success is not happiness, that the love of money is evil, that desire brings disillusion, that youth and strength are vulnerable; Malamud adds to these lessons a debate on the self and, still more interestingly, on time. The characters are aware of their relation to time, from the opening section in which Roy's train crosses America, losing an hour as it passes across different time zones, through Roy's visit to a fortune-teller who finds that "the future has closed down" on her (138), to the fate of the team members as the end of the season approaches when they feel that "Time was after them with a bludgeon" (177), and to Iris's confession that she is "tied to time," not to past or future but to "here and now, day after day" (211).[4] Ambition is pressure of time; love is a stoical acceptance of the everyday, which may—perhaps—eventually be transformed, without magic, into happiness and may produce a stable future through the parenthood that Roy seeks to reject.

All this is thoughtful and perceptive; it creates a morality of patience. (Perhaps we are to see Roy's weakness for the bad ball as a sign of impatience.) Critics have often stressed, rightly, the quality of endurance in Malamud's characters: the shoemaker's assistant waiting years to win the love of his masters' daughter in "The First Seven Years," Frankie Alpine accepting the weary duties of the grocer's shop, Yakov Bok surviving years of arbitrary imprisonment. But why does Iris have to stress that her happiness with her daughter is "more a reward of standing it so long than any sudden magic" (211)? Perhaps because at one point in the novel time is subject to magic. Roy's train journey is interrupted by the arrival of a doctor, summoned by a telegram; during the halt Roy defeats the Whammer and accidentally injures Sam. But the doctor couldn't find any patient; the only person who is sick is Sam. The presence of the doctor—which might seem to be the effect of the injury—is in fact its cause.

The reader, then, may start to grow unsure about how straightforwardly the author is reproducing the standard "realistic" pattern of ambition and failure. And there are other aspects of the narrative that may contribute to this uncertainty. The plot is very efficiently conducted, perhaps a little too efficiently. There are coincidences. By what chance does the neophyte meet none other than the champion on his journey of initiation? How is it that the champion is accompanied by the very same sportswriter who will dog Roy in his own time of greatness? By what chance do the apparently random prizes Roy wins at the funfair include the essentials of a game: a ball and a washboard (which ingeniously turns into protective clothing for the catcher)? So too with the narrator's handling of objects: Harriet's much-emphasized hatbox, which appears to be a normal accoutrement of a glamorous woman but proves to contain a gun, the black sedan that follows Roy and proves to belong not to Nemesis but to a detective hired by Pops to check up on Roy's extracurricular activities. Are these things a bit too neat? Is Malamud demonstrating that these are not the sort of things that happen through cause and effect, but through the ingenuities of a novelist? And what of the reverse, the apparent clumsiness of some writing? What of the sudden unmotivated shifts in character and event, such as Roy's unprecedented hunger in the latter sections of the book? The consistency of the book is not a consistency of logical development; it is a consistency of moral emphasis.

Similar points arise in the use of focalization. Of course much of the text is focalized through Roy; the reader wants to know what success means to the hero. But Malamud has no Jamesian puritanism about this (and Roy is far from the "most polished of possible mirrors" of the Jamesian ideal).[5] The novel opens, very memorably, with Roy's vision of himself and persists with his point of view for some pages in his efforts to get up and have his breakfast (these things are efforts because the train is an alien world to this country boy) and with his first sight of Harriet. Then the text suddenly shifts to Sam, paralleling Roy's naïveté with Sam's acuity and determination: young and old, hopeful and weary, passive and active, controlled and controlling, the complementarity of the two is forcefully spelled out. The reader is conscious that the author has imposed a viewpoint that illuminates this complementarity, which neither of the characters fully recognizes. Later we see things, in short passages, through the eyes of Memo, Iris, Pops and the other players, and once briefly of the rival Bump. A striking moment is when the text suddenly enters the consciousness of the Whammer to comment of the atmosphere of the contest with its "sensation of surprise and strangeness" (30); the character is there to tell us that the scene has a mysterious seriousness. Malamud stresses that the individual consciousness is part of a pattern, that the individual is not just an active intention but also a facet of the author's extended consciousness.

The personality of the narrator himself is at times conspicuous, too (despite the claim of one critic that "the author's point of view is almost always assimilated to that of the characters").[6] Often it provides a jokey distance from the characters: in the opening section, basically seen through Roy, the narrator interrupts to comment, when Sam is first sighted, that "he was an expert conniver where his comfort was concerned" (15). A little later, Roy sees Harriet for the first time and notes her "heartbreaking legs" (17). The epithet conveys Roy's desire and frustration, but not in Roy's words; this is a wisecrack that appeals, with a nice balancing of sympathy and mockery, to a standard image of the desirable female and the aroused male. It implies a world outside the story, the world of narrator and audience. The point is very clear when the narrator refers to Roy's "few weeks in the game" (93). The reader doesn't yet know how short Roy's career is going to be; the reader, enjoying novelistic tension, has been following it with the same hope and anxiety as Roy himself. The narrator is the detached commentator who knows it all already.

There is too a sense of artifice in the way some of the moral points get very explicit formulation (and some critics have reproduced these formulations as keys to the work, presenting it for instance as an account of the "spiritual rewards of suffering" [7]): Roy's recognition that his "fate" has comprised "defeat in sight of the goal" (158), generalized by Pop's remark that a whole lot of people "will go the same way all the time, without them getting what they want, no matter what" (216); Iris's assurance that "suffering is what brings us towards happiness" (159), ironically echoed at the end of the book by Roy's recognition that "I never did learn anything out of my past life, now I have to suffer again" (237); Roy's surprising quotation to the corrupt Judge, "Woe unto him who calls evil good and good evil" (210); even Roy's sense, as he waits to bat in his last game, that saving the game is "the most important thing he ever had to do in his life" (229). Such comments ensure that the text reads coherently—as a lesson, as a picture of what life is like and what it should be like, as a display of the priority of goodness. In making his characters into tutors or textual commentators, Malamud reduces their role as agents; story is rivaled by a timeless wisdom.

The timeless is what is asserted by what is perhaps the best-known aspect of *The Natural*, its mythic framework: "[myth] links man in an 'ennobling interchange' with the permanent, while starkly reminding him of his mortality which alienates him from wholeness of being."[8] Such, at least, is an idealistic view. The mythic sense is introduced gradually. When the porter Eddie asks Roy whether he is carrying a foolproof lance, this may seem to be merely part of his generally fantastic style of conversation. When Harriet speaks of Roy's contest with the Whammer as a tourney, the hints are getting stronger. When she compares it to "Sir Percy lancing Sir Maldemer" the hints are getting forceful (despite the crude humor in the names) (33). When finally, fifteen years later, Roy arrives at Knight's Field, with its dusty dry earth, to meet Pop Fisher, veteran of Fisher's Flop and suffering from an incurable wound, no doubt is left for the moderately sophisticated reader.

Some readers might miss the whole dimension and, no doubt, feel a slight oddness about the book; perhaps it is this that leads Baumbach to comment that "the mythic superstructure" is "somewhat gratuitous, a semi-private literary joke between author and academic reader."[9] Certainly the jokiness does a lot to modify the gravity of Malamud's morality in this work.

But how is the Arthurian legend going to be used? The parallels with the career of the Grail knight are very far from exact. Sir Perceval is not shot with a silver bullet by a predatory female; he fails his first test by not asking the appropriate question about the Grail (Roy, as critics have pointed out, gets into trouble with Harriet by not *answering* her question).[10] Roy, like Perceval, brings rain to the wasteland and a cure to the Fisher King (and this looks very much like an infringement of the realism of the "surface" story of *The Natural*: either it rains by coincidence as Roy hits a homer or the heavens are alert to the game). In Arthurian myth salvation is irreversible; in *The Natural* Pop Fisher's sickness returns. And who are all the other characters? The ancient Fisher King had a niece. Her only contact with Perceval in the medieval versions was to send him a sword; there is no suggestion of a doomed love affair. In Wagner's *Parsifal*, however, the niece is Kundry, whose curse drives Parsifal away from the Grail castle before the issue of asking a question arises. The rival Bump may recall the malicious Sir Kay (though critics have found other candidates for this post), but Kay's malice is verbal and does not take the form of practical jokes, he has no romantic liaison with the Fisher King's niece, and he is wounded but not killed by Perceval. Sam, Roy's mentor, would appear to be Gornemants, who however survives unharmed in earlier versions (not having had to trust his life to a washboard). Perceval is deeply concerned with his mother, but she is merely overprotective and not malicious like Roy's. The various women in Roy's life seem to echo Blanchefleur in legend and are all associated with white roses, but the pure beloved has been divided into murderous college girl, mercenary baseball groupie, and saintly single mother. Roy himself is far from Perceval's virginity, vital for the Grail quest. "The point of the new version is to examine and often change the values presented in the old," says Helterman of Malamud's use of myth in *God's Grace*;[11] in *The Natural* there is perhaps less reexamination of the original values than an eclectic recasting of them. This is not the sort of mythical novel that we find in Joyce's *Ulysses*, where the story being referred to guides the reader's expectations as to the development — as well as the significance — of the events of the novel. The myth, for Malamud, is not a sequence of events but a repertoire of incidents illustrative of salvation and temptation. It tells the reader—if it is taken with full seriousness—that Roy's ambition is a quest, that it is for an ideal, that it calls for discipline and dedication, that it is subject to opposition and to faltering, and that it brings redemption not just to the individual but to the community.

Moreover, it is not all that easy to take it with full seriousness, because it competes with other myths.[12] Some are drawn from other aspects of the Arthurian world: Roy's sleeping with Memo while she believes he is Bump inverts an episode involving Lancelot, Elaine, and Guinevere; his returning to the game prematurely after an injury again recalls Lancelot; his reverence for the bat Wonderboy and the final destruction of it recalls the fate of Arthur's sword Excalibur. If Memo and Iris are the Lady of the Lake and Morgan le Fay, as some critics persuasively argue, they too are part of Arthur's fate and not Perceval's.[13] An elegant detail refers not to the original wasteland story but to its best-known twentieth-century avatar: as Roy defeats the Whammer, "the violet evening" falls onto the spectators, that "violet hour," which, in T. S. Eliot's London, is "the evening hour that strives homeward." Other references appear as well: real events from baseball, Homeric references, David and Goliath (33), and Cavemen (29, 76).[14] It is not surprising that some critics have found these elements confusing, considering that they "comically reduce [Roy] and all his mythical archetypes with him. The novel works . . . to crystallize a picture of Sir Perceval swatting homers against the walls of Troy."[15] They also afford a somewhat different emphasis from that of the Grail quest, not the hero's sanctity, but his strength, his celebrity, his vulnerability. Malamud is insistent on his concern with the idea of the hero, from the porter Eddie's kissing the hand of "my hero," Roy—though with his usual irresponsibility of tone (13)—through Roy's recognition of himself as a hero after his defeat of the Whammer (34), to the press's acceptance of him as "a throwback to the age of true heroes . . . a natural not seen in a dog's age" (170). As with other aspects of the moral code of the book, the crucial conversation with Iris makes it very explicit; she tells Roy that "I hate to see a hero fail. There are so few of them. . . . Without heroes we're all plain people and don't know how far we can go" (155). Heroes demonstrate what humanity is capable of. The inspiration Roy gives his team and his fans is short-lived, but at least he has shown that people are capable of pride and endeavor. In this, Roy has done what one kind of novel can do: he has given a model of human potential and he has added one more model to that vast gallery of knights and warriors. Perhaps this is why his failure is essential to the book (rather than the view that "to fail is to preserve one's moral integrity").[16] The important thing is not that the New York Knights should win the pennant; the important thing is that an example should be set of morally impeccable action as valuable in its own right, irrespective of success, of action not for gain but as an acceptance of responsibility.

Heroism excludes individuality. Individuality may well be essential to the genre of the novel, in its classic realist form;[17] the novel as romance or fable may reject it. Roy himself insists on his own individuality, because he sees individuality as success. He is bewildered by Harriet's questions about Sir Percy and Homer. Harriet admits she has a fantastic imagination (34): Roy the realist has none at all. Malamud, like Harriet, is an intertextualist. Harriet defeats Roy once. Malamud defeats him for good.

As Roy rejects identification with the heroes of the past, he rejects identification with his immediate predecessor, Bump, despite the wishes of his fans and of Memo. He wants to be unique, but the book insists on sameness. Throughout Malamud's works, as critics have often noted, characters are identified with each other, find in each other fated equivalents or predestined patterns.[18] Even Roy identifies Bump with the Whammer (54). He himself "fills Bump's shoes" in the team (91). He fills Bump's bed once and wishes to do so again. At one moment he thinks he sees Bump in his own mirror, and he becomes a practical joker as Bump was (if less maliciously) (171). Roy is the inheritor of Sam and of Bump, part of the stream of sporting endeavor, a being without uniqueness.[19] These are not the only parallels; his bassoon case (containing his bat) is the equivalent of Harriet's hatbox (containing her gun) (36–67); Roy imagines that red-headed Memo in her black dress might be replaced by a black-haired woman in a red dress (89) — and the imagination becomes reality as Iris appears. The wicked bookie Gus has one eye; at one moment Roy appears to have one eye (having injured the other) (132), and he blacks Iris's eye through misjudged batting (225), creating a strange grouping of the evil Gus, the good Iris, and the fallible Roy.

Everyone is alike, and events can be alike too. The novel is largely made up of anticipations and repetitions. Eddie produces a pair of strangely "bewitched" dice and throws them away, asserting that "I don't crave any outside assistance in games of chance" (16); Roy plays dice with the magicianlike Gus before he is offered financial assistance in return for cheating (175). Harriet watches the game with the Whammer "without fear of fouls" (29); it is Iris who should fear fouls, since she is seriously injured by one. Lola seeks Roy's future in a crystal ball

(138) and prophesies his love for Iris; the ball Roy pitches to the Whammer has been "a fortune teller's lit crystal ball" (31). Most obviously, there are dense patterns of symbolism that ensure the consistency of the whole work. Roy sees Harriet as a silver-eyed mermaid (18); hypnotized by Dr. Knobb, he searches in imagination for a fish or mermaid but sees only flashes of her green tail (75). There are the birds (studied by several critics), the moon and water, the forests and trees, the ghosts and haunting (21, 92, 117,162, 234), and the constant play of light and darkness, especially of lightning: the unseasonal summer lightning of the opening page, the lightning that Pop prophesies can cut down the tallest trees (58), which actually does split the tree from which Wonderboy is carved and in turn splits Wonderboy itself (71, 227), the lightning that anticipates Iris's attraction to Roy and which accompanies Roy's collapse in Memo's bedroom (191) — the lightning of passion and retribution.

It is fair enough to comment that this symbolism is intrusive and non-structural — if by "structure" one means plot;[20] the essence of *The Natural* is to challenge plot, to show storytelling as subservient to the brutal world of possession and desire. Some of the characters in the novel tell stories: Bump and the Judge, the figures of coarse domination. It is valid to say, as one of Malamud's most acute critics does, that "the story *The Natural* has to tell is the process of a sensibility forced to extremities in order to withhold acknowledgement of the world."[21] What one needs to add is that the world Malamud does not acknowledge is the world of realistic narrative, the world of action and ambition. The world of *The Natural* is one of threat, of solemnity and excess, of impracticable longing; it seems almost a supernatural world — almost a mythical world — because it reflects the inner self, the self of imagination, fear, guilt, and constraint, the self that Roy denies. This is barely a narrative world. The characters are made up less of strategies of action than of a sensitivity to sensations — sensations of fear, aspiration, nostalgia, sensations that hint at an absence.

The Natural, then, is concerned with the limits of the outer life; it presents action and success as secondary to the barely recognized inner life of nature and imagination. The paradox is impressive. Malamud succeeds in maintaining his readers' interest in the extroverted world of sport, a world that can be measured in batting averages and attendance figures. At the same time he undermines the quantifiable world by his insistence on the inner, the unchanging, the impersonal.

Finally one should note another undermining. Malamud — in this novel — has a hyperbolic energy of writing (perhaps he seeks irresponsible excess in writing as Roy seeks it in sport). At the funfair Roy wins a baseball and a washboard—and a kewpie doll, an alarm clock, a potty, a cigar case, a banner, a flashlight, coffee, sweets, and four kisses from the fairman's daughter. At his benefit he is given two television sets, a baby tractor, some garden hose, a nanny goat, and lots more, including the Mercedes in which he runs down his juvenile self. The text accumulates lists of fans (repeated in strict pattern) and Rabelaisian lists of food; it exaggerates (when Roy is ill, the Japanese government issues an Edict of Sorrow, 193); it plays on words, and repeats the play: early in the novel, Roy then a pitcher, "thumped down the pitcher" (of water, 182), and near the end, having become a batter, he "slugged the slug" (the odious Gus, 236); and it provides its own sound track: Harriet's shooting of Roy is accompanied by "thrum of bass-fiddle" (42). This hardly fits with the solemnity of the author's commitment to morality and selfhood. There is even mockery of the grail legend itself: Roy's status as holy fool is shown by his getting both feet into the same leg of his pants, a surprising clumsiness in a great sportsman; Pop's misfortune is not a grievous wound but athlete's foot on the hands. The novel is a performance. It shows an undisciplined enjoyment of imagination, not the imagination of the mysterious and solitary forest, but the imagination of the joker, of the tall story, of the fairground and the newspaper. The public life, after all, can be a refuge from the anxieties of the inner self.

2
Bellow: *Mr. Sammler's Planet*

ONE CAN LEARN A LOT FROM *MR. SAMMLER'S PLANET*: WHERE TO BUY chickens (Kresge's; you can get seersucker jackets, white caps, and spiral notebooks there too), what are the distinguished London tailors (Mr. Fish, apparently, and Turnbull and Asser, of course). One can recognize things too, if only partially; most obviously one can recognize substantial elements of recent history,[1] from the Holocaust in Poland to the Six-Day War (on which Bellow himself had reported)[2] and beyond to a future of space exploration—just begun when the novel was published, with the moon landings of 1969; more specifically, one can recognize various British intellectuals of the mid-century, in particular H. G. Wells, but also Keynes and Lytton Strachey, Tawney, Laski, John Strachey, Orwell. One can recognize, especially no doubt if one is a New Yorker, the modern city, with its crowds, dirt, crime, vandalized telephone booths, and need to mind one's own business. (Bellow's sense of the modern city, as Tanner points out, writing before *Mr. Sammler's Planet*, is akin to that of Dreiser, and "denser, thicker, more impinging and engulfing" than Whitman's world.)[3] One can recognize too the types of the 1960s: the radical student who abuses Sammler during his lecture (the episode is said to be based on a real experience of the author's, but even if one doesn't know this, one does know of many similar cases from the period), the displaced Third World academic, the dizzy pseudomystic.[4] The point is made explicit in some cases; Angela, for instance, on her first appearance, is described as "one of those handsome, passionate, rich girls who were always an important social and human category ... Angela sent money to defense funds for black murderers and rapists. That was her business, of course" (11).[5] "One of those": Sammler (whose consciousness this seems to be) is familiar with the type; Bellow expects his readers to be so as well. The reader can perceive, in other words, the plausibility, the verisimilitude of the novel; what happens in *Mr. Sammler's Planet* is the kind of thing that is quite likely to have happened to an intellectual Jew born toward the end of the nineteenth century in Poland, having prewar experience of Britain and migrating to the United States in middle life. The plausibility once recognized, the reader can enhance it by imagining what sort of feelings such a person is likely to have in New York in the late 1960s. Europeans (educated northern Europeans) have been inclined to cultivate reserve, distance, and privacy and found it difficult to accept American spontaneity and directness—and Sammler is very European, Polish-Oxonian and therefore polite, as the book several times reminds us. Old people are likely to feel estranged from the sexual adventures of the young (though some of Bellow's characters, in this book and in others, belie this general assumption), and especially those brought up well before the 1960s are likely to have felt disquiet or distaste at the much-publicized sexual revolution of that decade, the ease and explicitness of modern sexuality. Sammler has been comparatively rich, too, unacquainted with kitchens in his student days, and is a stranger to the vitality—and the cynicism—of work and money making. Knowing these things, the reader is not wholly surprised by Sammler's alienation from New York; he or she sees it as certainly an aspect of Sammler's identity and possibly something to admire or respect; imagination entails sympathy. There are then two major narratological concerns in the novel. One is the ambiguous distance of the narrator from the sensibility of Sammler, through whom the text is focalized. The other is the author's conspicuous imposition of a thematic pattern on what appears to be a realistic representation of the real world.

Bellow is close to the real as his readers know it, in fact, closer than most readers, almost too close. His historical and cultural knowledge—lavishly displayed—much exceeds what most of us possess. How many people are in a position to assess his preference for the mystics Suso, Tauler, and Eckhart over those fashionable "worthless fellows" Adorno, Marcuse, and Norman O. Brown (32)? Who was Clare Sheridan (44)? (Artist and sculptor, 1885–1970, according to the *Dictionary of National Biography*; she also gets a reference in *Ravelstein*, as Claire Sheridan). Bellow has, too, an intense capacity for conveying the responses of his characters to the outside world, which makes up much of the convincing nature of his books (as critics have often noted).[6] A case is Sammler's observation in the streets: "a delivery man with a floral cross filling both arms, a bald head dented, seemed to be drunk, fighting the wind, tacking. His dull boots small, and his short wide pants blowing like a woman's skirts. Gardenias, camellias, calla lilies, sailing above him under light transparent plastic" (37). The detail of the dented head, the semihumorous metaphor of tacking, the precision with which flowers are named, the hint of a symbol of beauty rising above the effortful world of work: the texture of the work is dense and persuades the reader that this sort of thing is there be seen. This, Bellow adds, is the work of a literary imagination: "the purposive, aggressive, business-bent, conative people" don't have it (38); perception depends on aesthetic distance.

But it may seem scandalous to talk of plausibility in Bellow. (Like Citrine, he "writes things that aren't so," *HG* 167). For one thing, there is a kind of excess in his references to real people such as Lucky Luciano, known to Gruner and Emil. H. G. Wells is very convincingly described, but his real biography does not include his acquaintance with Sammler. Senator Javits, whatever his other services to the state of New York, does not include amongst them saving Wallace Gruner from a Soviet prison. This reference to real people is very frequent in other Bellow novels. In the earlier works there was a sort of shyness about it: Joseph writes a letter to Jane Addams, but he doesn't send it (*DM*, 28); his friend Steidler tries to get an appointment with Lubitsch but fails (*DM*, 106); Augie March glimpses Trotsky and is offered a job with him, but he doesn't take it (*AM*, 481–3). There are, too, apparent historical references of which the reader may be skeptical: was there really a project for a world state, known as Cosmopolis, organized by the now largely forgotten Gerald Heard and Olaf Stapledon? Neither Fiedler's study of Stapledon nor any other source I have discovered mentions it.[7] Are there really dialogues of Wells with A. N. Whitehead, "which Sammler admired so much" (26)? No bibliography that I have found lists them, nor do the two appear to have had serious contact.

Much in his work, moreover, is extraordinary or incongruous; Bellow creates a strange world. A typical instance is Sammler's meeting with a gaucho in Israel: an exile like himself, but brutal, ready to kill the nutrias he breeds because they are stupid. Bellow goes on to comment on "the humiliations of inconsequence" (23), on the disturbing incoherence of life, but in the context of the novel this displacement is not just disturbing, it is also colorful, fascinating, entertaining; it promises a world of change and surprise, against the harsh ordinariness of the everyday. Similarly, the boldness of Wallace's enterprise to make a fortune by photographing people's trees and labeling them—would it work? It might, though the investment would be huge, as Wallace recognizes (and in fact it fails through Wallace's incompetence). Feffer, a little later, wants to buy a locomotive, which you can apparently do in a syndicate. Unreal they may be. But at least these ideas are bold, ingenious, and new (they verge on the purposive, aggressive, and conative);

it is Bellow's ingenuity that the reader marvels at. Are these things plausible? They are things rarely experienced or heard of in reality (at most in odd paragraphs in newspapers, the paragraphs that may be viewed as on the edge of reality); they are close to fantasy. Bellow in a sense is testing what can be accepted as an outgrowth of the known real, of the drab or ugly everyday; he challenges the reader's imagination for the variety and extremity of action. Or to put it another way, he insists on strangeness, the "strangeness of life" (*HG*, 439), "the strangeness of the world" (*HRK*, 212), the "queerness of the world" (*V*, 233), the intensity with which people seek to make their own fates. This strangeness, emphatically, is not just Bellow's invention. There are accounts of real but barely credible events: the prisoners in Buchenwald in 1937 being invited to purchase saucepans (48), and, most crucially, the astonishing career of Rumkowski, the theatrical "king" of the Lodz ghetto, with his royal robes and his gilded coach (185), the symbol for Sammler of the empty theatricality of the world, of "the bad joke of the self."[8]

Most astonishing, perhaps, is the pickpocket's act in exhibiting his penis to Sammler as a threat. The act is commented on and explained later, as Sammler seeks to understand the act and his own fascination with it (45, 54), but the explanation doesn't quite make it plausible. The penis, in Sammler's explanation, is a symbol of the Schopenhauerian will (168). The pickpocket may not have seen it that way, but Bellow surely did. He is offering his readers a symbol rather than an actuality.

All the verisimilar material is strongly and conspicuously organized by the author. At a certain level of detachment from the text we can admire Bellow's sheer narratological skill. While we are actually reading for pleasure and imaginative fulfillment, we at least recognize the organizing discipline of an author; we recognize that for all the vast variety of characters, places, and events in the novel, there is no chaos. They are all—sooner or later—relevant: relevant to the gradual crystalizing of Sammler's feelings about his life in America. This recognition of relevance comes, most obviously, from the way Bellow, to a large extent, focalizes the events through Sammler. The text, that is, contains an interpretation and judgment of the America of the 1960s; there is a rhetoric that is Sammler's view of the world about him (which is, then, also the world the reader can remember or the world he or she knows from history books). It is the judgment of an outsider, and not just any outsider; this is an outsider who is specially qualified to think of the ultimates in our history. On experiential grounds, in part, Sammler has experienced more than most of us do, and his experience includes what we may well consider to be the single most significant event of the twentieth century, the Holocaust, which proved the limits of liberal humanism, showing the barbarian within civilized humanity; he is, in Bradbury's words "a true experiencer of the modern apocalypse."[9] On a much more modest level his experience also includes his acquaintance with H. G. Wells, the voice of liberal and scientific progress, but also the sensualist and, in his last work, the voice of despair as war seized Europe. Sammler is morally qualified to judge: he is a survivor of the war, in which his wife has died, he has been half-blinded, his daughter has been partially estranged from him by being brought up in a Catholic institution, and he has himself killed a German soldier, in circumstances that are not exactly of self-defense. He has experienced guilt and victimhood and so knows at first hand what good and evil are. His present situation, too, is one of pathos, as he waits for the death of his relative and benefactor Elya Gruner; the gravity of the occasion solemnizes his thinking. He is mythically qualified to judge, too; during the war he has been before a firing squad, has fallen into a mass grave and escaped, and then has lived for some time in a tomb; he has risen from the dead and so can judge life. This last point is an important one; myth is the stuff of fiction and gets a hesitant, skeptical, partial assent from us in everyday life.

Overall then, it seems that the purport of the novel may be to endorse Sammler's view, desperately asserted in the last words of the novel, argued out explicitly against Hannah Arendt, at an earlier stage, his view that we know what goodness is—and that the world about him has ignored that knowledge. The novel, that is, may seem to imply certainty, but can fiction assert a truth? Bellow makes clear in the book that at least some fiction falsifies life; telling the story of Pierre Bezukhov in *War and Peace* being spared by Napoleon because of his "human look," Sammler admits that this was not likely to happen in reality: "Pierre Bezukhov was altogether lucky. Of course he was a person in a book" (151).

Sammler's rhetoric is a powerful and often memorable one and largely constitutes the very distinctive tone of the novel; Bradbury, for instance, comments on the "new voice" in the novel, and by speaking of Sammler as a "complex surrogate" of his author implies that the voice is ultimately Bellow's.[10] Porter, more severely, identifies Sammler's complaint with Bellow's, and so judges the work to be not a satisfactory novel; it is in his view "a novel in which Bellow's moral indignation seems to overshadow his artistic control."[11] The rhetoric is a form of energy; it is an energy that transforms the contemporary external world into the world seen by Sammler, in proud bewilderment and concern.

So, on the abused telephone kiosks: "The opulent sections of the city were not immune. You opened a jewelled door into degradation, from hypercivilised Byzantine luxury straight into the state of nature, the barbarous world of color erupting from beneath" (8). There is antithetical and picturesque imagery, an emphatic moral vocabulary, a sense of dynamism, learned echoes; this is a keen mind confronting a complex reality (or at least the worst of it). Sammler's rhetoric often takes the form of a concise and effective wit (boasted of a little too much in the text). So, complaining of the dirtiness of young people, he comments that "In their revulsion from authority they would respect no persons. Not even their own persons" (32). The pun is economical and pertinent: Sammler believes in discipline, and cleanliness is part of that. Jet-set preachers, Sammler thinks, cast "artificial pearls before real swine" (93). The scorn is elegantly compressed; the implied learning and mental vigor almost justify the scorn. If only it were addressed only to the preachers and not also to their audiences! The novel also often contains aphorisms claiming to illuminate human life in general, and the voice on these occasion seems not just to be Sammler's but also that of the author, who at the least is proffering a view of humanity for his readers to reflect on. Thus, in connection with Shula's perpetual frustration, he reflects that "You could seldom get people to long for what was possible—that was the cruelty of it" (211). The rhythm suggests a rather Wildean paradox, inverting the Romantic cult of longing for what is not accessible. Sammler—and, undoubtedly, behind him Bellow, continuing his engagement with a Romantic form of individualism—sharply combines a respect for desire with a respect for success.

But there is, too, a discreet counterenergy; the rhetoric is often ironized. The narrator's phrasing about Sammler occasionally suggests a criticism, as with his "bitter, angry mind" (39), and Sammler is often critical of himself: "he had his own view of everything, an intensely peculiar one, but what else was there to go by?" he wonders; "Europeans often misunderstand America comically" (55–56). Still more significantly, he reflects toward the end of the work that he is like his companions, that he shares their lunacy: "And was he himself a perfect example of sanity? He was certainly not. He was their Sammler. They shared the same fundamentals" (213). This self-awareness is deeply ambivalent—a creditable sign of his disinterest, but also an undermining of his criticism of the United States.

More important, the energy of his speech may reveal bias, prejudice, or ingratitude. Consider, for instance, his view of his daughter Shula (and the implied view of women): "Shula, like all the ladies perhaps, was needy—needed gratification of numerous instincts, needed the warmth and pressure of men, needed a child for sucking and nurture, needed female emancipation, needed the exercise of the mind, needed continuity, needed interest—interest!—needed flattery, needed triumph, power, needed rabbis, needed priests, needed fuel for all that was perverse and crazy, needed noble action of the intellect, needed culture, demanded the sublime" (30). This, of course, is not wholly negative; human beings all need the sublime, no doubt, and should need culture, but the gist of Sammler's thoughts is to condemn Shula for an ill-disciplined greed for an ill-defined sensation. The rhetoric is strong, even blatant; the repetition of "needed," finally modified to "demanded," the intense physicality of "warmth and pressure," "sucking and nurture" (and the patterning of the words) balanced against the lists of abstracts, "emancipation," "exercise," "continuity," the sudden harsh interruption with *"interest!"* This is virtuoso contempt, but it shouldn't convince the reader; these thoughts pass through Sammler's head as Shula is good-naturedly cleaning his windows for him, sitting uncomfortably outside on the window sill—and later, throughout the novel, we find she has done a great deal, if not always efficiently, to look after her old father (providing him, even, with the best-quality vodka). Her major concern in the novel is, in fact, to make him do something with his culture; she believes in him and wants to see the book on Wells he is too inert to actually write. Her father goes on to complain of her opening the windows and so blowing away "the personal atmosphere Mr. Sammler had accumulated and stored." The personal—here—is stuffiness; he dislikes his daughter because she brings fresh air. This speech is part of an ongoing oddity in Sammler; when, some time later, he reflects on Angela's attractions, including her eyes which are "dark sexual blue" (57), some readers may wonder what shade of blue is more sexual than others and suspect Sammler of rather too much susceptibility, and too little willingness to recognize it. When, conversely, the text refers to Gruner's "courteous Jewish baldness" (63) one may suspect Sammler of identifying goodness with age and masculinity.

The novel, also, dramatizes its basic conflict: it brings Sammler into conflict and debate with representatives of the world he dislikes. The characters are clearly conceived as opposites to the gentlemanly Sammler: Wallace, Gruner's self-seeking and ineffective permanently dependent son, Shula, whose Catholic contacts have left strange traces in her; Angela, whose sexual availability has led to a quarrel with her boyfriend; Feffer, for whom academic life is a source of hard profit and sexual advantage, even in his own generation and from his own race;

the singer and musicologist Bruch, his dignity lost in the pressure of ill-placed erotic desire. The tone of these contacts is often excessive; there are tears, confessions, laments, and harassment. Sammler's presence provokes his fellows to express their emotional confusions. The effect of the novel depends on these people being offered precisely as representatives, as typical, and not just as isolated and often eccentric individuals, on their confusions being those the reader can recognize as typical of their age. They are confusions of money, sexuality, and religion, all things that were changing fast in the 1960s. Confusion implies abnormality; one of the crucial undertakings of Bellow's writing is to present the extraordinary as typical.

Most sympathetic amongst Sammler's contacts is the scientist Lal. Like Sammler, Lal is a victim of the modern world (most precisely, wronged by Sammler's own daughter, Shula, who "borrows" the manuscript of his book and shows little willingness to return it). Like Sammler, he is a scholar with roots outside America, partially in the same British intellectual elite from which they can both drop names, but unlike Sammler, preserves a faith in science. Lal has varying impacts in the novel: an object of desire for Shula and Angela; a model of efficiency for Wallace; and a source of tempting ideas for Sammler, who is impelled into a lengthy defense of imagination, precisely because he sees in Lal's Wellsian prophecies of material progress on another world a misplaced idealism to which his own idealism provides a purer answer. Porter notes in Sammler's lengthy debate with Lal the quality of recital and sees it as symptomatic of the quality of the whole book as a "staged performance."[12] The observation is an acute one; there is theatricality in the work, in its conflicts and in its patterns;[13] the fact might have made Porter skeptical of his view that the novel essentially endorses Sammler's judgments.

The reader is also conscious of the way Sammler's varied discoveries in the outside world are formed by the author into a plot, a coherent sequence in which everything has a result. There is a convention of the novel as a genre that foregrounds this act of plotting: the coincidence. The most striking example is very close to the end of the book. Sammler's encounters with the black pickpocket open the book, dominate chapter 1, and are referred to occasionally afterward, usually to Sammler's embarrassment, as with Feffer's attempts to get him to describe exactly the pickpocket's penis. But they seem to have little to do with his major concern, the death of Gruner. As Sammler finally is driven to Gruner's hospital, he sees from his car an altercation in the street; he intervenes and finds that Feffer is fighting the pickpocket. Also present, by chance, is Sammler's son-in-law Eisen, a second-rate artist, violent husband, demanding acquaintance, and general nogoodnik. Urged by Sammler to stop the fight, Eisen does so—by striking the pickpocket with a bag of heavy metal medallions, the products of his art, which brings the man to the ground, bleeding. Sammler's preoccupation with the pickpocket, Feffer's wish to cash in by photographing him at work, Eisen's brutality and foreignness, the pickpocket's animal health and overpowering insistence—all come together in a way that embarrasses Sammler deeply, as he finds himself more or less responsible for serious injury to the criminal he has admired and feared. Coincidences do happen, of course, and in real life people laugh and wonder about them; in fiction they are seen as a sign of the narrator's artifice. In incompetent novelists they may be taken to be a sign of incompetent artifice; in Bellow they are a sign that he refuses to disguise fiction by excluding chance. Such conventions mark a certain paradoxical distance from the real. They mark out the work as being fictional, even while they use happenings that might well be actual. They make the reader see what might be unusual and random as being willed by the author.

The novel, moreover, imposes themes on its events. Sammler's thoughts return to a number of key concepts: humanity, death, the past, our assigned purposes. Why shouldn't they? Not many of us, no doubt, avoid repetition in our daily thought and speech; it may well be that it is precisely our tendency to revert to the same concepts as we respond to different events that makes us distinct personalities. Once again, there is a novelistic convention here. The recurrence of terms is not just plausible, it is also a patterning. (It is no chance that we speak of "themes" both in literature and in music; the repetition and variation that make the intelligibility and the delight of music also make for the seductiveness of fiction.) This patterning is perceptible because readers expect—though on reflection they may know that their expectation is wrong—that the novel will provide ever-new ideas. The patterning is especially perceptible when the repetition is emphatic, hyperbolic, and unsupported by plausible explanation. The most obvious example in *Mr. Sammler's Planet* is, of course, the moon. By the end of the first chapter, the moon has acquired three senses: it is the Wellsian fantasy, it is Lal's practical escape from the biological crises of this earth, and it is Sammler's imagined escape from the psychological problems of this earth. The second chapter, in a startling change of tone, opens with a great deal of scientific information (presumably paraphrased from Lal's book) that is curious but, as Sammler points out (44), irrelevant to his own anti-materialist aspirations. Shula, by stealing Lal's manuscript, has focused the novel on the exploration of a symbol, and from now on the moon appears with exuberant frequency. A few pages later, Sammler's continuing preoccupation with the pickpockets' penis produces a reference to Artemis and her lunar chastity (54). A little later again, Sammler imagines a perpendicular dropped from the moon to the grave; the moon acquires yet another meaning, associating itself with the death fixation of much of the book. In the same passage it gains yet another sense, a still more extraordinary one: the moon is a "white corroded pearl. By a sole eye, seen as a sole eye" (85). The moon is Sammler himself, the one-eyed man, and the single eye itself becomes a symbol of varying and not always clear purport. The insistence may seem excessive when Sammler later reflects that "There is nothing left remarkable Beneath the visiting moon" (157). We soon realize, too, that all the references to lunatics can be seen in a lunar perspective. The emphasis becomes almost a taunting of the reader when Wallace asks Sammler for a crossword clue, and Sammler not only knows the answer ("Morrice") — as befits his literary culture — but illustrates it with a quotation from Milton: "a wavering morrice to the moon" (79); less intellectually, Wallace himself, comfortably drinking in the Rolls Royce, indulgently approves of the moon ("Isn't the moon great?") and reveals that he has reserved a ticket to visit it (146). Nothing, the reader more and more realizes, happens by accident in this book; everything is justified by something else (everything is overdetermined, in Freudian terminology). This is a constructed world, a strange world, a symbolic world, as Opdahl insists, with its "lack of literal realism."[14] What must be stressed here is both that there is, despite this, quite a lot of literal realism and also that the unrealism is the emphasis of the author.

The point appears, not quite trivially, with Sammler's Augustus John hat. This hat is referred to several times (e.g., 70, 91–93, 122) and becomes a discreet leitmotiv. What is this hat like? Some photographs of John and some self-portraits show him in a battered straw hat, but can this be what Sammler wears?[15] Anyway, it insists on Sammler's foreignness, in antiquated European garb; in a moment of comic dishonesty (91) Sammler uses it to conceal the stolen manuscript (for which its wide brim is ideal). By the time of Gruner's death, in the last pages of the novel, this piece of European dandyism is not forgotten but has become a mild embarrassment: "he didn't lay it on the clean new-made bed" (237).

Repetition also creates the occasion for comedy. Much of the comedy of the book is directed at characters other than Sammler: Shula with her wig, Wallace with his harebrained enthusiasm, Feffer and his deviousness. It chiefly supports Sammler's attitudes, in fact, by mocking the excesses and self-indulgences of the young, as with Feffer's story of the would-be seducer who carries a gun to defend himself against jealous husbands but finds that it won't pierce a telephone directory (101). It is difficult to find Sammler funny, since we are so aware of the horror of the ordeals he has passed through; Bellow tests our tolerance of the comic to the extreme. But there are at least sections in which Sammler does appear in a somewhat absurd light. When Feffer exhibits (if the word may be used) pressing curiosity about the pickpocket, there is humor in Sammler's contortions in attempting to continue the conversation politely while actually evading a topic which is not a subject of "polite conversation" and which, moreover, he feels all too acutely. Feffer and Sammler both have their obsessions; the symmetry makes for an elegant comedy. Comic too, is one scene when Sammler attempts to flatter Lal over the telephone but starts by assuming that the manuscript which took three years' work might have needed only six months. So again is the scene in which on first meeting Lal (161), he tells him that his manuscript (which he knows in fact to be in a left luggage locker at Grand Central Station) is "not actually in the house." One more example inclining to farce (an example noted by Hyland): Mr. Sammler has given, in conversation with Lal, a long speech on the value of metaphysics, need, affection, and love, which culminates in the vision of a world of saints rising up to the moon, the object not of scientific truth, but of our heart's desires (190).[16] As he reaches these words, Shula notices that her feet are wet, and a dispute breaks out as to whether she has turned off the bath water. This is closely interwoven with the whole texture of the work. It reminds the reader, first of all, of the disturbing physicality of Shula, seen in the bath by her father, and it proves that the flood is in fact caused by Wallace, in a stupid and selfish attempt to find money in the plumbing. It is Sammler's opponents, those who accept the brutal physical reality, who are at fault. But isn't Sammler himself just a bit at fault too? How can he go on speaking about the flight of the imagination when his feet are wet? Does idealism mean impracticality? Similarly, and even more acutely, the morning after these excessive and absurd events, in the climactic section of the whole book, Sammler recalls the mass execution in which his wife has died (his reaching this lucid memory at last being one of the great climaxes of the work) and starts to formulate a key conception of the book, the "assignment" which is to make sense of his own life—and which is apparently the assignment of *Mr. Sammler's Planet* itself: he is "Assigned to figure out certain things, to condense, in short views, some essence of experience" (220).[17] He is interrupted with a query about the cleaning woman and then finds that Shula has scorched the shoes that have been a source of pride for him throughout the book.

How firmly does *Mr. Sammler's Planet* assert a judgment of the modern world? A Wellsian reminiscence may help to focus the issue. Sammler refers to his story "The Country of the Blind"—where the one-eyed man, according to the popular saying, is king (169). But he deprecates the obvious interpretation: "Anyway, I am not in the Country of the Blind, but only one eyed." We are being teased by this; we look for the author's intention in the reference (as we admire again the neatness with which the themes appear to coalesce—now Wells and the single eye). What is Bellow's intention? Is he saying that Sammler is the one person who can see the true values of civilization in a blind America? Is he remembering the Wells story, in which the seeing man is tempted to accept being totally blinded? Is he, on the contrary, stressing the deficiencies of Sammler's view?[18] Or is he, like his modest hero, rejecting significance and showing the loss of the eye as mere misfortune?

Kiernan acutely speaks of the tension in this novel—and in other of Bellow's works—between what he calls pronunciative and amplified styles, between, that is, a style for "annotating and explicating a stipulated reality" and one for "plumbing reality through the artifact's self-realization in a world of eccentrically drawn perspectives."[19] The opposition is a crucial one and underlies much of what we have been seeing. Documentary and fantasy, rhetoric and irony, realism and artifice, multiplicity and order: Bellow's writing forcibly brings together a record of the actual with a display of the writer's transforming will. The tension requires the reader to be alert throughout, assessing what is evidence of the world he knows or could know—and what is evidence of the author's temperament: his boldness of imagination, his ingenuity in construction, his delight in pattern and contrast, his discreetly shifting sympathy, his moral austerity. It requires the reader to assess what is history and what is fiction. The task is not an easy one. Bellow's is an extreme world, but we can believe that modern America is an extreme world too. Kenneth, in *More Die of Heartbreak*, hesitates as to whether his uncle suffers from delirium or a "fantastic reality" (*MDH*, 122); the union of the fantastic with the real is the fascination of much of Bellow.

3
Capote: *In Cold Blood*

In Cold Blood, AS EVERYONE KNOWS, IS A NONFICTION NOVEL. THE apparently paradoxical conception of a nonfiction novel has been much discussed, most importantly in Zavarzadeh's perceptive study.[1] What will be stressed in the present account is the issues the genre raises about the conception of an impersonal narrator. In the classic novel of the eighteenth and nineteenth centuries, impersonal narrators are often omniscient; they know everything about the characters the authors have invented, including their unspoken thoughts. Serious modern novelists are in general reluctant to claim such omniscience, since it seems alien to our real experience of other people, whose thoughts are essentially unknown to us. One might expect such reluctance to be especially strong when the author is committed—unlike the fictional novelist—to narrating only events that he can guarantee to have really occurred. But if the author did in fact meticulously confine himself to such provable happenings, how would his work differ from that of the reporter or historian? Capote's answer is to use lavishly the techniques available to the novelist: internal perspective, in particular through free indirect discourse and through focalization, and manipulation of chronology in such a way as to heighten the effect of the events and to present them as part of the author's sensibility, as things which are meaningful to him because they are shocking, startling, pitiable, admirable, and the like, rather than merely things that have objectively happened in the public world. This approach then raises a concern for the reader: who exactly is the author and what is his attitude to the story he relates? He seems at times almost like the author of fiction, who is communicating to his readers the events he has invented. He seems at times to be a neutral observer (but if he is so neutral, why does he think these dreadful events interesting enough to merit the reader's attention for so long?). He seems at times an observer fascinated with evil or fascinated with the unfamiliar ordinariness of a part of America new to him. He seems at times the aesthete, determined to subordinate a tale of violence to a recognition of the beauty and orderliness of an artistic vision. All of this means that the figure of the narrator—very discreetly but unmistakably present in the text of the novel—has to be related by the reader to the figure of the real author: the reader is intrigued and uncertain about the distinction between the narrator, the character adopted by an author to convey a story effectively and engagingly, and the author, the man who went to Kansas to find out as much as he could about a crime.

Capote's novel is described on the title page as "A true account of a multiple murder and its consequences." The reader needs the assurance; whereas most American readers can be assumed to know at least the essentials of the Rosenberg case, used by Doctorow in *The Book of Daniel*, few outside Kansas were presumably well informed of the Clutter case when Truman Capote published his book. Readers' knowledge of the case, that is, depends in practice, in the overwhelming majority of cases, on their trust in Capote. And Capote offers quite a challenge to his readers' credence. Not least there is the extraordinary minuteness of detail; can we rely on the author to know what sort of map Perry Smith used to locate the Clutter farm, what sort of pen Mr. Clutter signed his checks with, what exactly were the news headlines on the local radio heard in a Kansas prison on November 17, 1959, what sort of beer is drunk by Perry's occasional landlady?

Virtually every page is rich in the sort of detail most readers would have forgotten if it had arisen in their own lives. The effect is complex; if the information is true, it bears witness to a remarkable dedication on the part of the author to the minuscule reconstruction of "what really happened" (in the terminology of positivist historians), and part of one's feeling for the author is compounded of respect for his meticulous patience and thoroughness. But is it true? Well, the book goes on from the title page to a dedication and then to acknowledgments, and this is a book where it's useful to read the acknowledgments, because they start with the declaration that "All the material in this book not derived from my own observation is either taken from official records or is the result of interviews with the persons directly concerned, more often than not numerous interviews conducted over a considerable period of time." Biographers and critics have shown how considerable that effort was, in time, energy, and emotional cost;[2] it certainly seems that Capote may have sacrificed his artistic and personal well-being to this book. Even without consulting such secondary sources, the book itself makes it clear that there is a possible source for each piece of information in this vast kaleidoscope, sufficient to establish it with a high degree of probability: Perry must himself have told the author what map he used, the insurance agent who received Herbert Clutter's check must have remembered the signing (which was obviously a hard-earned business success for him at the time and must have become very solemn in retrospect); Harold Nye, the detective who interviewed the landlady, must have remembered the beer (and of course the good detective observes and remembers detail). The news broadcast is perhaps a little more dubious. Floyd Wells, the prisoner who heard it, was no doubt profoundly shaken by news of the Clutter murders, for which he had some responsibility, and had every reason to recall the announcement; one may be less convinced that he recalled word-for-word the information about Dr. Adenauer and President Eisenhower. Perhaps Capote had access to the radio station's recordings or scripts.

Some uncertainty remains, but one can accept the story as plausible for two reasons: the journalist's or historian's plausibility of the availability of evidence and the novelist's plausibility of the accumulation of phenomena that we regard as in general likely to be associated with the given situation. Of course Perry stayed at a cheap rooming house (and former brothel) and not a well-run hotel; of course such a house is run by a slovenly old woman; of course part of her slovenliness is that she is drinking beer from the can—and it is going to be a common, readily available sort of beer and not an expensive foreign import. This is the sort of life that is associated with the punk murderer, what Nye sums up as a "lonely, mean life" (181). In other words, the detail is significant detail; it doesn't just bear witness to Capote's industry, it bears witness to his perception of the characters.

This industry is suppressed in the text; the evidence that can be guessed at is not actually given. The point strikes the reader and perhaps shocks him or her time and again. Beyond the accumulation of physical detail there is the accumulation of differing points of view. Many of these arise from documents to which Capote has gained access, in which people say "I": prison reports, private correspondence, statements to the police, lengthy recollections of the characters transcribed, apparently verbatim, by the author or by some intermediary. Perry's account of the murders, which extends to over six thousand words given in a car returning to Kansas, must come from the arresting detective Alvin Dewey. Capote claims to have trained himself in verbatim recall to a 95 percent level of accuracy. It is not clear that Dewey had done so as well. In these ways Capote ensures that the crime appears as the focus of multiple viewpoints. He also provides the stereoscope effect by seeing through the eyes of his characters as the events unfold. An early example is the account of Herbert Clutter, introduced in the second subsection of the book: "The master of River Valley Farm, Herbert William Clutter, was forty-eight years old, and as a result of a recent medical examination for an insurance policy, knew himself to be in first rate condition" (17).[3] There is a great deal to admire here; the insurance policy neatly anticipates the visit of the insurance salesman on the day of the murder and his later dilemma in deciding whether his firm is obliged to pay out on a premium that has not yet been banked (an instance of the many incommensurabilities associated with murder; how does the letter of commercial law relate to the horror of arbitrary brutality?); the first-rate condition of Herbert Clutter contrasts with the precarious state of his wife, which will be introduced shortly. But what of that word "knew"? Can one ever, with this degree of confidence, say what someone else "knows"? Capote makes explicit the grounds for his assumption; Mr. Clutter knew it because he had been told it. This looks uncomfortably like a usurpation of the fictionalist's right to enter into the minds of characters. Dorrit Cohn lucidly argues that one of the distinctive features of fiction is that it allows the author to present the private thoughts of characters;[4] we feel no anxiety when a fictional author tells us what Maisie knew, but the historian or biographer is much more likely to tell us what a person must have known. A critic has acutely commented that Capote's use of documentation in *In Cold Blood* gives " a surface of persuasive immediacy and impenetrable omniscience";[5] what must be added is that in normal speech and writing immediacy and omniscience are incompatible. We only know immediately what we experience ourselves, and our experience is limited. There is a hard-line modernist argument against any omniscient narrator, summarized in Sartre's criticism of the omniscient narrator in Mauriac's novels: Mauriac seeks to be God, but God is not an artist. Clearly this argument is insensitive to the importance of convention in fiction, but it does at least focus attention on the problems of the God's eye view—problems which suggest that the essence of the nonfiction novel is that it is a story where the facts are true and the author is imaginary. Capote, in his years of research, may well have got as near as humanly possible to being omniscient about the events at River Valley Farm; what is humanly possible is knowing the perceptible actions of people and their appearance, possessions, and surroundings, not their inner thoughts.

But Capote frequently does convey their thoughts. A favorite technique, as with most modern novelists, is free indirect speech, as in Perry's reflections on Dick's mockery of his song: "Of course Dick was very literal-minded, very—he had no understanding of music, poetry— and yet when you got right down to it, Dick's literalness, his pragmatic approach to every subject, was the primary reason Perry had been attracted to him, for it made Dick seem, compared to himself, so authentically tough, invulnerable, 'totally masculine'" (28). The passage deserves close attention; the end of the sentence is often quoted because it acutely formulates the relationship of the two criminals and hints at a homosexual dimension. But who is offering this analysis? At the start of the sentence, it is clearly Perry who is speaking. As Perry's voice, it shows quite a lot of that defensive and rather feminine vulnerability that is implied in the latter part of the sentence: Perry, as much of the story confirms, is imaginative, albeit his imagination is of a second-rate kind fed by run-of-the-mill movies and magazine articles, and he defends himself against Dick's aggression by the deprecating "of course" and the vaguely elevated "music, poetry." Then what happens? Is it still Perry who provides the acute analysis of his own motivations, who uses accurately words such as "pragmatic" and "primary"? (Perry loves learned-sounding words, but he often gets them wrong.) If so, where do the quotation marks for "totally masculine" come from? The effect here is of a discreet slippage from Perry's thoughts, told in free indirect speech, through Capote's abstract analysis, to a brief direct quotation that confirms the analysis. Perry has told Capote that Dick is "totally masculine," but he must also have told him that he is "very literal-minded, very," and Capote has presented this comment as if it were Perry's immediate response to a specific past event. He has seduced us into entering Perry's mind for a moment of sympathy—partial sympathy, not unmixed with irony—and then skilfully distanced us as his approach verges on the clinical and on the evidence that supports that clinical view, a view of what many readers in 1968 would have regarded as abnormal feelings (and what Capote, one may guess, may have thought to be unrecognized feelings). What Perry knows is, for many readers, more interesting than what Mr. Clutter knows. Mr. Clutter is an almost monolithic avatar of Christian Republican virtue; Perry is a shifting mixture of helplessness and viciousness, and the mastery of Capote's writing is to mirror—or create—those shifts.

A picture of the author emerges discreetly from the work. Capote's aim was "to write it without ever appearing myself, and yet, at the same time, create total credibility."[6] But the aim isn't quite maintained. An almost explicit self-reference appears toward the end, after many pages in which Capote seems to be totally absent from his text, when Capote tells of Dick Hickock's speaking to "a journalist with whom he corresponded and who was periodically allowed to visit him" (331); later in the same conversation this person is described as "the journalist, who was as equally well acquainted with Smith as he was with Hickock" (335). Who can this be? One doesn't need to have read the biographies or Capote's own interviews on his preparation of the book to realize that the only journalist who can have had such regular contact with the killers is Capote himself; there is a conspicuous self-abnegation here. One point of comparison is with the nineteenth-century ideal of the impersonal narrator, who, in Flaubert's words, "no more appears in his work than God in his creation," and undoubtedly Capote is triumphantly successful in creating a Flaubertian perfection of language and form, in which the impact of the real is held at a distance, as if beneath glass, to be contemplated in its self-contained strangeness.[7] This means that in *In Cold Blood*, despite the usual precise distinctions of narratological theory, it is very difficult to distinguish narrator from implied author. The personality we perceive behind the book is above all the craftsman; his engagement with the events of the novel is (as Capote told Perry Smith) to make them into art. Critics often contrast the apparent impersonality of *In Cold Blood* with the blatant self-display—and self-mockery—in Norman Mailer's nonfiction writing of the same period. The restriction of self in Capote is very deliberate; it arouses curiosity as to what sort of person could live at such close quarters with extremity for a long period and avoid explicit comment. There is a clear contrast with the explicitness of most other people in the book: the vociferous denunciations of crime by the prosecuting counsel, the lengthy, self-pitying monologues of Perry Smith (and considerably less of Dick Hickock), the obsessiveness of the detectives, the baffled anxiety of the neighbors. The author is the person who has no explicit judgment to make, the witness who reproduces the observed facts and the feelings and language of other people.

More than that, the author discreetly places himself—and his reader—with respect to the events. He is an outsider who opens the book with an account of the village of Holcomb and its surroundings, a place strange even to other Kansans, who sees the grain elevators rising like Greek temples "long before a traveler reaches them" (15), who finds western Kansas—in its public manifestations—alien, drab, and primitive; he writes rather as an anthropologist, who seeks to establish for his readers a real way of life and a real set of people and invites the readers' wonderment. A striking example is the presentation of Susan Kidwell, a close friend of Nancy Clutter and the first person to see the bodies of the Clutter family. On the morning after the murders, "Susan, on this Sunday morning, stood at the window of this room watching the street. She is a tall languid young lady with a pallid, oval face and beautiful pale-blue-gray eyes; her hands are extraordinary—long-fingered, flexible, nervously elegant. She was dressed for church" (69). The bulk of the text is in the past tense (and that first sentence quoted could have graced many a novel of the most traditional type). As in a novel, Susan is a young lady of exceptional appearance. But that appearance is real and continuing; whereas Holly Golightly exists only in a novel and so appears only in the past tense, there is a real Susan, and contact with murder is only a small part of her life (the book indeed ends with an invented scene in which Susan and Al Dewey comment on the return of life to normality); the alternation of tenses gives the reader a slight shock as the flow of narrative gives way to an admiring recognition of the living person.

The author is however not only an admirer of the beauty, health, and innocence conveyed by Susan. He shows aesthetic aloofness when he recounts the Clutters' admiration of Nancy's performance in a play—because she hasn't forgotten her lines (19). He describes the Clutters' furniture and carpeting, the "spongy displays of liver-colored carpet intermittently abolishing the glare of varnished, resounding floors," in terms that imply little sympathy for the family's taste, and going on to comment that "this sort of furnishing was what Mr. and Mrs. Clutter liked, as did the majority of their acquaintances, whose homes, by and large, were similarly furnished" (21). It hardly needs saying that people like the sort of furniture they have in their homes—unless to express surprise; the end of the sentence hints at Capote's endless surprise as he enters more and more Kansas homes. He more explicitly judges the children's attempts at decorating a room; they had sought to remove its "unremovable dourness, and neither was aware of failure" (49). He sets up Holcomb as a character with unified views: Holcomb is impressed by the Clutters' large house, everyone in Holcomb recalls a plane crash, Nancy is "the town darling". Passages of the text abandon the principals—the Clutters, the detectives, the killers—to present a rural chorus of uninformed comment on the progress of the action, which images a community that is both ordinary and strange, ordinary because of its distance from the violence in which the principals are involved, strange to Capote and the sophisticated readers he addresses because it is so matter-of-fact and gossipy.

The urban sophistication of the text goes beyond this. The author is a wit, an ironist who enjoys relating the strangeness of the local people and their speech: the postmistress with her homely bossiness and eagerness to hear herself reported on the radio, the Englishwoman who finds Kansas "very *different*" from Paris and Rome. He captures acutely the appearance and manner of the large number of people who are affected by the crime, and with a discreet balance of politeness (since these people were likely to read the book) and reservations: Nancy Ewalt may have been delighted to find herself described as "a clothes-conscious girl with a film-star figure," but perhaps found her pleasure somewhat diminished a few words later when the author notes her "coy, tip-toe way of walking" (69). Nancy appears in the story because it is her visit to the Clutters on the way to church that leads to the discovery of their bodies. Her appearance doesn't affect her role in the events; it shows that Capote has met her (and so further authenticates the book) and it contributes to the picture of a society of nice people, people only slightly unnatural, which is disrupted by the alien force of violence. Capote's politeness declines sharply when he is dealing with a fellow writer, a local schoolteacher who "at least looks literary" (71). Mr. Hendricks's behavior at the discovery of the murders appears to have been exemplary; Capote's irony at his unpublished status serves to heighten the distinction of author and subject. The people of Kansas are there to be written about, not to write themselves.

With major participants, Capote's impersonality is far from total. He sometimes judges his characters very explicitly, as with the portrait of Dick Hickock, one of whose eyes has "a venomous, sickly-blue squint that although it was involuntarily acquired, seemed nevertheless to warn of bitter sediment at the bottom of his nature" (42). The author warns the reader, and so sets the plot in motion (in particular he anticipates the various references to Dick's risking recognition because of his malformed eye). He sets up a tension between the inner evil and the impression of charm and ease that Dick gives to many people in the course of his activity as a confidence trickster; he proposes the idea of sedimentation, of evil accumulating within a person till it reaches the point of action. He comments ironically on Floyd Wells's "several careers, as soldier, ranch hand, mechanic, thief, the last of which had earned him a sentence of three to five years in Kansas State Penitentiary" (162). It is this prison sentence that allowed him to betray the Clutters to Dick Hickock, a disastrous conclusion to what the author presents as a life of futile drifting, barely dignified as a career but earning something, after all. He can be ironic toward his own aesthetic sense: when first introducing Perry, he lists his accoutrements—guitar, shotgun, flashlight, knife, hunting vest and shells—"a curious still life" (33); in fact the items are combined not for the elegance of shapes but for their use in murder. He satirizes the defense lawyer, whose efforts for the murderers are perhaps not as dynamic as they might have been:

"a classic country lawyer more happily at home with land deeds than ill deeds" (283). A critic has spoken, in a striking and pertinent phrase, of Capote's "determined disinterest";[8] the disinterest merges into distaste.

The combination of explicit comment and focalization is crucial in the rhetoric of the book. A complex attitude, for example, appears in Capote's presentation of the first interrogation of Dick, which is narrated, in broad terms, from the point of view of the detectives, Harold Nye and Roy Church. Dick's actions are described from outside: he was "evidently proud," and he "seemed" not to understand a question. For some time there has been little on the thought of either detective. But then we see (in the present tense) an aspect of Nye's character that Capote must have later observed: "Nye is a short, short-tempered man who has difficulty moderating his aggressive vigor, his talent for language both sharp and outspoken" (222). Nye is not a writer; he has a talent for language, but not the indirect, patient, elegant language of Capote (the language that produces the witticism "short, short-tempered" in this very sentence). He is aggressive; he belongs in the world of crime, the world of action, with the dangerous Dick and Perry, and so his talent needs to be moderated. But Capote can enter far enough into his consciousness to know about the "difficulty" he feels. A page later we enter further into Nye's consciousness: "His poise, his explicitness, the assured presentation of verifiable detail impressed Nye—though, of course the boy was lying. Well, wasn't he?" (223). The narrator carefully paces the development of the story, leading up to Nye's abandonment of Hickock once he has been unsettled by the accusation of murder and to Nye's glimpse of Perry, in which Nye's sensibility occupies the text for a whole paragraph, as his fascination with Perry's small feet and exotic coloring is conveyed. The choice of Nye as (essentially) the focus in this scene allows Dick and Perry to remain outside the readers' sensibility—until we read their confessions and autobiographical reminiscences in the later parts of the book. They are strange to us, both cocky and vulnerable, the objects of Nye's control and of his curiosity. Morally, no doubt, we should see them through the eyes of the police; we should share Nye's eagerness to see justice done and the power of the law, of the state and the settled community of Kansas, restored. But the presentation is more confusing than that. We are a little distanced from Nye by his bad temper (as we have been earlier by his numerous prevarications in the course of his investigations). And we recognize Nye's own insecurity; he wants to know that Dick is lying, but he can't be quite sure. He is impressed by Dick (a fluent and plausible liar), and he is intrigued by Perry. Perry is "not pretty," unlike his sister, whom Nye has interviewed previously—but does the denial itself hint at the possibility of an attraction? We shift from the arrogant Dick to the apparently passive Perry, from Nye as protagonist to Nye as observer, from speech to silence. We anticipate the last pages of the novel, when Perry's feet will again be seen (though this time it is Dewey who recalls that first interrogation) not touching the ground—as he is hanged.

As Capote guides the reader's sympathies through focalization, so he does through temporal sequence and discontinuities. The section we have been considering ends with Nye deducing that Perry is still a "virgin," in other words, that he still does not know what he is to be accused of. The following section passes from Nye's view to the patient professionalism of his colleagues, Dewey and Duntz (a "patient professionalism" akin to Capote's own), and then shows us the reactions in turn of Perry and Dick as they at last realize the danger they are in. The passages recounting these reactions are conspicuously symmetrical, each introduced with the words "he later recalled," which justify the author in recounting their most private thoughts; they differ in that Perry continues to respect Dick, but Dick is contemptuous and cynical about Perry, and in the next section Dick will break down under questioning and blame Perry for the shootings. Capote's technique is a mastery of continuity and articulation. The questioning makes Dick and Perry insecure; insecurity makes Dick confess. Dick's confession is not recounted in detail; Capote cuts after Dick's words "He killed them all" (232), ignoring the question the detectives must have asked in consequence—and we later find that Dick has in fact told the detectives much the same as Perry does here. The author then cuts to a low-tension scene in which the people of Holcomb are hearing the news on the radio ("Just imagine," one of them comments, "I don't wonder the varmint fainted" [232]). The next cut takes us into the car in which Perry is returning to Kansas with the detectives; unusually, the narration is in the present tense, although it recounts the next event of this past sequence, which is Perry's detailed confession. The detectives' weary and at times discouraging endeavors at last here reach a climax, which moreover fills in a gap in the reader's knowledge; we have read earlier of the killers' approach to River Valley Farm on the Saturday night and of the discovery of the bodies on Sunday morning, but we do not know what happened during the killings themselves. What we have here is a compound of the skill and insistence of the detectives, of public opinion in Holcomb, and of the anxieties of the criminals, the result of their unsteady dependence on each other and, at least in the case of

Perry, their preoccupation with the crime. The climax is an achievement for the detectives, a (partial) reassurance for the public, a catastrophe but perhaps also a catharsis for the criminals.

The sequence ends with the passage that looks most like the book's authoritative assessment of the crime. Dewey reflects, having now heard both confessions, that they "failed to satisfy his sense of meaningful design. The crime was a psychological accident, virtually an impersonal act; the victims might as well have been killed by lightning." Yet he can feel a certain sympathy, at least for Perry, in his "ugly and lonely progress towards one mirage and then another" (248). Capote has placed his fullest assessment of the story in the mind not of the aggressive Nye but of the wise, efficient, and thoughtful Dewey. Dewey's sense of those ugly and lonely lives shows an impressive gravity and reflectiveness and corresponds acutely not only to what he has just been told but to many things he doesn't know, things the reader has learned and is yet to learn. Nevertheless the crucial sense—and one the book as a whole must endorse—is of incomprehension. There is no logic that fully motivates the shootings.

Critics have debated the difficulty of interpreting or explaining the Clutter murders, at the risk of providing their own explanations. Reed sees them as the outcome of a fatal determinism, in good nineteenth-century humanist style.[9] It is true that a lot of the characters speak about fate or doom, but there doesn't seem to be the recognizable chain of cause and effect that would allow one to think of determinism. Capote doesn't explain; he watches. Hollowell sees the random crime as characteristic of America in the 1960s;[10] writing in the 1970s, he was more conscious than readers may be now that the 1960s were strange and disturbing. The book, however, may suggest a more wide-ranging sense of the incomprehensibility of action, as indicated by Garson's acute comment that in this book there is not only an American tragedy but also "the human tragedy, the wanton as well as inexplicable nature of existence."[11]

But even this may seem to distort a book that refuses such great gestures as tragedy, a book which devotes much space to rejecting abstract theory or commentary. *In Cold Blood* is haunted by abstractions. We have the character of Perry, analyzed by his pious and complacent friend Willie-John, the moral exhortations of his sister's letter, the psychiatric evidence that would have been given by the expert appointed by the defense. The article by a psychiatrist, cited near the end of the book, that classifies such motiveless murders as a category of mental disturbance does little more than demonstrate that they indeed are motiveless and so inexplicable. The vague abstraction of the psychiatric jargon strikes the reader by the way it falls short of the intense precision with which Capote depicts the acts and words of the protagonists; the kind of evidence that might have been (but isn't) presented to the court as moral or legal argument is not the sort of thing that shows how events happened. That has to be narrative, and the fullest narrative is that which insists on the indeterminacy of meaning, on the multiplicity of sense impressions and vital expressions, on the tension or calm that arises from the harmony or conflict between the individual and the outside world or other people. In short, it is an aesthetic narrative, ordered to constitute "literary truth, with its invitation to the reader to share in an imaginative game."[12]

Which is why the text is full of scenes in which the significance of murder is displaced from what it reveals of people's potential for evil and from the ways it affects the need for survivors to continue, to disparate details; when Dewey searches the Clutter house, for instance, "upstairs in Kenyon's room, on a shelf above his bed, the lenses of the dead boy's spectacles gleamed with reflected light" (159). There is pathos in the abandoned possessions of the dead, but there is also a peaceful beauty in the gleaming object; things survive. It is such selected details in the work that make art, according to Capote, from a "distillation of reality."[13] And throughout the book there is another beauty, the beauty of the seasons, much commented on and enhanced by solemn metaphor: the whitest sunlight in the purest sky in autumn, immediately before the murder; the light the following Monday, "as glittery as mica" (85); the snow that starts to fall as the two killers are brought to Garden City; the fine but muddy conditions at the auction sale before their trial, with the trees—the elms that, throughout the book, have suggested the privacy of the Clutters and the hiddenness of the evil that was to confront them—"lightly veiled in a haze of virginal green" (271). The seasons display the passing of the time, which is also the time of crime and punishment; in a classic pathetic fallacy they correspond to the fullness of the Clutters' lives—to be antithetically disrupted by the brutal intrusion of the murderers—the bleakness of the process of arrest and the hope for a new life. More than that, they indicate that things go on. In the rural world that Capote discovers in Kansas, life continues in its eternal cycle; if evil can temporarily disrupt society, it doesn't disrupt nature. So the work ends with Al Dewey recognizing the permanence of life: in a scene set in May, four years after the crime, he reflects in the Holcomb graveyard on the death of the Clutters and also of the Judge who condemned the killers and of one of their neighbors, but he also recalls the marriage of Bobbie Rupp, formerly the boyfriend of Nancy Clutter. Then he meets Susan, beautiful as ever with her willowy figure and long, elegant legs. Susan is thriving; she has attained the local university, as she and Nancy always intended to do. She is, Mr. Dewey reflects, "just such a young woman as Nancy might have been." She is, to some extent, a substitute for Nancy; the type persists—the healthy, attractive, lively young woman—if the individual is destroyed. Finally he turns away from people, striking what Garson aptly calls "Capote's memorable elegiac note"[14] to reflect in the last words of the book, heavily emphasized by Capote's use of alliteration and of sentence rhythm, on "the whisper of wind voices in the wind-bent wheat" (343). Human voices are stilled as the book concludes, and the voices that remain take us back to the start, to "the tawny infinitude of wheat stalks" that Mr. Clutter sees on his last day. That day was in November; the half-grown wheat of May has a cycle to complete. Beyond the incomprehensible contingencies of the human there lies the infinity of the natural.

4
Barth: *Giles Goat-Boy*

BARTH STARTED HIS LITERARY CAREER WITH TWO WORKS CONCERNING private life, the life of family and sexuality, in modern America. He then changed his style considerably—and hugely enhanced his reputation—by producing the vast and exuberant historical mock epic, *The Sot-Weed Factor*. This novel provides an account, both farcical and bitter, of the development of literary culture in the early years of American history (which is also an account of a loss of innocence and of a resignation to the viciousness of life in general). The remoteness of the period, the unfamiliarity to most readers of the specific events of early Maryland, the legendary status of Captain Smith's very mad affair with Pocohontas, and the example of the frank or brutal explicitness of much eighteenth-century fiction: all these things justify the excessiveness of the work, the coarse physicality of the narration, the cynicism of much of the dialogue, the implausibility of much of the action, and the strangeness of many of the characters. This is a conspicuously fictional exploration of a world that impinges only very indirectly on the reader's own experience, and for this reason the reader can—to some degree— blithely accept the way it appears to abandon the dimension of decorum, restraint, and orderliness that is inescapable in actual social life.

Giles Goat-Boy marks another development, and a more disturbing one. This too is a work of excess, of exuberance beyond the bounds of seriousness, but it deals with serious and immediate matters. It offers very recognizable references to the major features of American life in the mid-twentieth century: the aftermath of war, the continuation of cold war, the uncertainty of moral values in a world where there is no ideological consensus, the shifting relationships of men and women and the changing visions of what women should want, the new demands of black people for full human rights, the rise of mass education, the concomitant student rebellions, and the growing importance of computers; in the background are the traditions of world and American literature and thought. A number of historical figures are referred to more or less identifiably. This is a novel then that appears to aim at reproducing a recognizable world, and specifically the intensely controversial changes of the 1960s, but it does so through farcical excess. The historical framework, of a society disrupted by the rejection of established norms, is not so different from that of *Mr. Sammler's Planet*, and many of the same factors are mentioned, but the tone of the narrative is utterly different. Barth, it seems, is not taking himself seriously. He has created a novel in bad taste, one in which the Holocaust, most conspicuously, is treated as material for absurdity. He has backed out of his responsibility; the framework that recounts the story of the manuscript containing the story proper creates a series of false origins for it so as to camouflage Barth's position as the author of the book. All of this seems to disrupt one of the most fundamental assumptions that readers make about fiction, an assumption that is justified by much fiction and in particular by most of the works discussed in this study: behind the novel there stands an author who has responsibility for his text and who has used it to make some serious comment on the world he or she shares with the readers. Barth *seems* to disrupt this assumption, but perhaps it can still be made, albeit in some much restricted form; at the least, the relation of author and reader—via the narrator—must remain the center of concern for an understanding of this novel, as it is, perhaps less conspicuously, of most other novels.

There is a lot to offend people in *Giles Goat-Boy*.[1] Black people may be angry at the portrait of Croaker, an African Caliban who alternates between mass rape and docile service to his roommate and master, Eierkopf, whom he carries around and generally tends to (the black person is body, the white is mind). Women may be infuriated that action and thought are almost wholly the responsibility of men, and that the most prominent female characters are the tough cookie Madge, who attends a party while totally naked and has mustard licked off her buttocks, and, much more centrally, Anastasia, who proves her saintliness by her willingness to have sex with virtually anyone (and almost with anything). Jews should be profoundly shocked by the presentation of the Einstein-Oppenheimer figure, Max Spielman, with his grotesque dialect ("Der goats is humaner than der men, and der men is goatisher than der goats") and by the frivolity of many of the references to the "Moishiocaust"—starting with the name, which is derived from the Moishian race that in this novel obviously represents the Jews, and perhaps reaching its nadir in the joke, admittedly attributed to the villainous Stoker, about the biochemist who wanted to fireproof the Moishians and so ate nothing but asbestos bagels. Intellectuals will be offended by the picture of Eierkopf, a vast head and shrunken body who entertains himself by watching coeds undressing though a telescope. Southerners, outdoor men, and pioneers will be indignant at the treatment of Peter Greene, the Huck Finn grassroots redneck who has blinded himself in one eye by smashing a mirror in which he thinks he sees another man ogling his fiancée. Christians will be none too pleased to find the Goat-Boy, a self-appointed savior of the fictional world, wondering if at his final humiliation people will "flip a penny for the golden fleece they dressed me in" (811). Even white Anglo-Saxon Protestants may feel victimized by the image of Ira Hector, the richest man in the world of the book, close to the seat of power since he is the brother of a former president, who is literally too mean to give anyone the time of day.

Not only does the novel indulge in coarse caricature of a number of stereotypes, it consists to a large extent of events that it would be an understatement to call tasteless. A climactic moment is the "memorial service" at the end of the "second reel" of volume 1. George, the hero and narrator, has been brought up as a goat. This situation has given him a good deal of experience of sexual congress with nanny goats but little understanding of the sexual attitudes of humans. On his way to become a Hero and Grand Tutor—in effect a savior—in the university campus which constitutes the whole of the known world, he sees Anastasia exposing her body in order to entice Croaker, by whom she is then raped. George's companion, George Herrold, a half-witted but kindly black man, plunges into the river and drowns. On arriving at the campus, George eventually finds his way to a large party where the body of Herrold is displayed, and he is maliciously advised that as an act of tribute to his deceased friend and guide, he should service Anastasia—in the animal sense of the word. This he does before a large audience, accompanied by solemn music (referred to as "the swelling organ").

The humor in the book, when not offensive, is often feeble. The low point comes in the implausible jargon of the Russian (or Nikolayan) characters, who are given to a haphazard form of English involving multiple suffixes. This culminates in the death of Chementinski, whose last word is "Gratituditynesshoodshipcy" (805). There is also brilliantly witty comedy in the novel. Notably the Oedipus parody, *Taliped Decanus*, if blatantly disproportionate in length to its place in the novel, is one of the most consistently inventive pieces of humor in any modern writing. The bad jokes are meant to be bad; the reader is meant to be embarrassed. This is voluntary kitsch.

These points are worth stressing because it is possible to write criticism of *Giles Goat-Boy* that gives the impression that it is a thoughtful and complex account of such things as postwar history, mythology, morality and personal salvation, rationality and intuition, ego and id, and culture and nature. It *is* an account of these things, and they are important things, but the first thing to be said is that it is an account written in the vein of farce and outrage. History repeats itself as farce, Marx said and Barth repeats (FB, 72). The farce here is not just an ironic judgment, like Marx's judgment of Napoleon III, an unworthy successor to Napoleon I; it is a blatant affront to the reader's sense of decorum.

Of course, this is one of the first things that Barth himself tells us. The story that constitutes most of *Giles Goat-Boy* is presented as a manuscript which has arrived at a publisher's by devious routes, and that some of the editors are disposed to reject; the first pages of the novel include four editors' reports. The first one printed warns the reader (and the editor-in-chief) precisely of the scandalousness of the book: "here fornication, adultery, even rape, yea murder itself (not to mention self-deception, treason, blasphemy, whoredom, duplicity, and wilful cruelty to others) are not only represented for our delectation but at times approved of and even recommended! On aesthetic grounds too (though they pale before the moral), the work is objectionable; the rhetoric is extreme, the conceit and action wildly implausible, the interpretation of history shallow and patently biased, the narrative full of discrepancies and badly paced, at times tedious, more often excessive; the form, like the style, is unorthodox, unsymmetrical, inconsistent" (9). We could hardly have put it better ourselves. Editor A has named a possible reader response in advance and made the reader self-conscious about the risk of repeating his views. This was the 1960s, of course. Much in the tone of this judgment no doubt suggested a morality and an aesthetics of caution or restriction, rather than the adventurousness that was readily confused with authenticity at the time. But even allowing for that, readers are being prepared to ask what sort of "delectation" there is in a literature of excess. The following—and more favorable—account still uses the word "excessive," applying it to the fictive author's previous work (which may be not unlike *The Sot-Weed Factor*), but puts it in the context of a new aesthetic: "he declares it his aim purely to astonish; where others strive for truth, he admits his affinity for lies, the more enormous the better. . . . He turns his back on what is the case, rejects the familiar for the amazing, embraces artifice and extravagance" (11). Critics have recognized Barth's own concern to "originate things that are not the case."[2] Do we judge by the moral standards of everyday reality (even if the reader's morality is a little more liberal than editor A's) or do we accept an amoral surprisingness as the essence of art? The answer has to be complicated precisely by the fact that the manuscript—as opposed perhaps to the author John Barth or to the author within the book, JB—does seem to lay claim to truthfulness. The reader is not of course likely to share editor D's view that the book doesn't need to be judged because it's a revelation. The reader knows it's a novel; if it reveals anything, it's what we think—already but inexplicitly—about growth and salvation, and this fictive sort of revealing—indirectly suggested by editor D's claim that "suffering the lie, we come to truth" (15)—depends on the reader's acceptance that the book speaks to us about ourselves.

Authors have been explicit about this relationship to the reader often enough, since *Tristram Shandy*, at least, and many modern critics have located the significance of fiction in the developing responses of the reader, and the extent to which the reader can identify himself or herself with the implied reader of the book. Given these things, the author of *Giles Goat-Boy* seems to have made his job as difficult as possible. The point is made toward the end of the novel, when George comes across someone reading. This is a "pimpled maid, thin and udderless as Mrs. Rexford but infinitely less prepossessing" who is "involved with" a large novel. Answering George's question, she returns to her reading, and George blesses this "mild, undistinguished creature" for her helpfulness, without which his text would be an endless fragment. At this point she reads aloud the words "-less fragment" (770). She is reading *Giles Goat-Boy*. The implied reader has become explicit, and a reader is obviously a harmless but unappealing sort of person to be. The point is nicely made; there is a sort of magic charm in the superimposition of the act of reading on the events one reads about, and after all, not many people could really object to being thought less glamorous than Mrs. Rexford (apparently Jackie Kennedy). In any case the reader is not likely to be really offended, this time; real readers are not actually like the fictive reader (many of them are not female, and those who are are not all pimpled or udderless). In fact Barth has been displaying his modesty; he has invented for himself a devoted reader (she has got to page 770, after all, as the actual reader has, and deserves approbation) but one who is not very remarkable. Barth has already shown his modesty in allowing himself to be denounced by editor C: "I see him at last alone, unhealthy, embittered, desperately unpleasant, perhaps masturbative, perhaps alcoholic or insane if not a suicide. We all know the pattern" (14). But perhaps this is not the real author either, but a deflection of the real author into the trivially malicious imagination of a reader.

The real reader may not wish to be mild and undistinguished, but is he or she the reader invoked by the editor-in-chief at the beginning, when he calls for faith and expects suspicion? All fiction reading depends on a sort of faith: not the faith that the novel is literally truthful, but the faith that our persistence in reading will be rewarded by some kind of interest or entertainment. (Barth elsewhere insists that history reading also calls for a sort of faith [L, 298].) A great deal in the book encourages us to constant skepticism, starting with the elaborate distancing of the authorship of the main story, which is perhaps drafted by George—whose memory is imperfect and whose sanity has perhaps been affected by his exposure to the Belly of the computer—amended by WESCAC, mixed up by a careless janitor with JB's own manuscript (which as Tanner points out has a close resemblance to the novel we are reading), and has acquired a "post-tape," which may be spurious, as indicated in a postscript that may itself be spurious (or has perhaps been written by George's son Giles) and has been revised to an unclear extent by JB.[3] The standard assumption that the author gives authority to his text is conspicuously undermined here.[4] Furthermore, personality is itself fictional: George comments on the "plaster fills" by which he has completed his self-image (113) and notes, in the same passage, that "self-knowledge is improvisation" (114), and much later that "I had invented myself as I had invented my name, and it was to myself I'd present my card (already 'properly signed') when I'd passed by the Finals" (739). George accepts no outside examiner, no standard of truth or rightness outside his own invention; the whole book is the spectacle of the fictional imagination at work, with the recognition that, absolute as this remark of George's may sound, his adventures are in fact based systematically on the model of the Hero of worldwide legend, as formulated by Raglan and Campbell (and elegantly systematized by Barth in his essay "Mystery and Tragedy" [*FB*, 41–54] and repeated in *Letters*, 646–50, debated in *Once upon a Time*, 313–16). The imagination—and the self of the narrator in whom the reader needs some kind of faith—is therefore a freeing from any test of objectivity (of the kind practiced by positivistic science or history) and a play of variations on a set pattern. And for Barth, once a jazz arranger, the idea of theme and variation is never far away.

Much of the brilliance of the text (as critics have pointed out) lies in the fact that Barth provides for the mythical cycle at least four kinds of equivalence in real life (the mythical structure, in Barth's own phrase, points *down* to literal reality, unlike *The Natural,* where the real points *up* to the myth): the structures of a modern university, the events of world and American history since World War II, features of European culture since the Greeks, including the legends and ethos of specific religions, and finally a series of images of separateness or unity which relates to a range of current conceptions that can be conveniently labeled as structuralism and poststructuralism, to the belief that significance comes from orderly differentiation and the belief that differentiation is artificial and restrictive.[5] This, in turn, implies imitation of a number of literary genres: bildungsroman, allegory, romance, religious tract;[6] the effect, it has been neatly said, is to make Giles a "novel-long pun."[7] The reader certainly finds a great deal of ingenuity and wit in these things, but he or she may have a lot of reservations and anxieties about them. So McConnell, overall an admirer of the novel, speaks of its "oddly bald, transparent allegory" and of its "clever, but painfully obvious" historical references—though he manages to find in them a serious "confrontation with history."[8]

We feel uneasy with the allegorical parallels partly because the equivalences may seem trivial, arbitrary, or partial, partly because they interfere with each other. Triviality: Aristotle appears as Entelechus, Christ as Enoch, the Japanese as Amaterasus; these tricks do little other than declare that the world of the novel is not the world the reader knows outside it. Arbitrariness: a witty passage describes the categories of student miscreant held in the campus's Main Detention: the ground floor holds loafers, procrastinators, and students who refuse to choose a major, together with the mentally defective and the invincibly wrongheaded. Below this ground-floor limbo are three subterranean floors arranged in circles around a sink hole, immediately above which is a single cell for "any who undid in flunkèd wise his professor, department-head, dean, chancellor, or—most heinous treason—his Grand Tutor" (493–94). Main Detention is, in other words, a transposition of Dante's *Inferno* (or, to confuse things a bit, of the *Campus Cantos* mentioned above, p. 150). The joke is a charming one, at least for academics, but it focuses on what is in any case a major limitation in the concept of the novel. The joke consists in finding equivalents for all the vices punished in the Christian hell. This of course means that they become trivial: betraying a head of department is betrayal, sure enough, but it may seem less serious than the betrayals of Judas, Brutus, and Cassius, who hold the corresponding position in Dante; it may even look like a normal bit of academic politics (of the kind satirized in many novels before and after this one)—so that the fact that the text places it as the most abysmal sin is an ironic pointer to the confined horizons of an academic author. Indeed, the whole vast and ingenious conceit of the world as a university is amusing and not entirely gratuitous given the recent great expansion of university education, but what strikes one very often is how strained and implausible it is. The campus is subject—as campuses were in the 1960s—to campus riots; these may seem a callous reduction of the world wars they supplant in the author's system, and they produce, as his imagination idles, the "quiet riot" that corresponds to the cold war. The reader knows what a cold war is, but what could a quiet riot have been? There isn't an answer; a neat oxymoron is its own justification.

What counts in a university, of course, is knowledge, not money (isn't it?), and the powerful people are those who have knowledge. But this has gotten mixed up with a satire on the primary importance of money in modern national and international history, so that the dictatorship of the proletariat advocated by Communists, a doctrine at least intelligible in its time, becomes the Sovereignty of the Bottom Percentile advocated by the Student Unionists (93), a doctrine without any conceivable foundation. Barth admitted in a later work the risk of trivialization in his mythical novels (*OT*, 120); in *Giles Goat-Boy* the whole work integrates triviality into imaginative vitality. The point is powerfully put by Tanner, who speaks of Barth "going to perverse lengths to demonstrate how he can equivocate about, trivialise and undermine his own inventions" in a "constantly dissolving plurality of versions and combinations."[9] The admirer of Barth has to accept a lot of this and to like literary perversity and dissolving plurality.

The problematic nature of all these equivalences is announced at the very beginning of George's story: "George is my name; my deeds have been heard of in Tower Hall, and my childhood has been chronicled in the *Journal of Experimental Psychology*." The tone is heroic. There is the proud declaration of the name—which may be either an everyday given name or the name of a saint—the deeds, the chronicling, and Tower Hall sounds like the site of some medieval celebration, until we discover that it is an academic address. The bathos comes sharply with the title of the journal. George knows enough about the world of learning to provide proper citation. So who is he? A hero, with a hero's simplicity and his right to boast? Or is he an experimental subject, usurping the pride of a scholar? We are warned that the central voice of the book is going to be one that shifts, not just from sentence to sentence, but from phrase to phrase. The comedy is the author's superiority, it is his teasing of his reader, who is being compelled to read provisionally, to hold the natural interpretation of a sentence (as the sign of a certain kind of mind) in abeyance; he or she has to learn to read fictionally. The reader has to be conscious that the author has invented multiple voices to formulate visions, of which none may be true or decent. (The similarity to the thinking of Bakhtin is clear enough, though I do not know if Barth is familiar with Bakhtin's work.) *The Sot-Weed Factor* and *Giles Goat-Boy*, Barth says in his famous essay "The Literature of Exhaustion" are "novels which imitate the form of the Novel, by an author who imitates the role of the Author" (*FB, 72*). The phrase elegantly defines Barth's work, as well as a lot of what is called postmodernism; in fact it suggests a lot about previous novels too, where there is perhaps always some sense that the voice of the implied author is not fully endorsed by any real person (whereas in everyday practical activity real persons have to "stand over" the things they say). Putting this another way, farce, parody, ingenious allegory, excess, and offensiveness are ways of writing that train us to reject the words we read.

So why should one continue to read? Isn't the easiest way to reject Barth's (or George's) words to throw the book into the corner of the room? It is true of course that the unreliable and objectionable narrator has been common in fiction (especially since the mid-nineteenth century, with such works as *Notes from the Underground*): Barth provides an instance in his Tod Andrews in *The Floating Opera*. One reads on in *The Floating Opera* in part because one is fascinated by Tod's impressive lucidity and humor, and because he exercises wholeheartedly the egoism most people repress, and in part because one knows that behind the malevolent Tod is an author whom one can assume to be more nearly normal. But what if the objectionable character appears to *be* the author? At this stage let us hazard an hypothesis: the reader reads on because people do like being astonished, as editor B suggests, and because one can be astonished by the variety, as well as by the extremity, of Barth's voices. He is not simply the pornographer depicting rape after rape, not simply the crude humorist satirizing simple targets such as the redneck and the Russian, not even simply the eccentric stylist producing exotic vocabulary and overwrought syntax and morphology. He is also the writer who is capable of what appears to be gravity of feeling, dignity of phrasing, and subtlety of argument. The model that comes most readily to mind is that of Rabelais, with his alternation of humanistic solemnity and crude banter. Barth, that is, sets us the task of comprehending a sensibility capable of embracing both ready-made prejudice and original and precise thinking. Burlingame, in Barth's previous work, chose variety from distaste for what "ha[d] been the case"

(*SWF*, 432); in *Giles*, a similar mingled love and distaste for the given gives rise to constant mobility of tone and reference. The parodic form of the novel, Ziegler acutely points out, is a way of reconciling the unchanging form of myth with the actual changeability of experience.[10] But even parody, it seems, can include gravity: much of the novel appears to discuss important issues in a way the reader might find informative or persuasive.

Here is perhaps the most elusive aspect of the work. Clearly Barth is very well informed about a mass of theories of life, formal and informal, such as came to the fore in great variety during the intellectual and social ferment of the 1960s: amongst others, the Pre-Schoolers, the Curricularists, the Evolutionaries, the Ismists, and the neo-Enochians (Romantics, the equivalents of the rationalists, the evolutionists, the Buddhists, and the modernist Christians). Does one learn to assess these ideas in reading the novel? Does the novel have, as Conrad claimed all true novels should, a "moral discovery" to communicate, and if so does the frenetic discussion of ideas contribute to it?

The first answer is that, to a large extent, the reader doesn't learn from the ideas in the book but recognizes them. Just as the reader recognizes that Reg Hector is "really" Dwight Eisenhower and that "The Campus . . . hath not anything more fair" is "really" Wordsworth, he or she recognizes that the diabolical sensualist and seducer Maurice Stoker, stoking the fires of Hell in the Power House that is essential to the survival of the Campus, is the libido, the id, the Dionysian power of will which underlies the rationalized ideologies of East and West; Nietzsche and Freud are reduced to the banality they have become by the later twentieth century. The brute Croaker carrying the almost disembodied intellectual Eierkopf is the body linked to the mind and detested by the mind: thousands of years of puzzlement and tension are reduced to absurdity. The animal naïveté of George facing the corrupt sophistication of almost everyone else tells yet again the story of innocence and experience, of the fortunate fall (so Max—debatably—explains the moral of Taliped Decanus by reference to the biblical temptation to "be like Founders . . . with knowledge of Truth and Falsehood," 383). Of course there are no new ideas. Humanity is subject to cyclology, in the book's own term; as the hero repeats the adventures of all previous heroes, the novelist repeats the systems of twentieth-century thought.

In one way at least this view of culture as kitsch comes to a special acuity, and that is in the characters' search for the Answer. The university depends on a final exam; there is a Question, and so there has to be an Answer, which is right or wrong. Or so the characters think. The allegory of *Giles Goat-Boy* implies that life too has a final exam and a Question and Answer, and the characters are eager to assert what the Answer is. For Stoker "the Answer's power" (226); for Sear it is beauty (though this amounts in practice to a perverse sexuality), or on another occasion "Knowledge of the University" (436); for Rexford, "light and order" are what make for a Graduate School (446). Peter Greene thinks (before he is disillusioned) that his wife is the Answer (278). Eierkopf quotes the saying that "Graduation is a state of mind" (511). Max, faithful to a certain sense of Jewishness, declares that "Suffering is Graduation" (497). George suspects that "There's more than one road to Commencement Gate" (212) but later comes to think that Graduation is the recognition of failure (450), and the protean or postmodern Bray asserts that all the divisions of the university are equally irrelevant to the Answer (480). Or then again, the Answer, in Buddhist style, may be unutterable (which would make conventional examination very difficult, 677, 673).

The whole framework of the book prevents us from asking if there is an examination at all and who is grading it, and that framework is in itself absurd. The multiplicity of Answers that people seek corresponds to the fragmentation of modern culture, manifest through the world in which Christianity has lost its hegemony. What we have here is a comic demonstration of the incoherence of the modern mind, implying that the search for a solution to life is a sign of a vital individual commitment and is inevitably mistaken. Life is error, the book nearly says. JB's (possibly abandoned) novel is about a Cosmic Amateur, "a man enchanted with history, geography, nature, the people around him—everything that is the case—because he saw its arbitrariness but couldn't understand or accept its finality," a person in short who treats the world as comic fiction. But the Amateur is to learn—through "the fiascos of his involvements with men and women"—to "aspire to a kind of honorary membership in the human fraternity" (24). The implications are complex. George never sees the world from outside, like the Cosmic Amateur; he does gain some access to human fraternity, but his starting point is goatish spontaneity of action. The figures that do regard the world as comic spectacle are the author and the reader, for whom the author himself is a comic spectacle. Comedy means rationality, Scholes notes; he also comments that the "fabulation" of *Giles Goat-Boy* arises from the clash between the philosophical and the mythical.[11] Does comedy lead author and reader to greater humanity in the course of the novel? Or is that the work of the mythic? Perhaps. The final—admittedly apocryphal—words of George invite sympathy for aging and isolation (one critic even sees them as tragic).[12] More debatably, the execution of Max, in the last pages of the Revised New Syllabus proper, has seemed to some readers to be a moving account of a sacrifice; others may feel it to be a ludicrous and perverse piece of theatricality, in which Max's death is overshadowed by the multiple illusions of Harold Bray. What one must add, certainly, is that the real author John Barth came to a positive, healthy morality in the later works from *Sabbatical* on, with their celebration not only of storytelling but of marital love, friendship, and adventure, and their denunciation of arbitrary power.

There are some aspects of *Giles Goat-Boy* itself that call for a sobriety of response like the kind that *Sabbatical* invites. Already there is the intensity of deeply felt sexuality, in George's minute examination of Anastasia's body; there is the clearly formulated denunciation of the postwar United States, with "its oppression of Frumentians, its lawless Informationalism, its staggering wastefulness, its pillage of natural resource and despoil of natural beauty, its hostility to learning and refinement, its apotheosis of the lowest percentile, its vulgarity, inflated self-esteem, self-righteousness, self-deception, sentimentality, hypocrisy, artificiality, simple-mindedness, naïve optimism, concupiscence, avarice, self-contradiction, ignorance and general fatuity" (508). The opening is still in the vein of the fantasy, and the Frumentians as black people and Informationalism as capitalism do something to distance the reader from real judgment. There are more problems as the list goes on: can America suffer both from capitalism and from an apotheosis of the poor? Can it be both artificial and naïve? Perhaps it can, or perhaps the charge is of a shotgun variety, but there seems little doubt that this is a patriotic — albeit conservative — American facing the failings of his own country. The voice, that is, is neither that of the Goat-Boy nor that of the creator of the Cosmic Amateur; it is a voice to which the reader can respond with real seriousness.

A like seriousness appears, too, in many elegant and suggestive phrases: if George's shift from a policy of unlimited distinction to one of unlimited merging and thence to one of unlimited ambiguity is the matter of a parable, schematic and thinly motivated, Max's comment that it is Mind "that tells you there's a you, that's different from me" is an acute hint at the nature of individuality (even if the tone returns to the grotesque in midsentence as Max adds that Mind "separates the goats from the sheeps," 85), while the later anxiety as to the distinction between "flunkèd Contradiction" and "passèd Paradox" (778) focuses a great deal of contemporary thought. So too does Max's biblical slogan that "Self-knowledge is always bad news" (121). And what could put one of Barth's deepest loves more eloquently than the Goat-Boy's discovery, at his very first contact with human civilization, of "the miracle called story" (54)?

So valid speech, the speech that installs a community of accepted values between author and reader, comes occasionally in *Giles Goat-Boy*, amidst a mass of words that are repellent, incongruous, or banal, words that fascinate only by their lack of restraint and by the energy and enterprise of sheer accumulation to which they bear witness. How can they be recognized? The way effective speech is usually recognized: by the precision and wit of their images, by the control of their rhythms, by the accuracy of their vocabulary, and by their handling of the key terms of the languages that exist outside the novel. The reader needs to be alert to identify these things; he or she needs to discriminate them from the crude, inert, and unreflective matter that surrounds them. The reader needs to see how far the author of *Giles Goat-Boy* has attained what the author of the "Anonymiad" hopes for: "Whimsic fantasy, grub fact, pure senseless music—none in itself would do; to embody all and rise above each, in a work neither longfaced not idiotly grinning, but adventuresome, passionately humored, merry with the pain of insight, wise and smiling in the terror of life—that was my calm ambition" (*LiF*, 198). Giles perhaps comes closer to the idiot grin than is comfortable, but discomfort is precisely what variety calls for, and discomfort makes for discrimination. Discrimination in language is surely what the novel does teach us; if there is an "ultimate seriousness" in this "gigantic hoax," it must lie in the experience of reading.[13] Precise reading is the humane value the novelist and the reader bring away from this "great trifle," as Barth—perhaps regretfully—noted that some readers thought it, from this "brilliant frivolity," in Tanner's phrase.[14] The key to attaining a clear evaluation of Barth's writing is in a heightened sensitivity to reading. Or in the words of the later novels, "the Key to the Treasure is the Treasure."

5
Doctorow: *The Book of Daniel*

G*ILES GOAT-BOY* OFFERS A VAST PANORAMA OF THE CONDITION OF the modern world—political, cultural, personal—and deviates immensely from the known reality. E. L. Doctorow's *Book of Daniel*, on the contrary, is extremely closely tied to one specific incident in history and reproduces many of the real circumstances with great fidelity. It is an incident that caused intense controversy at the time and was still a matter of passionate debate when the novel was written: the Isaacson family, who are the central figures of the novel, are unmistakably (despite some departures from fact) modeled on the family of the Rosenbergs, executed as communist spies in 1953. The execution of the Rosenbergs is an issue of major political importance (and aroused strong feelings throughout Europe as well as in the United States) for two reasons: if the Rosenbergs were innocent (which the most recent historical research suggests was not the case) or if their punishment was disproportionate to the gravity of their crime, then the quality of American justice is undermined, and justice appears to be subservient to political expediency; and if this is so, the wave of anti-communist feeling that was manifest at the time of the trial and executions, and which is clearly allied to the McCarthyite processes of elimination of suspected communists that were being carried out at the same time, can be seen as a hysterical product of a cold war mentality which is a blemish on American civilization rather than a proper response to Russian aggression.

Doctorow discusses these issues with a strong sense of how painful they were for individuals concerned, and for America, but he displaces the discussion. First, he refuses to answer the central question of the couple's guilt. Second, he focuses attention not on them, but on the effect of their notoriety on their son as an adult some years later. Third, the presentation of the son and his generation—the generation of the rebellious 1960s, the same generation mocked by Barth—uses a range of the fictional techniques of the novel so as to stress the absence of objective knowledge in this matter and the painful imaginative construction of a past by the derelict son. There is frequent variation of forms of language, each form implying its own set of values, which may be incompatible with those implied in other parts of the book. There is the shifting of focalization. There is the slipping from first- to third-person narration. History becomes fiction, then; uncertainty about the real gives way to a conspicuous inventiveness that richly exploits the resources of fiction.

The distancing of the novel from any simple sense of the factual is apparent in the perspective of the son, Daniel Isaacson, as it is presented to us through his own consciousness. On his way to a demonstration against the execution of his parents, Daniel, aged about ten, stops to admire two mounted policemen (19).[1] But he feels guilty about this, because he knows they are reactionaries. How many other children would know they are reactionaries? Daniel does, because his parents are communists and have taught him the right vocabulary. Language divides him from mainstream America and from his own feelings. The point is made more explicitly later. Traveling to a Paul Robeson concert—at an even earlier age—Daniel knows that Robeson is "a proud black Communist" and that the event will be "a great moment for the forces of progressivism and civilization" (48). He knows, as the adult Daniel reflects in the next paragraph, because his father has told him. Language is the product of an older generation; it forms sensibility. Daniel, as an adult, is seeking to write an account of his past, without making himself a slave of the past or of his parents: he specifically rejects "liv[ing] in faith or memorial to the people who had betrayed you" (64); like many Doctorow characters, as many critics have noted, his dilemma is to find a language in which to do it.[2]

One language he tries is that of scholarship, and especially of objective research: he reflects, like a biographer, that people "must have" acted in such and such a way (8, 63). He quotes authorities: Horowitz, Shannon, Kennan, E. H. Carr (a whole paragraph on Bukharin, 55). He comments that "many historians have noted this phenomenon" (25). He includes documents: letters of various characters and essayistic writing on general matters such as the history of American literature and a reasonably well-documented and distinctly polemic account of American foreign policy in the 1940s and 1950s, which implies an explanation of the victimization of the Isaacsons. All this may seem to imply a "real" perspective, within which Daniel's private life can find its place. But does it? Is writing record, interpretation, or imagination? Whichever it is, is the act of writing founded in the individual, in the myths of society and tradition, or in the objective world? If the objective world, is it the objectivity of Marxist theory or of scholarly discipline?

Daniel's objectivity may seem a tribute to his father's Marxist respect for impersonality and for the historical process: "he claimed to believe in the insignificance of personal experience within the pattern of history" (33). But this novel, like Doctorow's other novels, refutes that view; he writes about the significance of personal experience within the pattern of history. Daniel himself is skeptical. In fact, the very passage in which Paul's view is cited is a meditation, acute and almost cynical, on the way in which the acceptance of communism fulfilled the personal needs of Daniel's parents. The radical lifestyle is a "justification": they adopt it as part of a rush for self-esteem. Daniel, in irresponsible adolescence, can justify his indifference to his parents' fate (at the time) with more open cynicism: "Whatever they did, whatever view they took, it was merely historical process operating" (65). This attitude, of course, will excuse anything; everything is inevitable and nothing is a matter of personal responsibility; "what occurs is right" he reflects a little later (73). Essentially, he rejects history, unlike his parents and sister; for him history is a threat, "that pig biting into the heart's secrets" (104). History means revolution, but revolution itself is failure: "no revolution is betrayed, only fulfilled" (56).

So the novel does not purport to be objective reporting. It is a bundle of different kinds of writing, all related to one of the poles of Daniel's experience, the beleaguered communist community of the 1940s and the bold new radical climate of the 1960s, creating not a consistently argued interpretation of them but a many-faceted context for both. Daniel also writes from personal experience, often sensitively capturing the partial impressions of a child (as when he comments on the way "fathers talked to each other in big words" [91]—though this fits strangely with his ability to quote apparently verbatim a lengthy speech by a political contact of his parents about the role of the Communist Party in the late 1940s). He reflects on his present situation, when he is concerned with his sister Susan's attempted suicide and later death in a mental hospital, with his relationship to his wife, Phyllis, and with the radical movement of the new Left, including the great demonstration in Washington against the Vietnam War, and he sometimes gives poetic expressions to his emotion. He includes a substantial and very colloquial discussion with a journalist on the fate of the parents, and a speculative assessment of their qualities or those of other characters. He reproduces (apparently in imitation of the Yiddish press) the voice of his grandmother, an immigrant whose knowledge of hardship and stoical moral sense, conservative and religious as she is, have formed the moralistic communism of the parents; he reproduces the "motherfucker" rhetoric of the radical 1960s, in odd, unattributed voices that appear in the text to upbraid Daniel. (By imitation he brackets the experiences of the 1940s communists between the immigrants who formed them and the hippies who forgot them.) The limits of his impersonality are most painfully shown in his comment on his sister, "Objectively she's dying" (215); Stalinist impersonality clashes with real anguish.

Is one of these voices Daniel's own? Is there a true Daniel? There are no true feelings that define him: he reflects ironically that his sister Susan monopolizes the family gift for having definite feelings (9); his own are uncertain, provisional, speculative. What is distinctive in him is his aestheticism: when the communist concert goers are attacked in their bus, he notes the driver's face "decorated in blood" and the "beautiful pattern of shatter" in the windows beside his mother's head (50). He is especially a literary aesthete, or pedant. Reflecting on his parents' possible guilt, he notes that they went to their deaths for crimes they did not commit, or did committ, and starts wondering about the spelling of "commit" (42). Quoting their jail correspondence—a skillful pastiche of the Rosenberg letters—he wonders if he can suspend the aesthetic judgment he feels at their outdated romanticism (they are formed by the language of the past, as he is, 198). He reflects often on his own writing (interrupted on the last page by the student demonstrations of 1967). He frequently instructs himself to "do" subjects, to "flesh out," to "strike" or not to strike drafts. He criticizes his own work as "a cheap effect" (9). He is a humorist, his black comedy extending to his parents' death: "Does Dick Really Love Liz?" a movie magazine asks. "I think if they were put on trial for their lives, he might come to love her," Daniel answers (8). He is an ironist, who recalls the photographs of himself at a White House demonstration for his parents and notes that "I played Washington when I was a kid" (260). He is conscious of the expectations implied by a style of writing (and often dismissive of them), so he rejects "this David Copperfield kind of crap" (98). He seeks to produce a text detached from the past, from politics, from selfhood; he seeks in writing to repress himself. He offers Poe as the true American revolutionary, the archetypal traitor, "that scream from the smiling face of America" (183); subversion is not scientific socialism but the irrational imagination. Daniel seems to seek, as Girgus says, a "triumph of art over ideology," but it only gradually becomes clear that art is sympathy and not negation.[3]

Daniel's artistic nihilism is not maintained throughout the book. He seeks early in the text to analyze with bleak resignation an overall disastrous course of things: "the pattern of our lives is deterioration ... the movement of our lives is towards death" (13) — and the book ends by superimposing the funerals of Susan (in connection with whom the remark is made) and of the parents (of whose death Susan's is a belated consequence); but the story of the book is that of Daniel's maturing, from the cruelty, bitterness, and aesthetic aloofness of the beginning to a gradual acceptance of responsibility and continuity, symbolized by his hiring mourners at the funeral to pray for his parents and sister according to the Jewish rites. To this extent the novel fits more with Girgus's view that art goes with maturing than with Morris's claim that Doctorow perceives a universal inauthenticity.[4]

One sort of writing that focuses the ambiguity of Daniel's development is the biblical Book of Daniel. Its relevance is strained. On the one hand the biblical Daniel is a "Beacon of Faith in a Time of Persecution" (12). The phrase might more naturally suggest the parents' steadfast faith in communism despite McCarthyite persecution rather than Daniel himself, whose capitalization of the letters in the above quotations indicate that he doesn't take the phrase very seriously — although the book perhaps tells how he seeks to attain some faith in his parents. On the other hand the biblical Daniel resembles the twentieth-century Daniel in the grievance of his heart (12) and provides a leitmotiv in the narrator's constant awareness of the vulnerability of the heart (and, often, of his own heartlessness).

Because there are so many types of writing in the novel, the text is characterized especially by transitions.[5] "The sense is not in the lineal column", a journalist in another Doctorow novel asserts[6], "but in all of them together." A case in point is the opening of the second book, "Halloween" (101). The book starts "July–August, 1967, I was very careful with Phyllis" and carries on for a paragraph about Daniel's tense relationship with his wife. The paragraph is neatly ironic toward both Phyllis and Daniel: "We considered me as our mutual problem." It ends by veering back to the production of the text itself: Phyllis dreams of moving away from New York, where Daniel can make progress with his dissertation. "I didn't disabuse her. Perhaps she could summon up my dissertation, actually create it, just by imagining me here in the library." The text then turns to the narration of a crucial event, the arrest of Paul Isaacson. It begins quite casually, even vaguely, "One autumn day, with the wind slicing through the chain-link fence around the schoolyard, and ghastly grey clouds racking into each other over the rooftops of apartment houses, Rochelle went shopping with her son, Daniel, and her baby daughter, Susan." So the story is back in the 1940s. Daniel, the apprentice writer, is setting the scene for a sinister event. The reader will know that the chain-link fence is associated with two things: separation (of the minority culture of the Isaacsons from the mainstream of the school) and death (Daniel observes a car accident in which a woman is forced through the fence by a vehicle and killed). Does the narrator Daniel know it is a symbol? Or is the reader reacting to a hint of the more crafty author Doctorow? Daniel, be that as it may, introduces again the main characters, himself and his mother and sister, as if they were all new to the reader. The narration continues for another paragraph in what is to prove to be a comically misleading way; Rochelle suddenly exclaims, "My God, it's happened." What she can see is a crowd gathered round the father's radio shop, but it is not there because Paul has been arrested, but because he has a television set in his shop (this is 1949; television was new). There is to be another twist: the Isaacson's friend Selig Mindish has been arrested. Paul, of course, reacts to this with blasé confidence in historical inevitability: "It's only the coming of Fascism so why should we be surprised" (107). Before reaching these developments, the narrator offers more historical reflections on "the shock of the supermarket," (104) which was weakening small stores, and on the relative social status of the East Side and the Bronx. Shifting briefly to his own poor progress in school, he goes on to an account of the way that schools reproduced the cold war hysteria of the time, with their atom-bomb drills—and of the way that his father had instructed him not to participate in this capitalist war mongering. He then notes "one other thing I will have to work on" (106) before getting back to the story of the television, of Mindish's arrest, of visits to the Isaacson house by FBI men over the next few days, ending with the child Daniel's sense of victimization and his shock at the dying woman in the chain-link fence. Daniel the narrator now gives up storytelling and reflects on the implications of this episode: "If they had something on them before Mindish was arraigned, why didn't they pick them up?" (112) From this he is led to an account of the Japanese form of execution known as "smoking," a paragraph that looks as if it might well be cited directly from an encyclopedia, and which anticipates painfully the detailed description of the death of the Isaacsons by electrocution in the final pages of the book.

In the space of ten pages the story of the Isaacsons has progressed through a critical stage, preceded by the writer' reflections on his writing, and interrupted by his placing of the event in historical context, from the child's eye view, by his attempt to understand—in other words, to treat his own narration as evidence of guilt or innocence—and by his horror at persecution and death. All this adds up to a picture of the writer: sophisticated, well informed, scholarly, self-aware, confident in handling his memories as evidence of historical process and of psychological development, and seeking with conscious desperation to face up to the evils of death, betrayal, and his own egoism. But this is not an integrated self; this is someone trying on different ways of being a self, speculative, reminiscent, confessional, creative, symbolic. Daniel, it has been well said, has various "selves";[7] his selves are not just those of son or husband, but those of the registers of writing he adopts.

Within this kaleidoscopic manner of writing, the issues of focalization are particularly significant. Daniel is attempting to write a coherent narrative in the third person but keeps lapsing. The novel starts by appearing immaculately objective (though this manner is interrupted by the writer's notes on his pen, notebook, and place in the library); it slips into Daniel's own consciousness ("although Daniel hadn't wanted [Phyllis] to come along, he was glad he relented"), and then into that of the drivers who pick them up: "they were inquisitive and obviously entertained to be driving these young American kids who probably smoked marijuana even though they had a baby" (4). "Obviously": the thoughts of the drivers are presented through Daniel's observation of their demeanor. But when Daniel reaches a reference to his (adoptive) father, the pretense breaks down, and he notes: "He didn't like my marrying Phyllis, neither did my mother, but of course they wouldn't say anything" (4). Daniel is no longer writing to interest an audience, but to explicate things for himself. Later the changes become sometimes very rapid, as Daniel's different personae become less distinct. Close to the end Daniel confronts Linda, the daughter of Selig Mindish: "'I don't want anyone to be afraid of me,' Daniel said. He seemed offended. . . . He massaged his forehead. I looked at Linda Mindish and saw the premature middle age at the corner of her mouth and under her eyes" (276). Daniel *seems* offended, because he is viewed from outside—by an impersonal narrator or, strangely, by Linda, his opponent. Suddenly this external viewpoint yields to Daniel's memories of former intimacy and his awareness of the great difference that has arisen between them. Even when the third person is maintained for some time, it may be blatantly artificial. For instance, the narrator recounts Susan's words to him after her suicide attempt and continues: "He listened alertly. He was not sure if she had said goodbye or good boy. He hung around for a while after that but she didn't say another thing or even acknowledge that he was in the room" (9). The first sentence is normal third-person narrative; so is the second, allowing for the novelist's prerogative of seeing into the consciousness of his characters (but is Daniel a novelist?). The third sentence goes wrong: "hung around" is the kind of word you use about yourself, partly because it is informal in register, and partly because it implies an attitude that an objective narrator couldn't safely attribute to another person; and "didn't say another thing" and "even" both imply frustration and annoyance, which are all too characteristic of Daniel's self-centeredness. The third person is a pretense. Similarly, there is a feeling of alienation in the use of free indirect discourse about oneself: "Suddenly Daniel was overwhelmed with a strong sweet sense of the holiday. . . . He was thankful to Susan for relieving the dangerous tedium of his graduate life. She would be all right" (15). Daniel's attitude is outrageous; you can't feel grateful to someone for committing suicide. "She would be all right" is his let-out. The reader knows that free indirect discourse is often ironic—since it can be its palpable falsity that shows it to be indirect discourse and not the sincere thought of the author. But in this case the ironized character *is* the author (some months earlier); the distancing of the thought entails an uneasy literary virtuosity.

The elements of narrative that most strain the reader's acceptance of the text are perhaps those in which the narrator enters into the consciousness of his parents. There are two essential passages. The first is the beginning of the trial: "His trial is held is a large, shadowed hall. Voices echo. Gestures are solemn, oratorical. In attendance are all the world's history of dead heroes of the Left" (190). The solemnity of a major historical moment is forcefully asserted. And questioned. Who is it who is aware of the presence of the dead heroes? Perhaps it is the narrator, and behind him the author; the names of Tom Mooney, the Scottsboro boys, Sacco and Vanzetti have echoed throughout the book, and the sense that the novel is one more account of a martyrdom is never far away, but it is never quite asserted either. So perhaps the dead heroes are only in Paul's mind. The next paragraph clearly shifts to his consciousness: "He sees a large square room, but a room, not a hall, and the raked jury box has leather chairs of green" (190). The solemnity of the previous vision is a mistake; this is an ordinary occasion, not a glamorous one. Paul continues to observe the people in the courtroom, the judge and counsel, and becomes aware of his own feelings: "They are counting on just the feelings I am feeling now. I will show them they can count on nothing" (192); from this he slips into a memory of his childhood. The picture of Paul's frame of mind is impressively complex:

pride, vulnerability, the patriotism of the first-generation American child, disillusion with an America that doesn't reward his kind of patriotism. This complexity is Daniel's work. He cannot know that his father was recalling his teacher Mrs. Goldstein as he sat in the courtroom; he can only combine what he knows of his dignity, what he assumes of his anxiety, what he grasps of the historical context, and what he either knows or can invent of his father's youth, and so create plausibility.

The second crucial moment comes very late in the book. Daniel has outlined to Linda an explanation of the trial and verdict. The theory is that Paul and Rochelle were deliberately sacrificed by the party to protect the identity of the real spies, and that Paul knew this, that he was in effect conspiring with Mindish to sacrifice his life for the party. Having spoken to Linda, Daniel goes on to describe his mother's feelings in the courtroom, her eagerness to make Mindish look at her as he gives evidence against her, her wish to be recognized (a recurring theme in the novel); then, as Daniel's narrative continues, Mindish looks "for one fraction of a second" (287) into her eyes: "She saw the comrade's life of terrible regret, of sad determination, one to another, and the assumption of their shared knowledge, the sexuality of it." Then she looks at her husband and sees that he knows too. Paul is not looking at her or at the witness: "while she had been shielding him from her dread he had withheld from her his one crucial perception" (287). This last phrase has a Jamesian ring, apt in the context of betrayal and exploitation and in the mind of the aesthete Daniel. A great deal is communicated by minimal means; Daniel presents us with his interpretation of Rochelle's interpretation of Mindish and of Paul, which includes their view of her own feelings. Daniel is increasingly entering into the mind of other people. He is growing into a better person; he does so because he inherits responsibility not from his parents but from his dying sister, and he does so by becoming a writer of fiction. Writing is no longer irresponsibility; it is, as for James, an assertion of moral weight (216).

But if Daniel is a fictionist, it's not quite clear how far Doctorow is. It may be possible in twenty or fifty years to read the novel as about the *kind* of situation in which the Rosenbergs and their children were placed; Doctorow in more than one interview points out the analogy with *Robinson Crusoe,* where the readers know that there was a person called Alexander Selkirk who had had the same kind of experience as Crusoe.[8] But it is difficult to believe that this is just the same *kind* of experience. To a large extent it is the *same* experience. The Isaacsons are executed for conspiracy to commit espionage, and only one couple in the United States has ever been executed for this offense. Behind

Daniel imaginatively recreating the life of his parents there stands Doctorow, systematically translating the life of the Rosenbergs into that of the Isaacsons.[9]

There is a great deal in the novel that the moderately well-informed reader will recognize: the arrest of the husband after a number of FBI visits; the brutal search of the house; the arrest of the wife after she has given evidence to a grand jury and while her children are left in the hands of a neighbor; the charge of conspiracy and the arguments in court that refer to treason rather than espionage; the prohibitive bail demanded; the location of the trial at Foley Square; the apparent sympathy of the judge for the prosecution; the Jewish background of judge and all the counsel; the listing of large number of witnesses who do not in fact appear; the arrest of another alleged conspirator (in reality William Perl) in the course of the trial; the reliance of the prosecution essentially on the evidence of an alleged accomplice who had already confessed but had not been sentenced, even the "moronic smile" of this witness; the biased charge to the jury; the use of the accusation and sentence as a lever to oblige the accused to betray further associates; the criticisms made of the defending counsel's tactics; and the presence of the children at the large-scale protest demonstrations and their regular visits to their parents in Sing Sing. All these things are taken very directly from the real history.

This ensures verisimilitude: of course this kind of thing could happen; it has happened. Furthermore, there is an efferent effect.[10] Our feelings toward the real world are affected: we feel angry that people could have been condemned to death on evidence that was debatable and by legal procedures which were not irreproachably just, and we feel curious as to whether, imperfect as the proof adduced in court may have been, the Rosenbergs were in fact guilty. (When Morris claims that for Doctorow texts do not necessarily presuppose a reality outside the text, the word "necessarily" calls for a lot of emphasis.[11]) The book doesn't answer our curiosity; we share Daniel's doubts. Frustration is part of the point of the novel (so we learn through the novel that acceptance of uncertainty can coincide with growing wisdom).

But there is also a great deal in the novel that doesn't support this efferent sympathy. The Rosenberg sons, one must say, though deeply disturbed by their parents' arrest and execution (and apparently somewhat hyperactive before), seem to have matured soundly, have no doubts as to their parents' innocence, and are deeply appreciative of their adoptive parents and of all those who campaigned for the Rosenbergs. (Robert in fact reproaches Doctorow for his criticisms of these people.[12]) These facts may not be relevant to an attempt to assess Doctorow's imaginative response to their situation, since they were not publicly known at the time of his writing; they simply emphasize that his novel is a conception of what their experience plausibly *might have been*. The novel is not about—or not just about—the Rosenbergs; it is about the Isaacsons. It is quite proper to say, as Bloom makes Doctorow say in his fantasized dialogue with a Rosenberg son, that the Rosenbergs are the *occasion* for the novel.[13] Levine provides a brief summary of the ways *The Book of Daniel* diverges from the known facts.[14] The main differences are these: the Rosenbergs had two sons and not a son and daughter; they were denounced not by an older friend of the family but by Mrs. Rosenberg's brother; and the charges did not involve copying atomic plans onto dental photographic plates. The Rosenberg were not excluded from the Communist Party immediately after their arrest, since they had nominally left it some time before. Julius Rosenberg did complete college and Ethel didn't, whereas the situation of the Isaacsons is the reverse. They did not break off contact with each other after the trial. Ethel's mother did not die before the arrests. The Rosenbergs were tried with a third defendant, Morton Sobell. Their advocate, unlike Ascher, was already associated with left-wing causes. The changes emphasize the child's partial comprehension, sexualize motives (the relationship between Daniel and Susan has an uneasy air of sexual connivance, and Selig Mindish's hostility to the Isaacsons is attributed to his frustrated attraction to Rochelle, as well as his insecurity about his citizenship), integrate the decline of the Isaacsons into a natural sequence (the arrests in autumn fit in with the pattern of the book, which moves from Memorial Day through Halloween to the end of the year), and make the accusations less plausible than they were in reality (Julius Rosenberg was not an accomplished scientist, but he did not need to be in order to reproduce the information given by his brother-in-law, a technician in Los Alamos; Paul Isaacson would have needed some scientific expertise to reproduce diagrams on dental film). They foreground Daniel's present at the expense of his parents' past: confused as to his own origins, resentful both of his parents and of the state that destroyed them, sexually insecure, less concerned with facts than with his role as an outsider to everyone, to mainstream America and to his family, to the Old Left and to the New Left.

Of course he is an ironic outsider to the myths of America reproduced in the kitsch art of Disneyland, a kitsch however that is not entirely alien to the true art of Doctorow: the West, the future, childhood, the colonial explorer (and we may recall that Doctorow had started his literary career by reproducing—and criticizing—the myth of the West). Daniel, with savage wit, summarizes the truths of American life that are manifest in these pop myths, ending with the view that "we are able to walk on air, but only so long as our illusion supports us" (294). Daniel himself, for the reader, is a myth; he has replaced the real children of the Rosenbergs, and in doing so has enabled us to grasp something of the deprivation they must have lived through. Daniel, like all fiction, is an illusion. Bukharin, he points out, has become a character in a novel (presumably *Darkness at Noon*) (54); Daniel is a Rosenberg who has become a character in a novel. In a book about loyalty, betrayal, and acceptance, Doctorow is both loyal and disloyal to history, and perhaps that means that he accepts history, not as in itself purposive, but as a place to contemplate our vulnerability and the multiplicity of our needs. Doctorow is writing a new kind of historical novel, it has been rightly said;[15] it is one where there is neither fiction nor nonfiction, but only narrative.[16]

The balance of loyalty and disloyalty, of truth and poetry, is most elusive when we have neither reproduction nor avoidance of fact, but inventions that are compatible with reality, what Doctorow calls a speculative history.[17] Were the Rosenbergs at Peekskill when communist concert goers were attacked by a mob? Quite possibly. Did Julius play a heroic role on that occasion? Who knows? Who is the communist leader who attends the grandmother's funeral? He speaks of the Browder heresy, and so is presumably a member of the Foster group that had replaced Earl Browder at the head of the Communist Party, but the hint is of a closer possible identification that the child Daniel can't make. (Similarly, who is the Catholic gang leader who assassinates Dutch Schultz and his gang in *Billy Bathgate*?) The reader is conscious of the author at work: it is not Daniel inventing here; it is the author who is ingeniously combining his invented characters with real events.

So too when Doctorow attributes to his fictional characters acts or qualities that the reader can verify in the historical record. The novel appears to place us in a fictional world where the Isaacsons have replaced the Rosenbergs. But in several instances the reader is both left within this fictional world and also closely reminded of the real world, in which the Rosenbergs do exist. What Jewish critic accused the Isaacsons of exploiting a religion in which they didn't believe? Leslie Fiedler, in his article on the Rosenbergs.[18] What attorney does Paul Isaacson describe as "an unctuous little b——"? Roy Cohn, later notorious as an assistant to Joseph McCarthy. Who is called Talkative Tom? Harry Gold, a frequent witness in the series of spy trials at the time. And what of the hypothesis of the "other couple," which Linda rejects as a "tenuous, fragile piece of nonsense" (288)? Daniel tells her that "a lot of mythology grew up about them," and this mythology seems to be the basis for the sacrifice theory (and sacrifice is one of Doctorow's own myths, right up to *City of God*). Can the reader find any justification for it? Well, it could be a reference to the Cohens, American communists who left the United States at the appropriate time and were later arrested in Britain under the name of Kroger (but did they have children? No press reports from the time indicate that they did). Or it could be the best-known couple of young communists who had two children and were associated with spying: the Rosenbergs. Are we in some alternative world in which the imaginary Isaacsons save the real Rosenbergs? The point seems to be obscurely hinted in the remark, much earlier, that "the couple in the poster got away" (43), but one may be reluctant to accept this, since this imaginary world includes McCarthy, Baruch, Truman, Eisenhower, the march on the Pentagon, and many more aspects of the world we know. Especially one may be reluctant to believe it because the Isaaacsons clearly *are* the Rosenbergs. The reader is left with a sense of ambiguity, the ambiguity that Doctorow, referring specifically to historic trials such as that of the Rosenbergs, considered to be characteristic of the true novel.[19] The hidden truth fascinates. The reader wants to know more; he or she perceives that one can know no more. The reader may long to know who is truthful, who is good, how one learns to be true and good, and the longing for certainty is perhaps what history can finally give us.

6
Morrison: *Beloved*

Beloved is a reminder of the past. It reminds—or, sometimes at least, informs—the reader of the crucial period of American history around the Civil War, from the development of abolitionist feeling and of opportunities for black people of escaping slavery and the South, to the postwar epoch in which black people had attained freedom but were far from attaining integration into any coherent American society. It brings home with passionate outrage the horrors of cruelty and humiliation visited upon black people by whites at that time and the deprivation of personality and self-respect these could produce. It displays the reason that black people may still have to feel that they are no more than the object of a white perception and to resent the demeaning power of that perception. It revives the history of the United States as it tells the story of a woman who has to cope with the revival of her individual past, with its burdens of guilt, isolation, and deprivation.

The story, as is well known, is both true and barely believable: Morrison's Sethe is based on the real Margaret Garner, who killed her own daughter rather than allow her to fall into the hands of a slave owner.[1] This is a story of a woman driven beyond what we generally consider to be the limits of the natural; it concerns an act of excess that is difficult for readers to understand imaginatively within the normal sequence of history, and which is difficult for the character to integrate into the natural sequence of her own life. But Morrison's aim is to present, precisely, an exorcism of the past: not simply a forgetting of the past, but a recognition of the past and a transformation of it from private obsession to public commemoration. The effect of this is dual. On the one hand, it means that the novel has to be largely concerned with making the reader experience the confusion, isolation, and alienation really suffered by black people; on the other hand, it has to produce a sense of growth in community and understanding, which depends to a great extent on the specifically fictive—or magical—forms of fantasy and of a perception enlarged beyond the limits of individual vision.

The novel concerns a break in a routine. For eighteen years Sethe and her daughter Denver have been isolated from the black community of their home near Cincinnati, which has been first of all indignant at the hubris Sethe shows in throwing an overelaborate party to celebrate her escape from slavery and her arrival in the North, and then horrified by her killing of her baby as the slave catchers arrive to take them back to Kentucky. The novel gives clear and serious voice to their disapproval through the comments of the wise and mature Ella: she thinks Sethe's action prideful and misdirected and disapproves of the independence that has led to her living "as though she were alone." More recently, they have lived alone after the death of Sethe's mother-in-law, Baby Suggs, and the departure of Denver's two elder brothers, upset by the activities of a poltergeist-like spirit assumed to be the ghost of the murdered baby. This stasis is interrupted, first of all, by the arrival of Paul D, an acquaintance of Sethe's from the slave plantation of eighteen years ago; he is a link with the past, then, but also brings new life as he becomes Sethe's lover. Paul D brings about a first exorcism, freeing the house from the ghost by sheer force of will, and he makes a first step to returning Sethe and Denver to society by taking them out to a carnival. But as they return, they find what is to be a still more painful haunting: they find waiting at home Beloved, a young woman of no clear origins who eventually is taken by Sethe and Denver to be a reincarnation of the dead baby, a "miraculous resurrection" (105).[2] Beloved lends herself to this identification, though she also makes a number of remarks implying a different identity (which may not imply any supernatural factor); on either view, she is very much attuned to the past, remembering her lost mother (who may or may not be Sethe—and indeed there are moments when she may appear to be Sethe's own missing mother), remembering the slave ships, and fragmentarily remembering her experiences immediately before her appearance at Sethe's home; idle and self-indulgent, she has no plans for the future and encourages Sethe and Denver to remain inertly with her, telling stories of the past. They turn away from the outside world: "The world is in this room," Sethe feels, "there is no world outside my door" (183–84). Finally Denver rebels against Beloved's monopolizing of Sethe and the impoverishment this brings when Sethe loses her job. The culminating scene of the novel has a group of black women coming to free Denver from the domination of Beloved as Denver is about to take up a job with the white liberal and former abolitionist Mr. Bodwin, and having to rescue Bodwin from an insane attack by Sethe, who takes him for a slave catcher.

This crucial scene is a complex balance: the central concern is of a black female community, the community that Furman aptly describes as fulfilling "their natural function as refuge and reservoir of knowledge for the individual," including Sethe, Denver, Ella, and Lady Jones, the schoolteacher who has been an inspiration and protector for Denver.[3] On the periphery are Bodwin and Beloved, who appears proud, naked, and pregnant but slips away unnoticed. The whole scene is under the spell of the past. Bodwin is recalling the heroic days of the abolitionist campaign (in which he was responsible for saving Sethe from execution) and is nostalgically interested in seeing again Sethe's house, his own childhood home. The women are seeking to undo the domination of the past: Ella, in a crucial phrase, "didn't like the idea of past errors taking possession of the present" (256). But as they approach, what they see is their own past: they see themselves, "younger, stronger, even as little girls lying in the grass asleep"; they have their own ghosts, seeing their dead mothers and Sethe's dead mother-in-law. They see the day of the party, in fact, "not feeling the envy that surfaced next day" (258). So they are ready to start again. Ella, in particular, remembers older and worse things, her injuries from slavery and her bearing a "hairy white thing" after sexual abuse by her owners. Bodwin arrives and sets off in Sethe's mind the reactions she had on seeing the slave catchers arriving eighteen years earlier: the white man "coming into her yard," the sensation as of humming birds stabbing her hair with their beaks. This time she does not attack her daughter, as she thinks Beloved to be; she attacks the white enemy. And the white man then turns into "the man without skin," Beloved's perception of the masters on the slave ship, and the crowd seeking to intervene between Sethe and Bodwin becomes a hill of bodies, like the mound of the dead amongst whom Beloved remembers making her dreadful voyage.

Two realms of experience are coinciding: the imaginative world of memory, in which the consciousness of Sethe, Baby Suggs, and Beloved merges and parallels that of the community, and the practical and moral world in which a crime is averted. We learn more about the practical events and their results in a conversation, in the following pages, between the two kindly, humorous, and pragmatic men, Paul D and Stamp Paid. It is Stamp Paid who has rescued Denver from her mother at the time of the killing of the baby. He now sees her saving of Bodwin from her mother as a repetition of his own humane action; whereas Sethe has remained in the thrall of past suffering, Denver, at last, learns from past achievement. Beloved, meanwhile, has disappeared (Grewal convincingly argues that she reappears as Wild in *Jazz*), her disappearance marked by the return of Here Boy, the dog driven out by the malice of the baby's ghost (so perhaps Beloved was the ghost, after all).[4] Her disappearance is half regretted by Denver, it seems, and very much regretted by Sethe, who regards her as "my best thing"- at least until Paul D tells her, in the last conversation of the narrative proper, that she herself is her best thing, that she can learn to live for herself, restored to the community and enriched by his own love. Sethe and Denver at the same time, through the crisis of public violence, attain freedom and resoluteness; they have lived though private suffering and conflict and have come out strengthened. Jackson interprets the literature of fantasy as a transgression of the unified self.[5] In the person of Beloved, Morrison's novel engages with this dissolution of the self, but finally it asserts the integrity of the individual in society.

This account of the structure of the novel implies an overall perspective of coherent growth in the characters and of the healing of a division in society. It shows "a reclamation of a sense of community and solidarity in the face of fragmentation and isolation."[6] But this perspective is not the one the reader has at first. The initial impression is of a world of fragmented, dramatic, and alien events. The opening sentence tells us that "124 was spiteful." The number is startling enough; we soon find that 124 is a house number, and that the house's spite, "full of a baby's venom," is shown by a series of small but inexplicable events: chickpeas spilled without cause; tiny handprints appearing in a cake; most cruelly, the dog Here Boy being picked up and thrown against a wall. The readers don't know why these events are attributed to a house and not a person within it. They don't know why a baby is relevant. The incidents are conspicuously presented as outside the normal—and even outside literary norms, since ghost stories do not usually start with these grotesque incongruities, but gradually introduce hints of a hidden world that is governed by some principle: passion, revenge, the desire for restitution. The novel will eventually make this spiteful baby disturbingly intelligible. It will play, further, on the personification of the house, as the second part of the book opens, "124 was loud," and the third "124 was quiet." There *is* a pattern in the novel; it is a pattern that integrates the hostile and unnatural into an experience of learning, of the discovery of harmony. The ghost story is an episode to be passed through; the reader's difficulty in adapting to a ghost story that is not solemn is an image of the characters' insecurity in solitude and maladjustment.

What is true of the supernatural dimension is at first also true of the presentation of the characters' consciousness. This too appears fragmentary, arbitrary, inexplicable but intensely felt. One striking aspect of this is the tendency of the novel to start new chapters in medias res: the second chapter (20) follows on directly from the narrative of the first, but the third starts with the comment that "Denver's secrets were sweet" (28), a comment that has no relation to the recollections of Paul and Sethe which conclude the second. Where is the scene? What time is this? It is actually a flashback; we have to learn to adapt to discontinuity. More fundamentally, there is the presentation of specific detail. On the second page, Sethe speaks to Denver of her love for the ghost baby and suddenly recalls

> the welcoming cool of unchiseled headstones; the one she selected to lean against on tiptoe, her knees wide open as any grave. Pink as a fingernail it was, and sprinkled with glittering chips. Ten minutes, he said. You got ten minutes I'll do it for free.
> Ten minutes for seven letters. With another ten could she have gotten "Dearly" too? (4–5)

Much in this must be obscure for the first-time reader. Eventually it will become clear, through repetition and variation in the later parts of the novel. Sethe is recalling the interment of her daughter; she has acquired a headstone on which is carved the word "Beloved" by consenting to hasty sex with the memorial mason. The feeling is complex: primarily for the reader, there is the indignity of a memorial that can only be attained through prostitution—and this, no doubt, is why Sethe keeps this memory to herself, sparing Denver the knowledge of her debasement. But also there is the sense that this is, after all, a sacrifice for the dead, the reproach that it is an imperfect one without the word "Dearly," the sense of pleasure in coolness and in color (we have already been told of Baby Suggs's love of color, and specifically of pink), and the sense of the clumsiness of the act and of sexuality as an equivalent for death. Symbolically, emotionally, this is rich, though the full sense is suspended: there is here a personality that is capable of deep and many-faceted sensation and emotion, and the reader realizes how partially this intense feeling is manifest in her communication with her daughter. Matus comments that Sethe remembers too much and too well, but that "a fragmented and discontinuous narrative performs a repression of memory."[7] The paradox is a real one, but it might be more useful to say that there is not a repression but a delaying of intelligible memory. What is not touched on here is how the baby died: the novel does not yet pose the moral dilemma (can Sethe be excused? or can readers attain the "unforgiving/loving" attitude Morrison elsewhere advocates?) or the puzzle of motivation (does the death explain the ghost's spite?);[8] the reader may feel disquiet at not yet understanding.

What is true of this detail is true of much else in the book: Why does Paul D, on his first meeting with Sethe, decide not to tell her about "the churn"? When he refers to Sethe's pregnancy eighteen years ago, why does she recall (but not mention) "that girl looking for velvet"? The answer comes eventually. For a long time, however, the narrator displays the seriousness with which the characters define the turning points of their lives through concrete memories but implies that these memories are not available to other people or to the reader, until the slow and complex working out of the text illuminates the total cohesion of the story. Toni Morrison wrote a thesis on Faulkner and Virginia Woolf; strange partners, except that that they have in common a concern with the way that private memories can contribute to the evolution of a shared sensibility. A crucial pair of passages in *Beloved* concerns Sethe's marriage to Halle and two ways of remembering it. The passages comprise more continuous narrative than those we have just considered. But continuity still allows incommensurability. In one passage, Sethe tells Denver and Beloved of her disappointment that there would be no formal wedding ceremony, of her making a wedding dress out of odds and ends, and of her and Halle going to consummate the wedding in a cornfield (58–59). It is a memory of hardship and innocence, one that can be shared with her daughters. But this event has already been recalled. As Sethe lies beside Paul D on the night of his arrival, she is reminded by his tenderness of Halle and their marriage (26–27). The same story of the dress and the cornfield is told briefly, without the detail and the enjoyment of memory that are appropriate in conversation. The telling of the story fluctuates; it must overall come from Sethe's memory, but for a moment at least it seems to slip into impersonal narration as it recounts that "Both Halle and Sethe were under the impression that they were hidden." The narration, at any rate, recounts what Sethe knows and endorses its accuracy. She has, too, come to mature understanding of one point: she and Halle were not hidden. So there appears Paul D's memory of the same event: Sethe, the only girl on the plantation, has been an object of desire to all the men; Halle is much envied, and the sight of the moving cornstalks has intensely frustrated them. So the same event is seen from two perspectives, female and male, affectionate and shameful, public and private. But they are seen because, a little strangely, the two characters are subject to the same stimulus of memory simultaneously: the separation of consciousness has been diminished. It is still more diminished when the text shifts to the symbolic: Paul remembers the feast of cornstalks the men ate, plucked from the stalks broken by Halle and Sethe. The feast has clear sexual import, and it is a female voice that makes this most explicit: "The pulling down of the tight sheath, the ripping sound always convinced her it hurt." *Her* must be Sethe—for once privy to Paul D's memories.

Coming to terms with the past, then, is a major concern of the novel. Like psychoanalysis, another retrieval of a past, it is, in more than one way, a matter of story-telling. Before Beloved's arrival, there is reluctance to talk about the past: most significantly, Denver has been so shocked by a schoolmate's question about her mother's murder trial—which Sethe has obviously not told her about—that she becomes deaf and refuses to leave her home so that she can watch the yard where the white men have once appeared. Inability to listen goes with loss of society and contributes to the impression in the earlier parts of the book that Denver is of inferior intelligence. Even in the events of the narrative proper, there are restraints on telling: Stamp Paid shows Paul D a newspaper cutting about the murder, but being unable to read Paul is reluctant to grasp what the story is and still more so to believe it. He himself is slow to tell Sethe the full story of the cruel punishment of having a bit in his mouth, which he suffered when the two of them were escaping from Sweet Home; he is even more reluctant to tell her that her husband Halle has been driven mad by seeing her, on the same occasion, being subject to sexual abuse by white men sucking her milk. Most crucially there is the feeling that the past is unspeakable (58); Sethe is reluctant to remember (70), and she seeks to beat back the past (73), to keep the past at bay (42). Denver too, for her own reasons, turns away from the past (with some exceptions), but when Beloved appears, "she had her own set of questions which had nothing to do with the past" (119). The feeling is understandable; it is understandable because the text, despite Sethe, does tell us of the thoughts that continue to preoccupy her. Just so, the American past may seem to be unspeakable, but the task of the novel (as of the historian) is to speak of the evils of the past, to show what they have done to the present and how they can be lived through.

Sethe finds her intelligence at odds with her wishes: her brain is "loaded with the past and hungry for more" (70). And *Beloved* is at least in part a celebration of the intelligence (despite Rigney's implication that Morrison seeks to escape the "dualistic, objective posturing of western rationality"), a celebration of the extension of knowledge.[9] Characters may wish to control knowledge, to keep it private, to rely on sensation and intuition: so Sethe, once fairly respectful of the more humane whites, after her quarrel with Paul D, "didn't want any more news about whitefolks. . . . She didn't want to know what Ella knew and John and Stamp Paid, about the world done up the way whitefolks loved it" (188). Denver, on first suspecting that Beloved is her sister, avoids putting the questions that most concern her; she appears uninquisitive for fear of losing the satisfaction beyond hunger that Beloved seems to promise (119). Moreover, she implores her not to tell Sethe who she is (76); she wants knowledge to be confined to herself, so she can retain a power over her mother and Beloved both. Paul D, despite his impulse toward openness, finds himself unable to reveal to Sethe his "coldhouse secret" (165), his sexual intimacy with Beloved, and Sethe's telling him of her killing of the baby—the knowledge he has previously rejected—is at first catastrophic: it leads him, despite his own more recent guilt, to condemn her as animal-like. Only at the end do they come together in frank conversation. Division allows reconciliation; after such knowledge there is forgiveness.

There is a fascination in the book with the private, "the private pleasure of enchantment" (37); the baby ghost has cut off number 124 from civilization at large, and Beloved adds to the intensity of private feeling in the house, driving out Paul, the male who has offered new life and wider perspectives. The supernatural elements in the novel, that is, appear to be expressions of a private world of female intimacy, which are put to the test of the realism and moral judgment of the wider society. (Rigney insists that in Morrison, "there are no polarities between logic and mysticism, between real and fantastic."[10] But the story of *Beloved* is precisely that of an elimination of the fantastic by a real community.) It is consistent with the sense of this society that there is a countervailing tendency to insist on full communication. Most crucially, Denver precipitates the final events because she realizes that "nobody would help her unless she told" (253); she recognizes that the self-sufficiency of Sethe and Beloved has become a sort of helplessness and that she must call on the outside world to reinvigorate them. So, after turning to the middle-class black Lady Jones, she goes to the white Bodwins and tells her story to their black servant Janey. She recognizes that people—of both races—are interdependent and that interdependence imposes a need for openness.

And so, more and more, stories do get told. Beloved gains "profound satisfaction" from hearing stories (58), and much of the novel is concerned with people coming to tell the story of the past. Denver tells the story of her own birth (76), and very gradually we come to hear a clear and coherent account of the stories of the killing of the baby (more than halfway through the book) and of the escape and the punishments associated with it; it is in this context that Sethe tells Beloved that "someone had to know it. Hear it" (202). The novel, Pérez-Torres points out, is both a telling of a story and an account of the telling of stories, of stories as "a means of articulating the accumulated wisdom of communal thought and of hearing the voices of the dead through the living";[11] it not only gives voice to the dead, it also asserts the finality of death condemning Beloved herself to final oblivion.

Beloved does not tell stories; at first she appears to have no memory (55). More than anything else she asks questions, and when she refers to her past it is in brief and obscure allusions. The longest passage of discourse we have from her is the disturbing passage of interior monologue in which she recalls the slave ship, with the loss of her mother, her hunger and thirst, and her contact with the bodies of the dead, and especially with the man whose teeth fascinate her (211). The passage is an extremely impressive one, forcefully complementing the monologues of Sethe and Denver that precede and follow it. But these comprise coherent narrative. Sethe has laid claim to Beloved as her daughter and has gone on to recount the story of the escape from Sweet Home, her relationship with the kindly but ineffectual white woman Mrs. Garner, and her beating by the schoolmaster and his nephews, and then goes on to reminiscences of her life in Ohio, including the discovery of Beloved, in other words, to the matter of the novel we are reading. Sethe repeats what we know but repeats it as her own possession and dedicates her memories to Beloved: "But you know all that because you smart like everybody said because when I got here you was crawling already" (204). The dead baby has been frequently referred to as "the already crawling? baby." What is being said here—apart from the important temporal enrichment given by Sethe's references to her own missing mother—is not new either to Beloved (or so Sethe assumes) or to the reader; the important thing is not to provide information but to solemnize the sharing of knowledge.

Denver, too, lays claim to Beloved and recalls the moment—a point of origin for the whole novel—in which she drank Beloved's blood together with her mother's milk, before going on to remember her own childhood experiences: the haunting by the baby ghost and then her relationships with Beloved and Paul D. The memories are fantastic and horrifying: she has dreamed of her mother cutting off her head every night, and this horror itself becomes part of the rationality of the novel, since it is the explanation for Denver's generally withdrawn character.

Denver, moreover, does not address her story to anyone. She is formulating what she has learned about herself; she keeps her distance from the frightening mother and, in a different way, from the "greedy ghost," greedy for love, which has become Beloved. Her acute psychological observations, her knowledge of her father, and her recognition of the objective time scale of the war show Denver as potentially one of the most rational characters in the book—aptly she is contemplating university education at the end, and she is rightly identified by Rushdy as the "site of hope" in the book—and she exemplifies also the desire for continuity that the book persistently asserts.[12] (Sixo's triumphant cry of "Seven-o" as he dies is a proud male boast of continuity through fatherhood [226]; Beloved seeks to establish continuity through motherhood.) The experiences of mother and daughter, with their increasing lucidity and respect for chronology, show the text coming to approximate to the model of an objective world, in which the subjective perspective of each character illuminates a facet of a shared life. The text approximates this coherence and does not yet fully attain it—Denver's second-hand knowledge of her daddy (acquired from her grandmother) emerges only gradually from her dreams of him.

Beloved's voice challenges narrative coherence very radically. She starts by echoing Sethe and Denver: "I am Beloved and she is mine." This is already confusing. The others have asserted that Beloved is theirs, and it seems for a moment as if the "she is mine," once again, refers to Beloved—so she would be speaking of herself in the third person. In fact, we soon learn that this refers to someone else, whose actions Beloved is describing in the present tense; she is having a vision of a scene she does not quite comprehend—from a child's perspective she is watching flowers being picked—but that has an intense emotional significance for her, affecting her very sense of identity: "I am not separate from her," she says, "her face is my own and I want to be there in the place where her face is and to be looking at it too" (210). *Her* is Beloved's mother, undoubtedly, but whereas Denver has the developed sense of selfhood that enables her to judge mother and ghost even while she loves, Beloved—though she hints at the impossibility of seeing what you yourself are—feels her identity to be indistinguishable from that of her mother. She is still in the stage that psychoanalysts such as Lacan attribute to the infant—the stage, perhaps, of the already crawling baby. Lacking the sense of a self, her sensibility formed above all by desire, the desire for the mother's presence, Beloved has no sense of time and little of distinct persons; her monologue then—instantly perceived as different on the page because it is punctuated only by spaces, not by the rational array of commas and stops that the adult Sethe and the adolescent Denver have used—consists of a series of impressions, which the reader can piece together into a deeply distressing account of a period of deprivation and cruelty. This period, of course, cannot be the experience of the baby; it seems that Beloved, lacking individuality, can be the voice of her ancestors' experience as well as her own.[13]

The fantastic in *Beloved*, Peach rightly points out, destabilizes the sense of identity and therefore the textual coherence of the novel.[14] This experience is not an articulate one. In psychoanalytic terms the baby is at the stage of the imaginary not the symbolic, of pictures not words, not the ordered code of adult communication;[15] "How can I say things that are pictures?" Beloved asks (210). Just as the voice of the slave has been largely unheard in history, so Beloved refrains from giving clear order to this bewilderingly, tragically different suffering. But Morrison ultimately asserts that language does transcend images: she speaks in her Nobel Prize speech of "the language that tells us what only language can: how to see without pictures. Language alone protects us from the scariness of things with no names."[16] So Beloved does, eventually, come toward the events of the story we already know, as she recalls following her mother into water and emerging from it to see Sethe, whom she now claims as "the face that left me." There are symbolic suggestions here, clearly enough (in the non-Lacanian sense of "symbolic"): birth, baptism, the oceanic; Beloved's immersion and resurrection is another point of origin for the events of the novel, an alternative to Denver's sense of her own birth or of the killing of the baby as origins, and it is an origin that implies its own continuity with a historic past: Beloved's hunger for contact arises from the deathly alienation of slavery. But there is nothing in this to allow change; Beloved's desire is for contentment with herself in the mirrorlike love of Sethe, and contentment turns to decadence.

The text, however, progresses to another monologue by Beloved, in standard syntax, which then gives way to a series of dialogues of almost ritual or liturgic form involving the three women—though it is not always clear that the three are systematically distinguished. Beloved's monologue, this time, is a coherent but fantastic narrative in which Sethe is the mother on the slave ship, whom the whites push into the sea with the dead but who then is seen near the bridge that Beloved connects with her coming to Bluestone Road. Affecting as this still must be, the reader is encouraged here to view Beloved as deluded, to suspect a natural sequence of events behind the dreaming or mythologizing that still obscures much of it, and so to query the historical consistency the novel is attaining: the identity of the slave child Beloved and the desired adolescent is the work of a fictional imagination.[17] What follows is a lyrical celebration of the togetherness of the three women, in their physical closeness and in their divergent fantasies: it is Denver who claims that "Daddy is coming for us," Beloved who records "A hot thing," and Sethe who asserts that "I have your milk" (215–17). The phrases and concerns that have characterized them throughout the book are woven into a fugue; the dense texture of varied frustration that has made up the novel so far makes an elaborate aesthetic pattern here, but it illustrates also difference. Each voice enters into the pattern as it demonstrates what it wants of the others, but what it wants is not what the others can offer.

"Anything dead coming back to life hurts," Amy says, as she helps Sethe at Denver's birth (35). Beloved's coming to life—if that is what it is—has hurt all those she comes into contact with. But the hurt has been productive, for memories have come to life with her and have become part of thriving common experience. Because finally the past, like everything else, has its limits. Fiction, like ghosts, reanimates the past. But like Beloved herself, that reanimation is ambiguous: does it restore a fixed past, or does it transform it in such a way that overcoming that past is a first step to new living? The wisdom of the book is implied in the account of the chain gang leader, who was able every morning to give the signal to start work and so to put an end, for the time being, to the cruelties to which his men are subject: "he alone knew what was enough, what was too much, when things were over, when the time had come" (108). Suffering is not endless; things come to an end. *Beloved* traces the way we can come to recognize when that end has come.

7
Oates: *Blonde*

A NOTE ON THE REVERSE OF THE TITLE PAGE OF *BLONDE* INSISTS THAT "the characterizations and incidents presented are totally the products of the author's imagination. Accordingly, *Blonde* should be read solely as a work of fiction, not as a biography of Marilyn Monroe."[1] But they are not *totally* the products of Oates's imagination. The central character is called Norma Jeane Baker (with some variations) or Marilyn Monroe, she marries an ex-athlete and a playwright, she makes films called *The Asphalt Jungle*, *Niagara* (directed by H), *Gentlemen Prefer Blondes* (with Jane Russell), *The Seven-Year Itch* (with Tom Ewell, directed by W). Anyone can tell who this is, despite some odd suppressions of names. And anyone can, very easily, think they know quite a lot about who it is; they remember what they have seen, the mixture of charm, beauty, boldness, joie de vivre, timidity, and tenderness. This *is* a book about Marilyn Monroe: it tells yet again a story often told, and one readers will know—even if they haven't read any of the real biographies—as an American myth, as an instance of a woman's vulnerability in a life of celebrity (and that vulnerability also people have already seen in those not quite immaculate features).[2] The risk, obviously, is that Oates is going to be telling her readers (at great length) what they already know: that Marilyn Monroe was destroyed by fame.

But this apparently simple and familiar point becomes the basis of a disturbing reflection: what is a personality? How can it be destroyed? What is fame? What does it show about the nature of a society, and especially about the view of womanhood that prevails in it, and what does it show about the dependence of the individual on society? These questions are posed, of course, not in abstract sociological terms, but through the imaginative creativity of fiction. Indeed this is a virtuoso work of fiction; it manifests its fictionality by its ingenious and startling extrapolations from the known facts of Monroe's life, by an extension of her life, and it exploits the ways in which fiction can convey significance beyond any fixed and known objective truth: by shifting points of view (sometimes shifting with confusing rapidity), by a complex layering of symbols, by unstable time frames, by the inclusion within the total narrative of fragmentary narratives that themselves may or may not be presented as true, by discontinuities of style and rhetoric, and by modulation into fantasy.

A purely literal transcription of the known life of Marilyn Monroe, of course, wouldn't exclude serious interest. There are telling moments in the novel that are taken direct from the real life; one may recall, as one astonishing example, the tie clasp she gave to her makeup man, inscribed: "To Whitey, while I'm still warm." It is the biographies, not the novel, that tell us of the immense pathos of Whitey making up her dead body; the novel chooses to focus finally on the moment of death, but it has already suggested a fascination with death on Monroe's part that can be documented.[3] Another detail of a haunting strangeness: Monroe's final home really was embellished with the words "cursum perficio": I finish my course. Some readers will recall only the best-known elements of Monroe's career and read in a state of uncertainty, unable to distinguish (and perhaps not needing to distinguish) the literally true from the imagined. Those readers who have read the biographies recognize the literal authenticity of these details; whatever else the novel may be doing, it is identifying, and foregrounding, a disturbing element in her character. It is an element that has thematic significance: the novel implies that her death was not accidental but a culmination of an attraction which was part of her and of the deathly culture of America in the 1950s and 1960s, a culture of nuclear warfare, lost children, sickness, and natural disasters. Elsewhere Oates writes on "living creatures in thrall to the indecipherable drama of their times" (*AA*, 9); *Blonde*, too, seeks to convey that subjection to history.

This use of detail may show a simpler affection for its subject. The photograph of eight starlets of which Norma Jeane is proud exists (200). It is reproduced in Mailer's book, and it does show Monroe "gazing dreamily off-camera"; Oates has shown a nicely sympathetic interest in the star's developing image. The detailed reference to reality can also highlight the author's ingenuity. On the last day of Monroe's life, various mysterious events occurred, one of which is the arrival at her home of a parcel by which she was apparently deeply upset. Oates makes this the starting point of her novel, in conspicuous and perhaps ironical rhetorical elaboration: the messenger who delivers the parcel, an ordinary youth in a T-shirt and baseball cap on a rusty bicycle, carrying a parcel labeled "handle with care" and childishly addressed to "Brentwood California USA Earth" (and to Monroe's real street address) is also Death—an absurd, grotesque, disproportionate Death, Death without dignity. This is justified in the development of the novel: Oates invents a plot strand that makes the day of her heroine's death into a culmination of deprivation and of male malevolence. As a child in an orphanage Norma Jeane is given a toy tiger by a visiting film star. She is delighted; the toy becomes a symbol of the affection between parents and children that is lacking in her life. As a teenager, looking after a child for a friend, she makes a toy tiger for it (for which the mother is far from grateful). As an adult, she passes a toyshop window with her two lovers and admires a toy tiger. With brutal energy they break the window and hand her the toy. When she leaves the ménage with the two lovers, she leaves the tiger behind, because she thinks of it as a plaything for the baby she has aborted. Now a new development occurs, by which she is very moved; she starts to get letters from the father she has never known. Shortly before her own death, one of the two lovers dies; the parcel is sent by the other and contains the tiger — and a message indicating that the "father's" letters were a hoax cruelly perpetuated by the dead man. Marilyn has revealed herself to her lovers; she has revealed her longings, not for artistic success or fame but for paternal love. Revealing yourself makes you vulnerable. The triviality of the messenger with his "goddam package" corresponds to the loss of human value that he brings, and that loss brings death with it.

All this might have happened. The uninformed reader cannot be sure that it didn't happen. The more informed reader will know that it doesn't appear in the biographies, and that what Oates has done is to provide a neat solution for a mystery, one which ties together various episodes in Marilyn's (imagined) life (for the biographies indicate that she did have affairs with the two men in question, but not simultaneously, and that one of them appeared in *Some Like It Hot* with her at a time when the novel implies that there was no contact between them). Moreover it ties them together with the themes of vulnerability, deprivation, and the cinema. It is fiction, in other words, not biography, that makes Marilyn into a victim. It is not impossible to see the real Monroe as ambitious, manipulative, egoistic; in *Blonde*, the novelist makes her weakly innocent.

A more detailed author's note comments on the major technique used in fictionalizing the Monroe story: "*Blonde* is a radically distilled 'life' in the form of fiction, and, for all its length, synecdoche is the principle of appropriation . . . in place of numerous lovers, medical crises, abortions and suicide attempts and screen performances, *Blonde* explores only a selected, symbolic few" (ix). "Appropriation," on the one hand: Monroe's life is Oates's property (the story of Marilyn is made to resemble the story of *Marya*, and the themes of physicality, vulnerability, deprived childhood, abuse of political power, and the limits of self-control may seem as much a syndrome of Oates's writing as a portrait of Monroe); "symbolic" on the other: the text does explore a preexistent reality. It does so, first of all, by elimination. Some readers may regret that there is no reference to the affair with Bobby Kennedy, which biographers indicate to have been a major preoccupation of Monroe's last months and perhaps a factor in her death. But the sense of Marilyn as a victim of a male sexuality oriented to power and control is given already—and with graphic force—in the narration of her relationship with the President, as her hero worship, her combination of political commitment and of openness to charisma, makes her prey to brutal contempt. Similarly the heroine of *Blackwater* is brought to her death by her satisfaction in being "the one chosen" by a powerful man. In both cases, there are historical models, and these give an air of authenticity, but what matters is the theme of destruction by power and passivity. An intelligent and respectful review of *Blonde* complains that it does not quite do justice to the real Monroe: "even this generous portrait of Norma Jeane feels strangely occluded."[4] The danger is not inaccuracy but simplification.

Synecdoche brings about compression—a compression quite in keeping with a classic expectation of artistic coherence and economy, even though the novel as a whole may seem far from classic decorum: it ensures an interweaving of themes to make up the texture of a life. Monroe had dealings with many photographers. In *Blonde* Marilyn relates to one photographer, Otto Öse; the same man who discovers her is the one who shames her by using the power of money to persuade her into being photographed nude, and he is also the quasi-Marxist cynic who denounces the corruption of American democracy by money. Photography is itself a major theme: in the orphanage, Norma Jeane fails to smile for the camera and is returned from the public world of the star, the magazines, the giving of presents, to the private world of the mirror; she is abused as she is sadistically exhibited by her first husband's photographs, but she comes to find the camera her closest friend as she attains fame as a model (188), and then to see it as a symbol of Death in Otto's hands. The camera superimposes the themes of power, of self-display, and self-alienation (Marilyn is reluctant to see the huge still of herself in *Niagara* outside the movie theater), of desirability and of the commodification of the person, "in a capitalist-consumer economy," as Otto reflects, true to his political understanding and to his male aggressiveness, "in which no body, like no soul, is inviolable" (223). Because of the camera, the body is political (and Oates is parallelling some modern film criticism with its suspicion of the male gaze). Moreover, the political leanings Marilyn acquires from Öse will make her an object of distrust to the studio, in these McCarthyite days, as she naïvely signs a petition for the suspected communists Robeson and Chaplin, only to have it snatched from her hands by her agent. The individual will to self-expression, whether it be in politics or in acting, is inhibited by a conformist commercial and inert society. The tension of the doomed individual and the dominant society is crucial to the work. A phrase attributed to the Playwright speaks of "the intersection between private pathology and the insatiable appetite of a capitalist-consumer culture" (542); it powerfully formulates Oates's judgment of her subject.

What here is done by economy is done also by elaboration. The author's inventiveness makes for a proliferation of symbol. It would be fascinating to elucidate the multiple images of nudity and being seen (both proud self-assertion and alien intrusion) of mirrors (return to the self, artificial doubling of the self in flight from other people) of doubles (the doll that is Norma Jeane, the night twin that reflects her [146, 173], her two lovers, the Gemini [and she is a Gemini astrologically too], the people "who're like twins" [in Montgomery Clift's phrase], the Brunette star [apparently Ava Gardner] with whom Marilyn is briefly identified but who also shocks her by her masculine assertiveness, even the crude parody of Marilyn by a transvestite in a gay bar); one can at least say that the novel is permeated by a sense (which one might call postmodern and relate to the writings of Baudrillard, for instance) that the individual is not unique, determinate, or self-contained, but is part of a network of images and reproductions, a sense that in the world of the mass media identity is ambiguous.

One much repeated symbol is that of the hummingbird. The phrase appears to originate with Paula Strasberg, Monroe's mentor, who commented on her friend and client: "She is a beautiful hummingbird made of iron. Her only trouble is that she's a very pure person in a very impure world."[5] The second sentence is not far from Oates's understanding of the character. But the iron disappears from the first image (as well it might; Monroe did not have "the constitution of an ox," as Strasberg claims, but suffered from constant ill health). Norma Jeane's happiest times are spent feeding hummingbirds with her grandmother (45). Her first husband feels "her wild heartbeat. Like a frightened bird in his embrace, a hummingbird" (146). A chapter called "Hummingbird" (205–17) recounts her visit to a Mr. Z, a senior official of the studio, in the hope of attracting a part in a film, in which he first shows her an aviary of dead birds (who are made to sing by recording, by, that is, an artificial reproduction) and then subjects her to a humiliating and painful anal assault;[6] the chapter is narrated by Marilyn herself, who awakes with the "*good happy feeling*" of her heart beating like something small and feathered. As she passes through the city she recalls the hummingbirds of her childhood, "so small and so hardy & bold & fearless" with their rapid heartbeat—and the fear that they might be killed by hawks or crows; she is relieved not to see any hummingbirds amongst the dead in the aviary. As she becomes better known in films, she feels more conspicuous and endangered, "a hummingbird observed through a rifle scope" (305). Humiliated by seeing a man (possibly her respected English teacher) masturbating while watching her in a film, she attempts suicide and becomes aware of "her heart beating! terrified she could hold it in her hand like a hummingbird" (487). On the last page of the book, in her dying moments, she dreams of accompanying her mother, lost in madness, to see her father, lost in illegitimacy, and "her heart was beating like a hummingbird held in the hand & frantic to escape" (738). There is a bitter echo to that bird caught in the rifle scope. The Sharpshooter, the CIA agent who watches her through much of the novel and finally kills her, enjoys shooting birds: they are "his beautiful prey" (644)—as Marilyn will be. The symbol combines delicacy, vitality, animation, and danger: the heart, escape, death. It links Marilyn's phases of joy (evanescent, in this case) with her feelings of despair; it links her consciousness with that of her husband and of her enemy. The novel, one might say, is a lyrical one; it transcends the orientation of the novel genre toward differentiation of character and situation.

So the text creates a consistency and a symbolism for the character out of Monroe's known or possible experiences—early marriage, a career in a Hollywood where men rule (286), public attention and perhaps official surveillance, death. Part of the consistency is also given by the framework of history;[7] the reader can see her life as constrained by the hardships of the 1930s, by war, by postwar anticommunism, by Korea, by Cuba, specifically by the history of Hollywood, effectively suggested by the spectacular and deathly public festival of Thalberg's funeral. "It's history. What happens to us," Norma Jeane says of the war, as her first husband leaves her for the marine service—and so sets her on the path to fame (174). Norma Jeane's life is to be—to some degree—an image of what has happened to America. (So Hilfer is right to stress that Oates's work is a clear response to historical and material circumstances, to a "nightmare of American history."[8])

But there is also a great deal in the novel that tends in the opposite direction, toward a fragmentation of the fictional texture, so as to offer something like the raw material from which we construct a life, whether it is a biography or our everyday informal sense of another person's identity. Characters in the novel are giving to telling stories, and the novel itself at times appears to be a complex of stories. Norma Jeane's mother, Gladys, tells of her love for the missing father, or of Fredric March's spinet; the grandmother Della tells the story of Gladys's childhood; Norma Jeane loves the stories of the movies, and she invents stories (the symbolic Walled Garden, to which "once upon a time" the child was admitted). And of course people love telling stories about Marilyn, the celebrity; we don't quite see her, "as Jesus in the Gospels is only seen and spoken of and recorded by others," but we do get a lot of "the witnessing and naming of others" (15). They are allowed to interrupt the flow of the narrative to interject their own first-person accounts: a fellow student recounts her first steps to studying acting; another how she anonymously attended an evening class to improve her literary understanding but was driven out by the embarrassment of being found to be a pinup model; another recounts a mime class in which she plays a dying woman. Or they intervene with brief—and often crude—comments (the change in voice signaled by italics). Unidentified groups get whole chapters to discuss Marilyn's career and love life. Press accounts of her are quoted. The President's brother-in-law passes on to him the unpleasant legends that have accumulated about her, such as that she has contracted venereal disease from Senator McCarthy himself. Substantial sections are told from the point of view of more or less incidental characters, such as the foster mother Elsie Pirig, for whom Norma Jeane, with her ripening physique, is largely an embarrassment, or—at much greater length—the Playwright, for whom she is a subject of puzzled and passionate concern and a complement to his own unresting self-questioning. Sometimes they are unidentified, as with the distant observers through whose eyes her first date with the Ex-Athlete is recounted. Within passages of third-person narrative there are sudden shifts of perspective: the first section of the chronological narrative, "The Kiss," starts with Norma Jeane's own viewpoint as an adult woman ("Her earliest memory, so exciting!" 9) but then slips to a vision of her through the objective abstract style of the novelist; the second section, "The Bath," again starts with Norma Jeane's perspective but slips momentarily into an external view ("her pudgy little hand," 13) and then into the voice of the mother (who is the *true mother* "when the demands of The Studio allowed," 13) and that of the grandmother (who finds her daughter "calmly maddening"), before assuming an impersonal visual notation, recording like a stranger the grandmother as "a mottled-faced fattish woman in a faded cotton housecoat" (14). Marilyn herself has long passages of storytelling, of stream of consciousness, of incoherent written ramblings, of letter writing; throughout she has brief comments on the action, not clearly related to any one stage in her life and often employing a style more sophisticated and theoretical than her spoken words. The opening of "The Kiss" is "This movie I've been seeing all my life, yet never to its completion," and the narrative of her childish impressions that then ensues is soon interrupted by the words referring to the movie screen: "This was the very universe upon which are projected uncountable unnameable forms of life" (9). This is the child's sensation, but it is the adult's language; Marilyn is reflecting on how she became enamored of the screen. When is she reflecting? No answer is given or is perhaps possible; the consciousness is incommensurable with the biography.

The novel is, then, a sort of mosaic of views of Marilyn. Some of the pieces don't fit into the mosaic because the view they give is obviously false. The list of her lovers supposed to be derived from FBI files in the chapter "Can't get enough of Polish sausage" contains some names that correspond to the rest of the narrative (Z, Richard Widmark, Charlie Chaplin junior), others which may be true of the real Monroe but are eliminated from the novel on the principle of synecdoche (Sinatra), yet others which clearly go against the logic of the novel (Öse), and many that are blatant fantasy (Roy Rogers and Trigger). The list is very funny and shows a hyperbolic energy of imagination. But there is a serious undertone. Marilyn is a public image; she has chosen to be a star and agreed to be a sex symbol. A predecessor in Oates's fiction, the actress and sex symbol Malvinia Morlock in *A Bloodsmoor Romance*, seems much happier with the role; for her it is a willed rebellion, a form of success. For both, the status of sex symbol is constituted by the legends that accumulate about her (Guiles's biography of Monroe is aptly titled *Legend*). And these legends are—at least in part—constituted by a scabrous fascination with promiscuity.

No single Marilyn emerges from the book. The opening pages, for example, of "The (American) Showgirl 1957" (562), which deal with the making of *The Prince and the Showgirl*, start with Marilyn's homesickness in the alien winter of England, present "the Blond Actress" through the character she is to play ("plucky"), and then have her "forced to" see herself through the "lusterless monocled eye" of the distinguished but unanimated British actor O: "the busty American actress, the cotton-candy fine-spun platinum hair and glossy red lips and shivery mannerisms"—a creature of conventional and superficial attractiveness (563). A little later, stung by his patronizing manner, she reverts to her prestar persona: "She was Norma Jeane Baker trussed up in a dress baring much of her bosom, her scalp stung from that morning's peroxide touch-up, mind slow as a winding-down alarm clock." She takes her revenge—conscious of herself not as the Desdemona that the Shakespearean actor O expects but as an Iago—by illness, which disrupts the shooting schedules. The text then shifts to the perspective of the Playwright. He is touched and astonished by her passionate sense of solitude, alienation, and dependence on him—and he notes the chemical smell of her peroxided hair. Marilyn is superficial in O's eyes but profoundly (if not quite lucidly) self-aware; she has girlish enthusiasm in the Playwright's eyes but sees herself as an embittered revenger. She sees herself as a victim of illness and of cosmetic routine but is seen by her husband as struggling for communication, almost demanding, and yet made unattractive by that same cosmetic process. Is she nature as opposed to English corruption? Immaturity as opposed to intellectual assurance? Has she artfully assimilated a model of beauty or made herself into a repellent creature of artifice? Does she represent spontaneity or hysteria?

Blonde, like other of Oates's works, partly shows the defect of its heroine, her destructiveness to others and to herself, as stemming from her disappointment in the image others have of her, from her sense of being unloved.[9] But it also stems from her frustration at there being no consistent image. The child Norma Jeane is puzzled by her mother's hints about her father: "So Norma Jeane was left to ponder what the truth was, or if in fact there was 'truth,' for life wasn't anything like a gigantic jigsaw puzzle really; in a puzzle all the pieces fit together, neatly and beautifully together, it didn't even matter that the landscape-in-the-puzzle was beautiful, like a fairyland, only just that the completed picture was *there*; you could see it, you could marvel over it, you could even destroy it, but *it was there*. In life, she'd come to see, even before the age of eight, nothing was there" (42).

The themes of beauty and destruction show how close the novel comes to a jigsaw puzzle that does fit neatly together, but the overall sense of the novel is that nothing is absolutely *there*. In particular, personality is not *there*. "I guess there isn't any 'Norma Jeane,' is there?" she asks later (200); "Marilyn Monroe," she reflects, is "not the real name of any real person" (256). Marilyn is created by the studio, or by her agent ("Marilyn was mine, you dumb broad," he exclaims when he discovers that her image has been threatened by the nude photographs, 306). She becomes her roles, identifying herself in turn with Angela, Nell, and Rose, to the extent that she is Norma Jeane playing "Marilyn" playing "Angela" (256). She acts much of the time; she sees the situations of everyday life as following a script or as requiring improvisation, as in a more or less difficult acting exercise. She is constituted by those around her and especially by men; "To be the object of male desire," she reflects during her first marriage, as she discovers sexuality and the threatening network of family relationships and family conflicts, "is to know *I exist*" (152). And yet she reacts against this later, writing in a poem to the Playwright—though apparently in a spirit of loving humility:

> Because you desire me
> I am not. (600)

She reflects in a crucial passage on the distinction between stage acting and film acting. The cinema she has come to see as exploitation; she escapes from Los Angeles to New York to find a more authentic art in training as a stage actress and tells her mother "The only true acting is living. Alive. In the movies, they splice you together, hundreds of disjointed scenes. It's a jigsaw puzzle and you're not the one to put the pieces together" (444).

The completion of the puzzle would be an act of personal responsibility, set against the fragmentation of commercial control in the film. But is this personal will a chimera? Not much later she entertains troops in Korea, singing songs that she has originally recorded "as Marilyn Monroe" (467) by a process of splicing together up to twenty-five takes. The direct contact with the audience of troops is one of the most fulfilling experiences of her life (as seems to be the case with the historic Monroe), but apart from this brief episode her live performances never gets beyond the level of the studio reading, and as her mental and physical state declines her film acting grows more dependent on multiple takes (to the great fury of some of her fellow actors). And there is another disquieting point: the text hints that living is acting, and, if so, any authentic self-creation, or self-composition, becomes difficult to envisage.

The self, as critics have noted, is a crucial concern throughout Oates's writing: Calla in *I Lock the Door upon Myself* speaks for many of her characters when she says that "My self is all to me" (*L,* 6). But it is essentially, as Creighton insists, "an elusive self."[10] If, in the earlier work, it is "individual, stubborn, self-reliant and ultimately mysterious," in *Blonde* the self-reliance has been largely eclipsed by the mystery. The female self that Creighton notes, constituting "inarticulate, imperceptive victims of an inadequate model of selfhood," has become more articulate, more self-aware, but more confused for that very reason and still in thrall to a false model.

The novel is then one that stresses multiplicity: changing points of view, changing time frames, changing stylistic levels, from the intense rhetorical narrative of the opening or the intensely patterned rhetorical account of the factors that drive her mother into madness to the drab and self-important style of the fake father's letter, the clumsy sincerity of Marilyn's own letters, the tense or lyrical feeling of much of the third-person narrative, the breathless and discontinuous excitement of Marilyn's consciousness, and the realistic accounts of simple, pragmatic male conversation, the literary and cultural quotations. The structure of the scenes tends to stress discontinuity: they can start suddenly in midconversation, with a striking anticipation of action (so section 1 of "The Bath" starts "See? That man is your father") and end with a shock discovery (so that this section circles round to the mother again pointing out the father, only for Norma Jeane to find that the father is not a man but a photograph). The novelist edits scenes like a director. One chapter is subtitled "a montage"; in fact the whole novel is a montage. As in classic film theory, the montage produces sense by contrast—and the novel partakes precisely of the slicing to which Marilyn objects.

In its display of multiple realities, the novel slips at times into hallucination. The Blond Actress goes to a restaurant on her first date with the Ex-Athlete, soon after she has aborted the baby of the ménage à trois. Visiting the ladies' room, she suspects that the attendant is a girl who was in the orphanage with her. She doesn't speak to her but starts to imagine this face from the past as implying a knowledge of the real *her*; the real her, as opposed to "the role invented for her," is the original Norma Jeane, the deprived child but also the passionate and sexual adult Norma—who because of the abortion is susceptible to judgment. Being known is being condemned. As she prepares to leave, the attendant says, "Miss Monroe? You forgot this" (402). What she has forgotten is something in a towel: "a red mangled gob of flesh," a recognizable fetus. The effect is nightmarish. The reader may take a moment to realize that this scene can't be literally true, since the fetus has been efficiently aborted some time before. The memory hasn't vanished; an evening of rather awkward personal chat with the athlete has obliged Marilyn to suppress her deepest immediate concern, even while—as if in an improvised scene in an acting class—she appeals to the family-loving Italian Catholic by telling him (truthfully) that she is crazy about babies. The memory returns. The awareness of poverty and of the body suddenly culminates in horror; the text briefly identifies itself with her delusion.

The novel will return to the Ex-Athlete, ready to pay for the meal from his full wallet and excited by a beautiful woman crying (401): it returns to the realities of male power, wealth, and consumption. But the delusion will persist and spread. In her dressing room, a little later, the actress will dream of seeking to refuse the abortion, of the baby surviving to be placed (as she was herself, in childhood poverty) in a bureau drawer and screaming. The chapter ends with a sudden cut to a different perspective (indicated by italics). This time it is the view of an unidentified subordinate in the film studio, who greatly admires Marilyn's professionalism and sees her as a true, full personality, not a role, controlling the animated image that is produced of her, but who ends his or her comments with a brief anecdote of hearing a baby scream in her dressing room (411). The speaker seems to be puzzled, or curious, recognizing that there isn't actually any baby there. What the sound shows is that Marilyn is not in control. Insanity is starting to get the better of her, and it is an insanity that takes physical, or ghostly, form, perceived by the onlooker as well as the subject and accepted by the novelist. The novelist, that is, plunges her readers into a world of excess and transgression, a world of multiple social contacts, of uncompromising and conflicting desires, of violence and exploitation, of the pressures of history, economy, and ideology, a world where the passionate wish to be a whole person is defeated by the divisive forces of economic and sexual dependence, a dependence in which one's view of oneself is constituted by one's image in the eyes of others; such excess is manifest in the cruelty, the fantasy, the dream and nightmare realm that makes up the gothic quality of Oates's writing.

But this is no ordinary gothic spectacle. It is a tragic spectacle, a manifestation of "the storm of emotion" that in Oates's view "constitutes our human tragedy, if anything does."[11] The Playwright reflects, briefly, that "Mercantile-consumer America" is a "Tragic America. For the counterminings of Tragedy strike deeper than the cheap quick fixes of Comedy" (634). One should not wholly identify the author's vision with the Playwright's comment, which clearly points to the sobriety—and perhaps the elitism—of the real Arthur Miller, but the clue is given that *Blonde* can be read as tragedy, as, in fact, the kind of tragedy envisioned by Joyce Carol Oates in a much earlier book: "We seek the absolute dream. We are forced back continually into an acquiescence in all that is hallucinatory and wasteful, to a rejection of all norms and gods and dreams of 'tragedy' followed by the violent loss of self that signals the start of artistic effort: an appropriation by destruction, or an assimilation into the self of a reality that cannot be named" (*EI*, 3).

The author and the reader contemplate the alien, excessive, anomic world that surpasses any sense of "tragedy" as order and survival: Oates's tragedy is a tragedy of violence, of will: "Art is built around violence, around death; at its base is fear" (*EI*, 6). The vision is a disturbing one. It makes for uncomfortable reading. But it enables the author to combine a fidelity to the reality of an individual with a constant sense of passionate significance.

8
Ford: *The Sportswriter*

FRANK BASCOMBE, THE NARRATOR OF RICHARD FORD'S *THE SPORTS-writer*, used to be a real writer. He published a book of short stories and started a novel. Sometime after he gave up the novel, he was writer-in-residence at a New England college. And that is his literary career. It is a career that nevertheless still follows him around, in undignified ways. When, toward the end of *The Sportswriter*, he visits the home of Walter Luckett, an acquaintance who has committed suicide, he finds that Walter has been in possession of a copy of his collection, *Blue Autumn*, stolen from the local public library. In *Independence Day*, the sequel, Frank finds a copy of *Blue Autumn* in the bookshelves of a hotel where he stays and is resigned to finding that it is covered with dust, though more regretful to find written in it both a loving message to the woman to whom it has been given and a vigorously resentful reply from the woman, dated some years later.

In his lapsed state, he's not quite sure what he thinks about literature, though he still thinks about it quite a lot; the "real writers" haunt his book. Alice Hoffman, in a perceptive and generally sympathetic review, comments that "his inability to write fiction, which should illuminate his inability to connect emotionally, instead seems trivial."[1] Perhaps "inability" is not quite the right word, but certainly his abandonment of fiction is crucial to his relationships with other people, and readers may feel that it is so central to Frank's concerns, and so richly developed in the course of the novel, as to be far from trivial. Ford's novel, in other words, is about fiction, and about the way fiction favors or restrains emotional connection. The novel examines this theme through the personality of Frank as it appears in the act of narration. He tells his story (mostly) moment by moment, apparently recounting events and his reaction to them as they occur. This might seem to be an extremely unsophisticated, literal form of writing, not far from the diary. For Frank himself, that is perhaps what it actually is. But for Ford and his reader, it is something else; for author and reader can see things in the narrator that he cannot see—or cannot make explicit—himself, and much of the interest of the novel lies in the gap between, on the one hand, the partial self-knowledge of a narrator who is intelligent and observant but whose capacity for self-criticism is underdeveloped, and, on the other hand, the judgment of him implied by the logic of the whole text, which the reader can perceive as a judgment intended by the author. In terms of narratological theory, Frank is an unreliable narrator; if his account of objective events is meticulous and precise, his interpretation and assessment of them are not endorsed by novel itself.

Frank is satisfied to be a sportswriter, though he has little interest in sport. His phrasing in *Independence Day*—which narrates a time when he has given up sportswriting as well as real writing—is, admittedly, less than enthusiastic: he has been "happily dedicated to giving voice to the inarticulate and inane in order that an abstracted-but-still-yearning readership be painlessly diverted" (*ID*, 146).[2] This looks satirical, or dismissive, but that "happily" is genuinely meant, and the state of being "abstracted-but-still-yearning," despite the difference in vocabulary, looks very much like the state of "dreaminess" into which Frank has fallen after the death of his young son Ralph, and that brings about strains in his marriage which finally lead to divorce. Sportswriting is precisely a diversion, with what that implies in classic terminology; it diverts from death and tragedy. The point is made more subtly in *The Sportswriter*: there he asserts that sportswriting, sitting in empty stands, talking to coaches and equipment managers, is his perfect calling: "How more easily assuage the life-long ache to anticipate than to write sports—an ache only zen masters and coma victims can live happily without?" (50). Anticipation is a key concept in this novel, and it has just been defined: "Anticipation is the sweet pain to know whatever's next—a must for any real writer" (49). Anticipation is a sensitivity to changing experience; it is felt at its most intense in sexual tension and given artistic expression in the music of Ray Charles, with its "four low minor-note sex-and-anticipation vamp" (280). It is lack of anticipation that brings Walter to suicide, in Frank's view: "He quit being interested in what's next, I guess" (334). Anticipation is specially linked with real writing and merely assuaged by sportswriting.

So what does Frank think of real writers? Once he shows serious respect at least for the greatest of them: the Tolstoys and George Eliots are great because they understand the feelings of others (52). Frank and his friend Bert Brisker, who has given up poetry for sportswriting and then reviewing, don't understand this. They suffer from a failure of imagination; they have lost their authority. Literature has authority; it is complicated and enigmatic (48). Frank, then, has a dignified, respectful, humanistic view of literature as expressing the complexities of common experience, and it may be that Ford endorses this view, even though much of the tone of *The Sportswriter* suggests a very different perspective, that of a more or less ironic solitude.

For Frank doesn't think respectfully all the time. What we see of the literary life in the book is unimpressive: Frank himself and Bert are has-beens. Walter, who considers writing a novel on the day he commits suicide and thinks of starting his novel with a suicide note, and who—in his real suicide note—sends Frank off on a wild-goose chase, "a novelistic red herring" (373) in search of a fictitious daughter, is a never-was. Frank's former lover, Selma, is a critical theorist and therefore is contemptuous of literature (232). If Frank were to drop his job as writer-in-residence, he would easily be replaced (231). Things have gone downhill since the days of Tolstoy and George Eliot.

Often, Frank simply notes that literature is not for him. His literary incapacity is apparent in the parodistic accounts of works he has written or might have written; the one about the bemused young Southerner who gets involved in sex and drugs and gun running and ends with a violent tryst with a Methodist minister's wife (42), or the unfinished novel *Tangier*, based on total ignorance of Tangier (44), or the crude dime novel that he imagines as he finds his girlfriend naked in their hotel room (174). More thoughtfully, there is the critique of his own work (and Bert's) with its "gross seriousness" (52–53). *The Sportswriter* itself, Ford's work and not Bascombe's, is serious but not grossly serious; Frank sees himself as a comic character, but his absurdity is of a kind that says something about a rootless self-acceptance. His literary exhaustion is a sign of his dreaminess: "Real writers have to be more attentive, of course, and attentive was what I wasn't much interested in being" (82). If he lacks attentiveness—and so, to a considerable extent anticipation—he lacks also concern for other people ("that alone would disqualify you as a writer right there, since what else is literature but somebody telling you what somebody else is thinking," 82) and confidence and perspective: "That we all look at [the world] from someplace, and in some hopeful-useful way, is about all I found I could say—my best, most honest effort. And that isn't enough for literature, though it didn't bother me much" (57–58). Here the emphasis is shifting. This is not about Frank's weaknesses; it's about his honesty, and about the falsity of literature. The view that literature is untrue to the real limits of authentic vision is one that is forcefully expressed elsewhere. Literature, Frank tells us, lies; it lies by imposing order, clarity, and uniformity of feeling and experience.

So he claims to have learned from sportswriting that "there are no transcendent themes in life. . . . The other view is a lie of literature and the liberal arts" (22). (Walter will confess in his suicide note that he can't succeed in writing a novel because he can find no themes in his own life [355].) Later he comments on "a minor but pernicious lie of literature, that at times like these [times of extreme emotion: touchdowns and orgasms] we are any of us altogether *in* an emotion, that we are within ourselves and not able to detect other emotions we might also be feeling, or be about to feel, or prefer to feel" (125). The example of falsehood he offers his uncomprehending students is Joyce's epiphanies. The term recurs in a crucial moment: the death of his son passes unnoticed by Frank or his wife (known in this novel as X and in *Independence Day* as Ann) until a nurse realizes what has happened. The event is almost an anticlimax, arousing no complexity of thought or feeling: "No lines of poetry. No epiphanies" (265). Elsewhere, the falsity of literature, of the belief in "the *oneness of the writer's vision*," is contrasted with another of Frank's key terms, "seeing around", the ability to "think of other ways I might be feeling about what I was writing, or other voices I might be speaking in." (70).

It is easy enough to comment that this view of the writer's vision is one that has largely been replaced by literary theorists such as Selma, who stress the multiplicity of the author's voice and vision; Bascombe fails as a writer because he doesn't know how post-modern he is. But we should stress too that the novel is not just his expression of envy for the real writers; it is also a sporadic but obsessive confrontation with one sort of literature, and it is inspired by an ethos that is both implicit in Frank's conduct and carefully formulated by him on many occasions, an ethos of contingency.

It is an ethos he continues to espouse in *Independence Day*, where he speaks of his ex-wife's concern with "truth's defeat by the forces of contingency, most frequently represented by yours truly" (*ID*, 253), and where he argues that society is not a persistent organism but "isolated, contingent groups trying to improve on an illusion of permanence" (*ID*, 386), but that his new life as a realtor helps him to see contingency as "father to true self-sufficiency" (439). *Independence Day*, that is, offers a rich and balanced account of contingency as an Emersonian willed self-reliance, as a freedom from the other and from the past, or as near criminal negligence: contingency here is the acceptance of accident that allows his son Paul to be struck by a baseball thrown at a speed of seventy-five miles per hour, at the risk of losing the sight of one eye.

In *The Sportswriter*, contingency is the view that "most things are better if you just let them be lonely facts" (100). The context is important. Frank is, in effect, rebuffing a confession from Walter. Walter, like Frank, is divorced and is shaken, confused, and resentful at the experience. Unlike Frank, he searches for a confidant; he chooses Frank, although he does not know him very well, and confesses to him a recent homosexual experience that seems to have confused him even more. Frank, indifferent to most people, particularly indifferent to Walter, whom he views as no more than a companion in time passing, and outstandingly indifferent to other people's sexual morality, seeks to dissuade Walter from any preoccupation with his own past. Facts should stand by themselves; they should be independent; they are not transcendent themes. They do not need to be placed in a framework of moral judgment, in a vision of common humanity or in a history of personal growth or personal guilt. Things just happen. Like the existential heroes of Sartre or Camus, Frank simply records one thing after another, and he does so in the name of an honesty that is akin to solipsism; only the moment contains reality. "As far as I'm concerned," says a character in another novel, "things just happen. One minute don't learn the next one nothin" (*PH*, 230). This is the contrary of literature, of any kind (so Sartre and Camus—and Ford—in fact develop a discreet but unadmitted framework): the most modest literature implies some cohesion in the life of its characters and some framework of values that enables communication between author and reader. Frank is consistent in his arguments (even if his views might seem to make consistency pointless): he rejects the past in general, and the novel of reminiscence in particular. He is a "proponent of forgetting" (150) who is "heartsick . . . when the novelist makes his clanking, obligatory trip into the Davy Jones locker of the past" (30); one of the vices of *Tangier* was the hero's search for his sense of history (44). "We all have histories," Frank reflects a little later, but they are only interesting if they are false or incomplete: "To the extent that it's incompletely understood or undisclosed, or just plain fabricated, I suppose it's true that history can make mystery" (47–48).

Mystery is another of the key terms of *The Sportswriter*; it is the sense of fascination that arises from a refusal of "full disclosure" and is essential to anticipation. So Frank is rejecting history as established fact; he accepts it as a work of imagination. The distinction relates to another, very pervasive theme of the novel, the praise of literalism and the rejection of factualism. Factualism is a grim recognition of unchangeable fact (above all the "bedrock factuality" of death, 67); literalism is the delighted welcoming of the immediate and the refusal of any beyond. The ideal literalist is Frank's current girl friend, Vicki, "a literalist from the word go, happy to let the world please her in the small ways it can" (134). And the novel is essentially the story of Frank's own desire to let the world please him, to "say yes to as much as I can" (58), to find "real wonder in the familiar" (136). If this attitude of wide-ranging acceptance is to produce literature at all, one is inclined to say, it will produce poetry (like the poetry of Roethke, which advocates "letting the everyday make you happy," 25, and which X rejects). It will not produce narrative, which depends, at the least, on desire and opposition. *The Sportswriter* is thus a conflict between Frank, the believer in contingency, the enemy of the novel, and Ford, who has produced a novel that recounts plausibly what the reader is likely to perceive as a significant section of Frank's life. More pedantically put, Ford has faced the challenge of writing a novel (and, eventually, two novels) about a character who is dismissive of the novel as a form—because he is dismissive of the values of personal maturing and social integration—and making him seem attractive enough to engage the reader's attention for nearly four hundred pages, while at the same time undercutting his perspective sufficiently to reinstate the values that he challenges. European and American thought have tended toward a simplifying hedonism, toward nihilism and egocentricity, toward a rejection of inner complexity and even of articulate consciousness. Works of literature have shown characters rebelling against the assumptions of responsibility and continuity. Ford's starting point is different: he starts with a character who takes for granted a largely accidental and irresponsible life and asks if such a life can satisfy.

An answer is given by Frank himself, in circumstances that typically combine the ridiculous with the pathetic and the reflective. Returning from a very unsatisfactory lunch with Vicki's family, a gang of eccentrics and oafs, he stops at a roadside supermarket to call his old flame, Selma. Since he has not seen her for a considerable time and left her without great emotion, the conversation fails to flow, and at first she does not even remember who he is. As the conversation struggles on, a teenage hooligan driving in the neighboring parking lot strikes a supermarket cart, which in turn strikes the telephone booth and breaks the glass. Continuing with a bleeding knee and a shattered fragment of glass resting against his leg, Frank tells Selma, "It must seem like I live a life of chaos and confusion"; Selma agrees but notes, humorously, that it doesn't seem to bother him (310). But it is bothering him a bit; as he speaks he imagines the dead face of Walter and regrets that he didn't think of warning him against ending his life. It *is* a life of chaos and confusion; it is so because Frank barely plans his life, living from sensation to sensation and from impulse to impulse. The chaos and confusion make for much of the comedy of the book, as does the equanimity with which Frank generally handles them. But the equanimity is not complete. He does aspire to something: on his way to interview a disabled sportsman, he observes in his hotel people who resemble his acquaintances, and regards these resemblances as signs that life is not random, but structured by the wish for rewarding contacts (149).

Yet the story of the novel is a series of encounters that are not at all rewarding: the disabled sportsman Herb Wallagher is not the model of courage and resilience Frank hopes to present to his readers—and still at the end of the novel thinks it possible to offer them in a spirit of stereotyped fiction—but an embittered and aggressive eccentric; Vicki is not the complaisant bimbo with whom he hopes to live on a level of undemanding pleasure, but shows her frustration at his failure to demonstrate real commitment; Walter is not the easygoing companion of the leisure hours that he looks for in his Divorced Men's Club (to which he thoughtlessly attempts to recruit the police officer who is investigating Walter's death, since Walter has created a vacancy). People are stranger and more demanding, or more remote, than Frank thinks. And his self-centeredness leads to a series of scandalous acts that contribute further to his isolation: he spies on X, interrogates their son Paul about her conduct and tells him to lie to her about his presence, invites Vicki to a motel after the fraught lunch and after the news of Walter's death, asks X to have sex with him in Walter's apartment, and avoids the person he takes (mistakenly as it happens) to be Walter's sister arriving from another town to cope with the aftermath of his death. A characteristic example appears in the conversation with Selma: although most of the conversation is amicable if a little strained, as he is about to ring off, he is resisting the temptation to tell her to go to hell, reproaching her for having rejected him in the past. But what sort of man would say that? he asks. The answer comes a second later: she says, "You should be careful," he says, "Go to hell," and she replies, "Yes, goodbye" and is suddenly gone (310–11). He does what he doesn't want to; the lonely fact of his old bitterness has overridden his concern for normal courtesy. No harm has been done, it appears, but he has lost a little dignity. Selma doesn't condemn him; Vicki and X do, Walter makes his disappointment clear enough, and Herb tells him he is full of shit. The novel, as has so often been the way of novels, shows not the isolated individual but the individual defending himself against society—and in this case often a justly aggrieved society.

Why is he phoning Selma, anyway? For a man who is a proponent of forgetting, Frank is extraordinarily obsessed with the past. In addition to Selma, there is the story of his attempts to get in touch with an old flame, Mindy Levinson (204). The episode is another charming instance of incompetence, deviousness, and nostalgia: leafing fascinated through what seems to be an Orvis catalog—for quite a protracted period of his life he is addicted to catalogs, that "literature of desire" (201)—he recognizes one of the photographic models as Mindy. He phones the firm, purporting to buy something, casually asks after the models, and when the salesperson quite correctly refuses to give him any information he cancels his order. He then makes his way to the town where the firm is based, and with some modest detective work finds Mindy and has a brief meeting with her, which he regard as "a brief love affair not quite" and a help to looking on the brighter side of things after Ralph's death. He has glimpsed perfection (208), just as he has briefly found perfection with Selma (234). Perfection is in the past, and it can only be remote or temporary: most Americans, according to Herb, believe that real life is somewhere else (164; many Ford characters believe this: "Where's the real life?" asks one of them (*RS*, 153). Only the violent basketball manager, Mutt Greene, an epitome of the short-term concentration that the novel often attributes to athletes, believes that "real life's going on here" (257). Life is lacking; the past is revived as a partial remedy for that lack.

But lost perfection is not the only significance of the past; there is also the past of suffering, the past of Frank's loss of X and of the death of Ralph, evoked with tenderness and a sense of dereliction time after time. This novel does its own trip into the Davy Jones locker of the past. The narrator asserts that Ralph's death must not be "entrapped by time and events" (24); one can respect the wish to give it a sacred, atemporal quality, to make it survive the breakup of the marriage, but it *is* an event in time and it does continue to captivate both Frank and X, their imaginations still overwhelmed by death, very strangely so when Frank encourages Paul in the belief that the dead Ralph can be contacted by carrier pigeon. It is significant enough that the visit to Ralph's grave is the starting point of the whole novel, for their shared loss is now the essential link between his parents—a link that will be strained toward the end of the novel by their visit to the site of a different death, that of Walter Luckett.

This affects the time structure of the narrative. The story, in many respects, looks like a close chronological tracking of the three days from Good Friday, 20 April 1984 to the following Easter Monday morning; the sequential presentation, the meticulous marking of dates and times, the precise recording of the geography of New Jersey, and the detailed presentation of observations and conversations reflect accurately enough the narrator's acceptance of the flowing present. In fact the sequence is much more complex. The story is interrupted by a flashback to Thursday evening, when Frank and Walter have a lengthy conversation (a conversation that takes us further back in time since this is when Walter recounts his homosexual experience of two nights before); scattered through the whole work are Frank's recollections of his life with X, the death of Ralph, and Frank's time at Berkshire College. The novel *almost* lives in the present, but the present is interwoven with the past, and, despite the narrator's ahistorical sense, life does form a continuum.

And these are no ordinary three days. It is no chance that the three days are the days of Easter, of Christ's harrowing of hell. (Herb's comment that real life is elsewhere echoes Rimbaud's *Season in Hell*, an earlier recasting of the harrowing.) The point is very persistently made. Vicki, the good-time girl, frequently refers to her conversion to Catholicism. Her stepmother works for a Catholic charity. Frank has an African lodger who is studying at the seminary that appears to be the major institution of Haddam, N.J., and Frank himself, to all appearances a thoroughgoing materialist, attends a church service on Easter Sunday. Two related issues appear in the mythical framework that is inconclusively hinted at here: Christianity is concerned with temporality (it is a religion of historical incarnation), and it is concerned—above all at Easter—with resurrection or regeneration. The lodger Bosobolo, the theological student (whom Walter consistently takes for the butler), asserts the first point: when Frank, who has drifted away from religion as he has drifted away from writing, failing to find in it the rapture he seeks, challenges him as to whether he reads Hobbes, he replies, "He was a Christian, too. Temporality interested him" (242). The claim that interest in temporality is a proof of Christian belief may seem tenuous, but it is picked up when Frank, immediately after, attends church. His reason for attending is not at all clear; his view of the usher (who addresses him as Jim) is distinctly satirical and his view of the minister, with his loud actor's voice, is not much better. But the minister's words promise that life begins again, and Frank responds to the myth with a sense of elevation, experiencing "a rare immanence"; he joins in the singing, "Rise my soul and stretch thy wings," and leaves before the

end of the service, "'saved' in the only way I can be (*pro tempore*) and
... ready to march on toward dark temporality, my banners all aflutter"
(244). Temporality, for him, appears to be the joyous acceptance of the
future; it appears to be anticipation writ large. Walter, he later reflects,
"gave himself up to the here and now, but got stranded" (340); Frank,
at this point, is not stranded because he believes in a promise, however
vague. His salvation is temporary. In other words he has not really risen
"from transitory things toward heaven, thy destined place" (244); to do
so would be to totally deny his life's strategy. For him temporality is a
renewal of vitality. To this extent it seems a resurrection of the kind
that he is to denounce a few hours later. Observing a kitsch crucifixion
ostentatiously displayed by Vicki's stepmother at their house, and disturbed by the news of Walter's death, he reflects mockingly on Christ's
irresponsibility. "He should try resurrection in today's complex world.
He'd fall right off His cross on His ass. He couldn't sell newspapers"
(300).

Irrelevant as orthodox religion may be, the period of the novel looks
like a period of resuscitation, but it isn't exactly. It goes from a death
on Good Friday to another death on Easter Sunday; the ending on
Monday morning is a mild and cheerful acceptance that life is going
on. On Sunday night Frank flees Haddam and all the failures he has
encountered there and goes, for want of anywhere better, to the sports
magazine he writes for. There he meets a new woman, a charming, sophisticated, self-confident Ivy League graduate who has started to work
for the same magazine and who makes her attraction to Frank very
clear. The main part of the novel ends with Frank anticipating again; in
the last lines of chapter 13 he waits expectantly as he hears her footsteps
approaching, reflecting with satisfaction that "no-one's noticed me
standing here at all"—that he has escaped Walter's melancholy view of
maturity: "when we get to be adults we all of a sudden become the thing
viewed, and not the viewer anymore" (191). The reader finds, without
surprise, from the concluding chapter (headed "*The End*") that this is
one more short-lived adventure; Frank's rebirth is simply the acceptance of his haphazard and temporary life. The three days of the novel,
in other words, are not quite a manifestation of the Easter story, and
not quite a refutation of it; they are a demonstration of an awareness of
pattern coexisting with a life of chance. The novelist, that is, imposes a
framework of established cultural values that are alien to the character's
ideology. He is respectful enough of his character—and perhaps skeptical enough of the great myths—to avoid a rigorous demonstration of the

pertinence of that framework, but its presence shows that life cannot be perceived as wholly random.

As indeed do Frank's own preferences. It is difficult, Walter says, to identify the themes of one's life. It is far from difficult to identify the themes of Frank's life. There are the themes entailed in his own idiosyncratic but consistent vocabulary: anticipation, rapture, mystery, literalism, full disclosure, and dreaminess. And there are the themes he's not quite so conscious of, but which the reader can grasp easily enough: his nostalgia for love, parenthood, and real writing, his courteous and good-natured avoidance of intimacy, and his moments of uncontrolled possessiveness. These are the ways in which Frank is unreliable as a narrator. (Alice Hoffman, in the review already quoted, criticized the novel on the grounds that "the authorial voice is so weakened that we are left only with the observations of an emotionally untrustworthy narrator," but surely the authorial presence is strongly implied in the interplay between Frank's voice and those of the people who surround him.) The reader understands him better than he does himself, sees him as seeking to insist on freedom while longing for fixity. Frank "hate[s] for things to get finally pinned down" (89); the form of the novel he lives in goes a long way to pinning him down.

The division within Frank accounts for much of the pathos of the novel, and for much of its attraction too. The character who knows himself too little is both a demonstration of wrongness and a demonstration of a comic energy; if one can sympathize with Frank enough to follow his adventures through the novel it is in large part because he has the gifts of a novelist while vigorously denying that he is one. He has the gift of acute perception of sensation, despite his claim to lack attentiveness; he has the gift of acutely indicating the feelings of others, despite his apparent insensitivity to them in his practical dealings; he has the gift of precise memory and sharp judgment, despite his living for the instant. He implies the relation of his own life to the history of his country, from Vietnam to Reagan. Above all, perhaps, he can use language creatively, developing with disproportionate precision scenarios and visions that live independently of the real. A delightful example is his entering into the world of the catalogs, the world of houndstooth sports coats, upmarket doormats and dog collars with names stitched in.

He can enter into the imagined world of a community that is not quite his own. What more could a novelist do? Frank, in other words, is a novelist who doesn't know it; the spontaneous innocence with which he creates fictions does a lot to disarm his criticisms both of the lies of literature and of his own incapacity as a novelist.

This leaves two criticisms of fiction, which appear not in *The Sportswriter* but in *Independence Day*, and which depend on his being not too little but too much of a writer. Ann reproaches him for using literature as a mode of control: "'You should go back to writing stories, Frank. You quit too soon. . . . You could have everybody saying what you wanted them to, and everything would work out perfectly—for you anyway. . . . You just want everything to seem perfect and everybody to seem pleased. And you're willing to let *seem* equal *be*'" (*ID*, 184).

And he reproaches himself not for having the writer's oneness of vision, but for having the writer's ambiguity: "(My greatest human flaw and strength, not surprisingly, is that I can always imagine anything—a marriage, a conversation, a government- as being different from how it is, a trait that might make one a top-notch trial lawyer or novelist or realtor, but that also seems to produce a somewhat less than reliable and morally feasible human being)" (*ID*, 226). And these reproaches, it seems, are not answered.

9
Smiley: *A Thousand Acres*

In *The Sportswriter* the gap between first-person narrator and author is apparent essentially because of Frank's morally limited sensibility. Jane Smiley's *A Thousand Acres* also employs first-person narration and similarly invites the reader to judge through the words of Ginny, the narrator, her complex and sometimes unclear emotions and reactions.[1] But this novel does something else with the conventions of first-person narration. It imposes on the experiences of the narrator a framework derived from one of the great literary classics, and with it a whole debate about the meaning of gender and authority that has been part of English-language culture for centuries and has recently become the object of special focus in feminist writing. The novel, that is, presents its character as exemplifying more than she is conscious of, and this means that the reader is constantly unsure as to exactly what kind of sympathy and understanding to give to her, and as to exactly what kind of verisimilitude to look for in the work. Reading *A Thousand Acres* thus challenges the reader to assess his or her own ideas of plausibility, of goodness, of community; the ambiguity of literary status corresponds to a questioning of social values.

A Thousand Acres is about sexual abuse of daughters by their father. The topic had rightly received much press coverage and scholarly attention in the years before the publication of the novel: apart from the inherent cruelty and irresponsibility of parents who endanger their children's later psychological health, it brings into question the traditional acceptance of the authority of the family and especially of the father;[2] it reinforces, therefore, the feminist hostility to patriarchy. Jane Smiley throughout her work has shown herself to be aware of issues of power, and not least of the ambiguity of power in the family—or between friends—where control may be difficult to distinguish from love. In *Barn Blind*, the power is that of the dominant mother. In *Duplicate Keys*, it is the more tenuous power of the charismatic personality. More recently there has been the power of a slave-owning society and of the apparently benign family that accepts it in *Lidie Newton*. Personal relations, for her, are likely to be based on power, control, and exploitation, and it is not surprising that in *Ordinary Love* and, still more crucially in *A Thousand Acres*, the emphasis is on the power of the father.

The story of *A Thousand Acres* is the story of a daughter who becomes self-aware and self-assertive. Ginny, the eldest daughter of Larry Cook, is incapable of criticizing him at the beginning of the novel. She is the daughter who has most clearly accepted his way of life. Whereas her younger sister, Rose, has married an outsider, a musician, even though she has settled down to farming like their father, and the youngest, Caroline, has refused Larry's wish that she should remain on the farm and has become a lawyer, Ginny has married a farmer, lives near her father, sees him regularly, cooks for him, and has no ambitions outside farming. When Larry decides to divide his farm between his daughters in order to escape death duties, she suspects he is drunk. She recognizes—indirectly—that the effect of this gift will be to keep her bound to the farm (so that for the lawyer Caroline it would be a "trapdoor plunging her into a chute that would lead right back to the farm"), but she nevertheless agrees immediately to accept: "Take it," she tells herself, "He is holding it out to you, and all you have to do is take it" (19). But Ginny is to change. She comes to recognize her father's increasing eccentricity, as he buys a set of kitchen furniture but leaves it outside in the rain, and as he starts driving about the country while drunk and is finally arrested and charged. She realizes, as does Rose, that she has to control him for his own good; authority is disappearing. The crucial moment comes when Larry, furious at his daughters' attempts to prevent his folly, insists on leaving the house during a storm and, after wandering for some time, finds accommodation with a friend, Harold Clark. The effect is to menace the daughters' reputation in the eyes of the public, who are inclined to think that they have driven their father out into the storm. They are isolated and are forced into self-reliance; the easy harmony of family and community is disrupted. Ginny learns to choose: "it was time to sit up, to reach out, to choose this and not that" (147). Ginny, moreover, has already started to discover her individual potential by starting a love affair with Harold's son, Jess, who has recently returned from exile as a draft dodger. This too contributes to her awareness of how she differs from society: she realizes that "to the eyes of almost any outsider, it would look like I had become my own enemy and the enemy of all my family and friends" (166). But she has still not realized one crucial fact about herself. She does not remember that, after their mother's death, while Ginny was a teenager, her father regularly abused her sexually. Rose has suffered in the same way and remembers it; her memory has made her bitter about her father and has led her to be acutely concerned to protect her own daughters from him, sending them away to school despite their reluctance and instructing them not to let him into the house. And it has made her a fiercely critical spirit, one who does not accept authority. When she seeks to remind Ginny of their father's behavior, Ginny refuses to believe; it is only sometime later, when she briefly rests in the bedroom she had as a child, that she has a sudden revelation of the truth of Rose's memory. There has been another clue: a family friend tells her that their mother was worried for their future, because "she knew what your father was like, even though I think she loved him," and because "Ginny won't stand up to him" (91). But even this friend, though she feels guilty at failing to protect the girls against an evil she doesn't name, praises her for her acceptance: "You're a good girl, and unselfish, and you will be rewarded. I believe that" (92).

Ginny grows more selfish; much of the fascination of the novel lies in its reflection on the extent to which what is called selfishness is ruthless pride and indifference to others—not so different from the father's—and the extent to which it is a legitimate wish for choice, freedom. Ginny tells Rose that she recognizes the truth of her memories when she chances to overhear her father and realizes that he can't tell his daughters apart, attributing the behavior of one to another—the joint effect, no doubt, of senility and of an exploitative attitude toward them. She is driven to decisiveness by the wish to be recognized. We need others, Smiley says elsewhere, "for the recognition of our identities" (*PG*, 111); Larry's abuse has been a failure to distinguish personalities. But Ginny's search for personal fulfillment drives her also to evil. Finding that her lover Jess has abandoned her for Rose and has told Rose of their affair, she again feels unrecognized; she feels that her individuality has been denied by Jess, the kindly, sensitive radical, as it was by her father, and she sets out to murder her sister. Fortunately the attempt fails: she gives her sister a jar of poisoned sausages, which Rose, under the influence of the vegetarian Jess, does not eat but stores indefinitely.

Ginny's final state is one of loss but also one of honesty. She leaves her husband, who has been, as she sees it, unduly critical of her and unduly indulgent to her father and to Caroline, who has taken the father's side, leaves the farm to him (as he asserts that "I gave my life to this place" [330]), and chooses change. The change is a drab but independent life as a waitress in a nearby town. Eventually she will divorce her husband and be reconciled, after a frank confession, with Rose, now dying of cancer, and take responsibility for Rose's daughters: a modest but healthy female family is created. The novel ends with an implicit dialogue on forgiveness: Rose is proud to remember that "I didn't forgive the unforgivable" (355); but in the final pages Ginny reflects with melancholy gravity on what she has learned, on the enrichment of self that has come from conflict, on the "inheritance" that comes not from patriarchy but from experience, from the "dead young self" that has enabled her to understand desire and evil (370).

The story, then, is one that is intelligible and, in general, convincing in realistic terms. The reader should be aware of the normal processes of aging and the accompanying need for children to take charge of their parents, of the divergent views that may occur between siblings, of the mixture of rivalry and affection that is common between siblings, of the frustration that may be felt by a woman whose husband is kindly and responsible but wholly unromantic, and of the pressures of familiarity and conformity that arise in small communities; the reader can see these exemplified in the novel and respond with the appropriate feelings of melancholy sympathy. The reader may well perceive also that these common problems take on a somewhat special form because of the countryman's concern to maintain land ownership, because of the intense demands of farm work in time and energy, and because of the slowness of change these things produce, and may feel that such restrictions form a complex balance with the farmer's pride of independence and closeness to the natural world (this is, in other words, a very restrained pastoral). The reader will, furthermore, have been alerted to the special problem of sexual abuse by recent public concern and will have little difficulty in feeling sympathy for the victims, as well as admiration for the extent to which Ginny and Rose are able to maintain self-respect in a situation that might have led to long-term humiliation. A feature that might have seemed extraordinary to the uninformed reader, the fact that Ginny can forget what she has suffered, is in fact no problem for anyone who recalls widespread accounts of suppressed memories (and, incidentally, of false memories). The whole psychological development of Ginny, moreover, follows a well-known pattern, that of self-development or self-discovery through an experience of extremes, including an experience of one's own guilt: the verisimilitude here rests not on everyday conversation, nor on newspaper coverage, but on a huge mass of novels, plays, and films that explore the consequences of facing up to unrecognized desires and conflicts.

In all these respects, then, the events of the novel convince us that they are the kind of things that could happen. The one point that readers may find difficult in this respect is Ginny's plan to murder her sister, with whom she has generally been on very close terms if not always in complete sympathy. The crucial passages show the author's acute concern to convey, through the first-person narration, a motivation that the character does not herself yet fully grasp. Rose, somewhat drunk, tells Ginny three shocking things: that she has had an affair with Jess, that she knows about Jess's relationship with Ginny, and that her husband Pete is involved in the accident that has blinded Harold. She further speaks openly, even brutally, of their father's "fucking and beating" them. And Ginny sees a betrayal in Rose's knowing selfishness and in her perception of Ginny's passivity. "I guess you want everything for yourself, huh," she says to Rose, and "You sound like you forgive yourself completely"; she comes to the conclusion that "Rose had been too much for me, had done me in" (304). Her disillusion amounts to recognizing that Rose is separate from herself (301–2). In the next chapter she starts to reflect with meticulous, housewifely efficiency on the availability of poisons on the farm and on the most effective way of destroying Rose. She destroys Rose because Rose has destroyed her vision of herself—a vision based on the concept of trust and moderation that the events of the novel have disproved. Ginny's crime is therefore a protest against disillusion. The most surprising event in the novel, then, the one that seems to introduce a major disruption into the character's motivation, is a response to the sudden disclosure, through Rose, of a world of amoral egoism, a world without order.

With this exception, the reader may be concerned that *A Thousand Acres* doesn't tell us enough about its subject; he or she may feel that precisely the factors that make the book easy to accept as a realistic account of how a person changes are the ones that prevent the author from challenging our preconceptions and offering us a fresh vision. In other words, they make this a middlebrow book. The answer, at this stage of analysis, lies in four things. First, the book is a contemplation of authority. One thing that focuses this theme in particular is the religious vocabulary. Larry is God: to distrust him is to break the First Commandment (109); he is "the living source of us all"(176), "the great I AM" (211). Second, it is a study or order and continuity and the ambiguities these bring. Larry, the biggest farmer, owns the biggest farm; that fits Ginny's sense of order (20). He "sought impossibility . . . to discipline the farm and ourselves to a life and order transcending many things, but especially mere whim" (46), and yet his wife has had to cater to his "whims and inflexible demands" (48). Later Ginny seeks to impose on him "a whole orderly future" (148). Larry insists on unchanging routine but himself disrupts the order of the farm by bestowing it (at least in appearance) on his daughters, and he is impervious to time: "Daddy thinks history starts fresh every day," Rose comments, bitterly, "that time itself begins with the feelings he's having right now. That's how he keeps betraying us" (216). But if order is often questionable, a mask for patriarchal power, if, as Ginny learns from Rose (342), the continuity of the ownership of the farm is not the grand history her husband sees but the blows she has suffered, nevertheless evil brings the need for a deeper order. Rose, with her usual uncompromising harshness, comments on the blinding of Harold as a sort of justice: "There's got to be something, order, rightness. Justice, for God's sake" (235). (The gods are just, she implies.) Third, it is a study of self-deception. "Had I faced the facts," Ginny asks herself—before the issue of sexual abuse has arisen, in connection with Rose's cancer. "Your own endurance might be a pleasant fiction allowed you by others who have really faced the facts" (90). Should you maintain, like the untransformed Ginny and her mother, "the unbroken surface of the unsaid" (94)? Fourth, it conveys with intense precision the rhythm of work, the planning of the farming economy, the variety of plants, of produce, of the seasons, the decline into senility. It shows the satisfactions of the rural life and the cruelties of the family. And to this extent, according to the definition in another of Smiley's works, it is a tragedy: "Tragedy did seem to me to be something that took place on one spot—at home perhaps, where all the characters were gathered together and all knew each other and the actions of each destroyed the others" (*LN*, 442). It is a tragedy based on a serious reflection on the destructiveness of power and on the insidious corruption that lies in accepting this power as normal and orderly, a corruption that permits exploitation and produces disillusion and loss of self-regard.

But this, as everyone knows, is not the only tragic thing about *A Thousand Acres*. If the reader does not know it from reviews or criticism, it is made clear as soon as he or she looks at the cover of the paperback: *A Thousand Acres* is a transposition of *King Lear*. Even if one didn't know before starting the novel, one should learn fairly soon. A rich man called Larry wants to divide his property between his three daughters, Ginny, Rose, and Caroline. The two eldest are married, the third is about to marry—someone called Frank. The youngest refuses to accept the share offered her. This happens within the first twenty pages, with some of the abruptness that marks the opening scene of *King Lear*. There is, then, a double reading of Smiley's novel. As has been shown so far, it is a realistic account of possible events in modern America. It can be judged in terms of its verisimilitude, its thematic subtlety and originality, its intensity of feeling. But also it is a rewriting of a familiar and much respected text, and so would seem to invite a quite different type of explanation and assessment: how can a work built on a coherence of social and psychological plausibility be any sort of equivalent for a Shakespearian tragedy built on a coherence of poetic symbolism and tragic gesture? And are the rather conspicuous ingenuity required of the author and the fairly easy decoding required of the reader justified by any serious relationship to Shakespeare and his world? If the novel is to be successful on this level, it needs to have a double motivation for much the behavior of the characters: Larry has to give away the farm both so that his family can avoid death duties and in order to replicate Lear—though of course the second purpose is not part of his psychology: the overdetermination implies that the work as a whole is authorial artifice, a text produced with a strong sense of previous culture. (Is it too fanciful to recall here the way the New Testament repeats the "types" of the Old, a structure to which Frank Kermode has drawn attention?[3]) Here lies perhaps the crucial critical issue concerning the novel. Conrad, for instance, who does not mention the death duties motivation and so finds Larry's decision inexplicable, is obviously uneasy with the fact that "the lives of [the novel's] characters have been predetermined by a Shakespearian text they know nothing about."[4] He doesn't quite say, as Sartre did, that the novel is the genre committed to personal freedom, but his disquiet suggests it.

The case that has just been mentioned is not too problematical. Larry's act is part of a complex set of feelings about the need to preserve: to preserve the farm, to preserve his own authority, and to preserve the continuity of the family (though, to Larry's regret, though the female line), to bring Caroline back into his own orbit while at the same time ensuring himself a leisurely retirement. Lear also wishes a leisurely retirement and is conscious of his "crawl towards death"; he wishes to prevent future strife in the kingdom. And he wishes to be flattered; his bestowal is a demand for gratitude. In both Renaissance England and modern Iowa, old men can act out of recognition that age and impending death make it politic for their control to be indirect, that the moral respect earned by apparent generosity will do more to maintain the set-up they wish to see than would any last-minute clinging to power. The most apparent difference is that the Renaissance was a period of verbal ornateness and that Lear therefore demands articulacy, where Larry requires only instant assent. Age and power go together now as they did four hundred years ago; the continuity of culture has been, in part at least, a continuity of authority.

But there are problems about this double motivation. One problem is that one may suspect mere ingenuity. People do not often have their eyes put out in modern America, at least not in the contest of unpleasant but restricted domestic conflicts. Smiley's Gloucester character, Harold Clark, is blinded by an accident with fertilizer, compounded by Pete, Rose's husband, who, in an attempt to harm Larry, has removed the water supply with which Harold might have washed out the harmful substance. How clever, one is tempted to say. The overall pattern is, however, made convincing and significant: like Cornwall, Pete has a "fiery quality." He is an impulsive and extreme character who has a history of conflict with Larry. He is remorse stricken at the effects of his action (unintended, unlike those of Cornwall: *A Thousand Acres*, bleak as it is in many ways, is a less harsh text than *Lear*; it lacks the sense of ultimate malevolence). Cornwall is killed in revenge for his cruelty; Pete commits suicide in a pond that has been a focus of intimacy, reflectiveness, and memory for him and Ginny. The episode is effectively integrated into the novel's concerns with conflict, environment, and the unpredictability of action, and yet it leaves the reader aware of a certain virtuosity, of an authorial effort to retrieve a modern meaning from the Shakespearian legacy.

It is in Ginny's poisoning of Rose that the problem of transposition perhaps appears most acutely. The unsympathetic reader may feel that the *only* reason Ginny poisons Rose is that Goneril poisons Regan. In fact, the patterning of the texts here is very different. Ginny acts from a sudden crushing sense of betrayal. Goneril acts out of sheer lust and rivalry, furious that Regan has had the effrontery to replace her as lover and benefactor to Edmund; a forceful and unrestrained character throughout, she has incarnated a passionate animal naturalness (whereas Cordelia incarnates a natural goodness) that has revealed itself in the play to be inherently evil. Caroline, toward the end of *A Thousand Acres*, tells Ginny that "Some people are just evil" (363), and Ginny is startled to realize that this refers not to Larry but to herself. Shakespeare does seem to imply that some people are just evil, that poisoning your sister follows more or less logically from flattering your father; Smiley shows that people are complicated, that single acts arise from multiple circumstances and so can have an almost accidental quality. In the last paragraphs of the novel Ginny comes to have some slight sympathy even for her father, subject to "the goad of an unthinkable urge" (370). This understanding of action can be stated in more than one way.

Morally, it is a recognition of a modern relativism that is reluctant to recognize unrelieved good or evil; aesthetically, it is a characteristic of the novel as a genre, which has room for chance, for ambiguity, for muffled effects and anticlimax. A novel, according to Milan Kundera, is "a realm where moral judgement is suspended. Suspending moral judgement is not the immorality of the novel; it is its morality."[5] In this instance, then, Smiley is asserting not the continuity of culture but the difference between our worldview and that of Shakespeare; she is reminding the reader that the unqualified condemnation that Caroline utters is part of our intellectual heritage, but a part that seems increasingly strange to us.

Smiley's novel therefore is both a transposition of *Lear* and a reply to it. As such it responds also to a major debate on the significance of Shakespeare that had concerned feminist criticism in the years before the publication of *A Thousand Acres*. Many feminists had welcomed his presentation of strong independent women, of female friendship, of the feminine values of family affection and domestic comradeship; others had perceived a distrust of women and a restriction of their social role. *King Lear* had been a particularly acute point of debate: if some critics stress the sincerity, openness and firmness of Cordelia, others see the play as essentially misogynistic, symbolizing in Goneril and Regan a hysterical fear of female energy and sexuality. A powerful (and, to my mind, convincing) statement of the latter view is given by McEachern, and a passionately balanced reflection on it by Joyce Carol Oates; a very sound survey of the issue is given by Ann Thompson.[6] Smiley has made clear her dissatisfaction with views of the play that prioritize the father's needs over those of the daughters;[7] against Shakespeare's concentration of evil in the female, she refocuses the story so as to concentrate evil in patriarchal power.[8]

This refocusing has some straightforward effects. Most obviously, Larry is unmistakably guilty. If some critics have seen an incestuous quality to Lear's relationship with Cordelia, there is no suggestion of previous sexual exploitation of any of his daughters.[9] Larry, by contrast, is obviously more sinning than sinned against. Furthermore, the characters who, in the original, serve essentially to assert the value of loyalty to the king or, at least, the centrality of the king disappear or are reduced in status. There is no Kent. The fool is the banker Marv Carson ("Marv Carson is a fool," another character points out, 49); his folly comprises only faddish eating habits, and he is in general an effective and dynamic (if not entirely reliable) businessman, who — to the relief of many readers, one may suspect — does not spend his time mocking Larry for giving away his riches. Harold, like Gloucester, is a loyal friend to the displaced monarch but is far from heroic: whereas Gloucester's blinding is the result of an eloquent denunciation of Cornwall over the storm incident, Harold merely creates embarrassment and ill will by an elaborately contrived denunciation of the daughters at a church social. And where Gloucester is misled by the evil Edmund, who shows all the spite of seventeenth-century bastardy, and so neglects the virtuous legitimate son Edgar, Harold has "damned and repudiated" the radical son Jess (69), and if he briefly appears to favor him over the innocuous elder son Loren, this is a dishonest contrivance that masks his real preference for order and obedience. Larry, moreover, does not gain in dignity but falls into an ever more profound helplessness; if he thinks that Caroline-Cordelia is dead, this is merely senile confusion.[10]

The most important transposition, however, lies in Goneril's barrenness. Lear curses Goneril, wishing her to be barren:

> Hear, Nature, hear! Dear Goddess, hear!
> Suspend thy purpose, if thou didst intend
> To make this creature fruitful!
> Into her womb convey sterility![11]

Larry, too, curses Ginny as a "barren whore" (181). And Ginny actually *is* barren: she has had a number of miscarriages, and these have not only caused major tension between herself and her husband but have also contributed to her sense of a lack of worth. But Jess recognizes that the problem is not hers but that of the environment; the miscarriages are brought about by the fertilizer applied to the land that has then made its way through the underground drainage channels to the wells from which the drinking water is drawn. The same system, it proves later, is responsible for Rose's death from cancer.

The implications of this are very wide ranging. The whole economy of the farm depends on the reclamation of land from water. "Water, at once absent and omnipresent, pervades *A Thousand Acres*," as Nakadate puts it.[12] Early in the novel there is an epic account of the heroic activity of the first settlers in turning apparently infertile ground into good farmland by a system of drainage, and this drainage remains one of the key concerns of the family in the present; throughout the novel there is the powerful sense—which constitutes the dominant symbolic system of the book—of the water that lies beneath the surface of the land, what the last words of the text call "the sea beneath the soil," offering fertility providing it is controlled. But whereas Lear calls on Nature to abandon its own normal purpose of fertility, in *A Thousand Acres* mankind has distorted nature and so destroyed fertility. Ginny, she realizes in her final reflections, is part of that cycle of environment and pollution, as she is made up psychologically of the pressures of community and exploitation, and also "the loop of poison we drank from, the water running down through the soil, into the drainage wells, into the lightless mysterious underground chemical sea, then being drawn up, cold and appetizing, from the drinking well into Rose's faucet, my faucet" (370). Individuals are not independent and so not entirely free; the characters, in Conrad's reading, are determined not only by Shakespeare but by "social tendencies or economic trends which tally individuals as statistics."[13] Specifically, the life of women is determined to a large extent by the domination of men. Ginny, in her final conversation with her husband, who has not lost his respect for Larry as a farmer, tells him that her father didn't come up with beating and fucking on his own: "No. I think he had lessons, and those lessons were part of the package, along with the land and the lust to run things exactly the way he wanted to no matter what, poisoning the water and destroying the top soil and buying bigger and bigger machinery, and then feeling certain that all of it was 'right', as you say" (343). As in a very different novel, Günter Grass's *The Flounder*, human exploitation of the earth is seen as parallel to men's domination of women; farming is violence.

The concerns here, of course, are the modern ones of ecology, of our recognition since the 1960s, since, especially, Rachel Carson's *Silent Spring*, of the dangers of human intervention in the natural cycle, and of the extent to which humanity is part of the natural world. Nakadate rightly identifies the novel as a "contribution to the literature of ecological vigilance."[14] Jess, in the novel, incarnates those concerns and the challenge they bring to the long-established and apparently successful methods of farming. Jess is the near outsider; unreliable, selfish, and calculating as a lover, as Rose points out, he is nevertheless the — ineffective — voice of wisdom and change for the community.

But this concern with the environment is of more than literal practical significance. The poisoned water is not only a danger to health; it is also a symbol of concealment and moral threat. It is what lies beneath the surface, "what is below the level of the visible" (9). Early in the novel, the child Ginny frightens her parents by playing on the grating that covers the drainage well. The vision of a repressed menace, from which she is protected only by the grid of order and control, matches the passion that is suppressed in much of her own adult life, the abuse her father can conceal from the wider public, her own forgetfulness. More generally it corresponds to a wish to preserve appearances that dominates the thinking of many of the characters (and Rose is important in part because she has less of this wish than anyone else). The world of the novel is largely one of surfaces, one where "appearances are everything" (284), where one can admire "the marvelous engine of appearances" (293), where Harold can exploit "the slippage between what he looks like and what he is" (109), and yet where "people don't believe what appears on the surface" (126). It is a world of illusion, a baroque world, perhaps, like that of Shakespeare, dominated by disguise and deception.

Finally, it is a postmodern world. "The same sequence of days," Ginny comments, "can arrange themselves into a number of different stories" (155). Because perceptions differ, because our viewpoint is constituted by our own passions, the expectations of our society, the deceptions of our associates, and the imperfections of communication, we can rewrite stories to suit ourselves. The point is a difficult one; *A Thousand Acres* is largely about the discovery of a truth, a genuine repressed truth, and about the demand for justice that goes with it. Truth and justice are realities. And yet the book is also about the variety of views that goes with that discovery of truth, and about the control of information: about the way Larry exerts a hegemony that prevents Ginny seeing things from her own point of view (212), about Ginny's failure to tell Caroline that her childhood innocence has been protected by the victimization of her elder sisters, about Caroline's respect for her father's suffering, about Ginny's anxiety as to the riddle Rose left her, "of how we judge those who have hurt us when they have shown no remorse or even understanding" (370), her anxiety, in other words about a reality that is not shared.

This arranging into a story is also a comment, a self-reflexive comment by the novelist, not the narrator, on the relationship of *A Thousand Acres* to *King Lear*. There is a dialogue here, stretching across the centuries. On one side there are an author and a culture who believed—if not quite without qualifications—in order and authority (so Kent finds in Lear's face "that . . . which I would fain call master": authority); on the other there is an author who challenges them in a culture where they are precarious. Shakespeare invites us to regret the replacement of reverence by self-seeking; Smiley asks us to welcome the replacement of reverence by critical self-reliance. But she also asks us to recognize what reverence has meant in the whole tragic tradition—which has given way to the more or less liberal and pragmatic tradition of the novel as a genre, but remains within the memory of our civilization—and to know what there is in ourselves that still sees some questionable grandeur in the suffering of the powerful.

10
Kingsolver: *The Poisonwood Bible*

MANY PEOPLE, NO DOUBT, HAVE A VISION OF THE CONGO BASED ON three things: Conrad's *Heart of Darkness*, which shows the country—as it was in the late nineteenth century—as constituted by brutal colonial exploitation and native savagery; memories of press and television coverage of the events following independence on 30 June 1960, when an army mutiny involved a number of murders and rapes of Europeans, followed by a series of political crises involving secession, tribal conflict, and bloody violence between the Congolese;[1] and impressions from the press and from hearsay (and from V. S. Naipaul's *A Bend in the River*) of the corruption and inertia of the Mobutu dictatorship, which succeeded the initial chaos. These impressions may be superficial ones, acquired without systematic study. They are profoundly negative ones: they suggest a country that shows that decolonization has failed, that the often harsh and inflexible rule of Belgium has been replaced by conflict, egoism, narrow local loyalties, and educational and economic stagnation. This whole perspective is, of course, one-sided. But one cannot assume that this pessimistic view can easily be rejected; it certainly seems very difficult to deny that the Congo has passed through chaos to a state of impoverishment and oligarchy, and to underestimate this would be to trivialize the grave problems of the whole continent.

Barbara Kingsolver's ambitious novel *The Poisonwood Bible* seeks to correct this perspective.[2] She is very aware of the stereotypes: a character asks, "May Africa talk back?" (338). She recognizes that we see Africa through a Western discourse; *The Poisonwood Bible* is—at least in part—an attempt to give a voice to Africa. It has three important points to make about the Congo: that there is much to admire in its traditional rural culture, that this culture was undermined by colonialism, with its apanage of missionary activity and majority democracy, and that its prospects for peace, prosperity, and African leadership in 1960 were destroyed by the activities of the colonial or neo-colonial powers—and not least by the assassination of Patrice Lumumba, the first prime minister of the independent Congo, which she attributes (as does one of the sources she quotes, Jonathan Kwitny) to the machinations of the CIA.[3]

The points are ones that are likely to be welcome to her readers. Many people in the developed countries would like to be reassured that there is a natural order in mankind that may be distorted by the forces of power and injustice, the forces which later brought the horrors of Vietnam, but which can survive such cataclysms as the 1960 crisis. The issues are presented forcefully and in some depth throughout the novel. But the wish to present factually valid political and ecological insights through fiction places a special strain on aspects of the text: it makes very special demands on the verisimilitude of the plot, it raises questions as to what information is excluded by the focalization adopted by the author, and it gives the author an acute challenge in plausibly creating a range of narrative voices, and especially in creating the voices of those characters with whom she feels little sympathy.

Kingsolver's view of the Congo is directed very explicitly against Conrad's view, which essentially is a metaphysical view of the nature of mankind: African savagery is for him a manifestation of the savagery that is inherent in the human breast. The point is made very clearly in the reporting of Lumumba's famous speech at the independence ceremonies on 30 June. In the Kingsolver version, Lumumba announces that "We are going to show the world what the *homme noir* can do when he works for freedom. We are going to make the Congo, for all of Africa, the heart of light" (210). This is to contrast with two later passages. In the first, soon after, a wife complains that being married to a tyrannical husband is like being "lodged in the heart of darkness" (228), not African savagery but American repression. In the other, much later, the same character who has reported Lumumba's speech reflects ironically on a futile prestige project to carry a power cable across "the heart of darkness" (518). Here, the heart of darkness is Conrad's impenetrable jungle, impervious to enlightenment or technical progress; the fall of Lumumba has meant a reversion to the wild. The whole pattern shows something of the problems of the novel. For one thing, the character who observes the independence day speech is a teenager who is not in a position to realize that it was widely regarded as very regrettable, since it contained much outspoken criticism of the Belgian regime and so may have contributed to the tensions between the Congo and the West, which formed one of the stumbling blocks for the new country. More crucially, what the character recounts is not quite what the historical Lumumba said. He spoke of Africans working *in* freedom, not *for* freedom, and he promised to make the Congo the *"centre de rayonne-*

ment" of Africa (accurately translated as "center of radiance" in Kingsolver's source).[4] Lumumba was not thinking of an English-language novelist when he addressed his liberated people; Kingsolver has dragged him into a European debate that was alien to him.

Which is simply to say, first of all, that this is a work of fiction. The author clearly asserts as much in the first words of her preface. Writers of fiction have the right to change and interpret history, but we may feel uneasy when what is changed is very recent and when it is an expression of a person for whom the novel as a whole seeks to arouse respect. The first of these reservations may be hard to justify; facts about Lumumba aren't necessarily more sacrosanct than facts about Napoleon. The point is essentially one of rhetoric, since modifications affecting facts fairly well known to modern readers are likely to be more conspicuous than modifications affecting facts less close to us. The second point is a more important one: is the reader expected to admire the real Lumumba, the victim of tribal and colonial hostility, or the figure created by the anticolonialist novelist?

The text is composed of five voices. The story concerns Nathan Price, an American missionary who arrives in the Congo in 1959 with his wife, Orleanna, and four daughters; the novel interweaves the voice of the wife, recollecting the events since 1959 from her old age in the United States in the 1990s, and the voices of the daughters, recounting the events as they take place. The four daughters are carefully discriminated. The eldest, Rachel, fifteen at the start of the novel, is concerned only with clothes, appearance, and the mass media. Leah, age fourteen, is a dutiful and serious-minded daughter. Her twin, Adah, suffers from hemiplegia; as a result of prenatal problems one side of her body has limited mobility, and she responds to her handicap and to her father's authority with silence, irony, and wordplays. The youngest, Ruth May, five, is a lively, curious, open-minded child, who shows real enjoyment of the new environment and adapts to it more readily than any other character. Through these voices, the novel, very explicitly, seeks to come to terms with history; the mother notes that at a time of depression and illness "History didn't cross my mind. Now it does" (368). Later she comments that the three sisters who survive have "their own three ways to live with our history" (438). Adah reflects that everyone is "trying to invent our version of the story . . . 'My life; what I stole from history, and how I live with it'" (558). The final passage of the novel declares that "Even the child Ruth May touched history. Everyone is complicit" (608).

The father, Nathan, is not one of the voices of the novel. The novel—

like for instance *A Thousand Acres*—is concerned with the establishment of a female community and the elimination of male power.[5] The mother reflects, in terms very reminiscent of Smiley, that "for time and eternity there have been fathers like Nathan who simply can see no way to have a daughter but to own her like a plot of land" (217), and like the West owns—or controls—the underdeveloped world.

This structure of narration, moreover, introduces a special tension. The mother addresses her reminiscences to one of the daughters, who has died in the Congo. It is only halfway through that the novel indicates clearly which daughter it is. Still more crucially the reader is likely to wonder if she was a victim of violence. In fact she is the victim of something like an accident, though it does arise from the intense conflict that has arisen in the small village where they live, a conflict which is only in the most indirect sense political. The novel, then, corrects the reader's probable assumption. More than this, the perspective allows a lyrical reflection on the importance of death and memory; it shows Africa as a place where death is accepted. Kingsolver has a deep sense of ecology, of the natural order in which death is a complement to life. Very near the end of the work, Adah, now a scientist, reflects on one of her most disturbing experiences, when a huge army of driver ants invaded the village, eating everything in their path and forcing all the inhabitants to flee: "If by chance a baby was left behind in a crib, or a leopard in a cage, it would be a skeleton without marrow, clean as a whistle. But for those prepared to move aside for a larger passage, it works. Loss and salvation" (598). For her mother, it is hinted, the act of composing these memories and dedicating them to the dead child is a kind of loss and salvation; accepting nature means accepting that humans are only one species amongst others, that to talk of a "tragic death," as Rachel does, is mere sentiment, convention, and insincerity.

The novel is in large part a tribute to the Congo (where the author spent part of her childhood) and it intensely praises the natural richness of the country. Leah expects "God's Kingdom in its pure unenlightened glory" (20), and that is what she gets, if the word "unenlightened" comes to have some complexity. And this sense of the ever-present and everlasting jungle pervades social life. The Congolese do not live like Americans because their environment doesn't allow it: "At home we have cities and cars and things because nature is organized a whole different way," Leah tells Anatole, the African teacher (322). "A jungle . . . supports no leisure class," she reflects more maturely (593). What it does support is a sense of a close, supportive, cooperative, and traditional community. In a striking passage, Leah observes Mama Mwanza, who has lost the use of her legs but does not suffer the indignities imposed on the physically imperfect (such as Adah) by Western society; Leah observes Mama Mwanza's two daughters pounding manioc together and envies them, as they "worked together in such perfect synchrony" (260). Rural Africa has a life of unceasing hard work, of poor diet, of danger from animals, sickness, and accident, but it is a life of harmony and order.

This is contrasted effectively with the behavior of the Americans in the scene of the invasion by ants. The Congolese act in spontaneous cooperation, running along to the river, carrying children and cooking equipment; Mama Mwanza is carried on her husband's back. The Americans run for themselves, even the virtuous Leah forgetting to help her disabled sister; only Orleanna carries her youngest child, Ruth May. Rachel coolly remembers the advice she repeats toward the end of the novel, which seems to encapsulate her attitude to history: in a fleeing crowd you stick out your elbows and lift your feet from the ground; you will then be carried along by other people's efforts (344, 585).

This is part of a general failure by the missionary family (as long as it is still led by the father) to learn from Africans. The point is touched on discreetly in Orleanna's opening reminiscences: the white girls, "pale, doomed blossoms," wearing shirtwaist dresses in the dense jungle (5). It is more simply illustrated in the career of Nathan, who refuses advice from his kindly housekeeper, Mama Tataba, and digs his garden in American style so that the earth is washed away by the tropical rain, plants American vegetables which do not fruit because there are no American pollinators, and insists on uprooting the poisonwood tree by hand, only to find himself covered in a painful rash.

The implication is that Christianity is an alien growth that will no more bear fruit in the Congo than Nathan's bean plants. The point again has a literary origin. Rachel, late in the novel, comments on her quarreling with her sisters, that in her family "things fall apart, of course" (548). The reference is to the novel of the same title by Chinua Achebe. Achebe's novel shows the effect of Christianity in destabilizing the traditional society. Some of the outstanding merit of *Things Fall Apart* lies in its complex balance; Christianity, in Achebe's view, does bring some merits, as well as forcing a difficult and perhaps destructive readjustment. One pertinent theme is that Christianity forbids the custom of exposing twins at birth. The same custom prevails in Kingsolver's Congo (as does female circumcision). Kingsolver perhaps simplifies the issue by seeking a justification for the custom in the imposition a multiple birth places on the mother (500), though admittedly the justification is deeply ambiguous in that it is formulated by Adah, herself a twin.

Allied with the disruptive effect of Christianity is the disruptive effect of elections. The villagers, it is explained, are not accustomed to the idea of majority decisions; they are accustomed to the gradual evolution of consensus.[6] They first of all make ironic use of this Western custom against the Western religion it is associated with, as their leader Tata Ndu insists on holding a vote, during a missionary service, to see if Christ is to be accepted as their savior (he is roundly defeated). But there is a more complex result of this distrust. A tribal gathering holds a vote as to whether Leah should be allowed to participate in a hunt, against custom. Leah is accepted by a small majority, but the vote itself constitutes a scission in the community, which leads to the witch doctor's introducing a poisonous snake into the missionary family's chicken coop and so to the death of Ruth May. It is Anatole, the *évolué*, the educated and liberal African, who proposes Leah's admission, though he opposes voting. He is to emerge as one of the most admirable figures in the novel and will represent the unfulfilled potential of independence, what a Belgian doctor welcomes in Lumumba, "the new soul of Africa" (138). But is Anatole actually a destructive force? Is independence—and the accompanying social change—a destruction of the real Africa?

It is moreover America that is responsible for the death of Lumumba. The point is made by the sinister air pilot, dealer, and secret agent Axelroot, who tells Rachel in advance that "somebody's going to die . . . somebody that matters" (333). It is then confirmed by Orleanna, from her later perspective, which has allowed her to study the Church report on U.S. intelligence activities in the Congo—which is then included in the bibliography of the novel. The very fact of a novel's having a bibliography is important; one function of this work is to draw the attention of the general reader to factual information that was in the public domain but not widely known. The novel, in other words, is a form of popularization. At the same time, the conspiracy becomes part of the relationship of Axelroot and Rachel, emblematic figures of wrong Western approaches to Africa.

In all these respects, then, *The Poisonwood Bible* gives a view of African life that is well-informed, complex up to a certain point, inspired by a sincere appreciation of the country, and at least plausible. But one must also consider the plot of the novel and the ways this contributes to its vision of how people develop. Here there is a simple distinction to be made. There are good people, who become more sympathetic to Africa, and bad people, who don't.

First and foremost amongst the bad characters is the missionary Nathan. His incompetence in the face of African ecology is a reflection of his refusal to relax his will for power. His insecure masculinity has contaminated his marital life, notably in his feeling guilt over his sexuality and in his blaming Orleanna for it; it also leads to a constant bullying domination of his daughters, most graphically illustrated in the frequently administered punishment of "The Verse," which consists of writing out one hundred verses of the Bible, the last of which proves to contain an admonishment for childish sin, a practice hardly likely to endear the Bible to the children but showing considerable ingenuity and close familiarity with the holy text. His inflexibility is most manifest in his dream of baptizing large numbers of Congolese in the river that flows through the village. This dream is hardly threatened by his discovery that the river is inhabited by crocodiles and that the local people suspect him of wishing to sacrifice their children to their ever-open jaws. This strand of the novel culminates in a powerful, almost hallucinatory scene in which Nathan, maddened by the death of Ruth May—herself still unbaptized—and by the dramatic pagan mourning of the villagers, appears during a heavy thunderstorm, announces that he is "one crying in the wilderness," and baptizes the African children by laying on his hands, calling on them to "walk forward into the light," into a Christian enlightenment, out of the heart of darkness (419–27). The children fail to understand the event and respond to his words with cries of "Mah-dah-mey-I?" their version of the game "Mother may I?" which they have played with Ruth May. The final words of the novel call on the characters to "walk forward into the light," ironically echoing Nathan's words and applying them to a lucid, secular self-awareness.

Nathan, now, is clearly insane; from this point he disappears from the center of the novel and is occasionally heard of wandering, bereft, in ever more remote parts of the country, till finally he is burned to death by villagers after an incident in which baptism has led to drowning.

The other character who fails to adjust is Rachel, and here the reader may feel a different kind of disquiet. Nathan may be disturbing as a monster, a figure of abnormal obstinacy, out of place in the comparatively realistic texture of the book as a whole. Rachel is worrying because the development of her character may seem arbitrary and excessive. At the beginning she is an attractive and funny character.

She is funny in part because of her malapropisms (though these too may go beyond the plausible), as when she refers to Gulliver and the Lepidopterans (327) and, even late in her story, when she comments that "We Christians have our own system of marriage, and it is called Monotony" (460). She is attractive because she refuses to take her father seriously. In fact she seems to have been extraordinarily impervious to the biblical atmosphere she has been brought up in; the explanation offered is that being a preacher's daughter in Georgia does not make you popular amongst other teenagers preoccupied with fashion and sociability. She has a frank recognition of the foreigner's situation in the Congo, apparent in her first words in the novel: "Man oh man, are we in for it now, was my thinking about the Congo from the instant we first set foot. We are supposed to be calling the shots here, but it doesn't look to me like we're in charge of a thing, not even our own selves" (26).

But this intelligence disappears as the family breaks up after the baptism scene. She elopes with the sinister Axelroot and settles down confidently in the racist and materialistic society of apartheid South Africa, eventually running a whites-only hotel in the former French Congo. Two points (amongst many others) illustrate her insensitivity: she despises the Africans of the Congo because "they're still struggling to get a decent telephone service" (521); the reader has just seen Leah's thoughtful explanation that the telephone service is dominated by bribery and corruption because this is the nature of the economy under Mobutu: "To an outsider it looks like chaos. It isn't. It's negotiation, infinitely ordered and endless" (511). Leah's point looks as if it's based on reliable observation, and Rachel isn't wholly wrong, only hasty in her judgment and inflexible in her standards. She is clearly in the wrong when, touring with Leah, she expects her to give priority to a visit to her hotel over being reunited with her husband, Anatole, who has just been released from a spell of political imprisonment—because Anatole is an African who cannot enter the hotel. In middle age, she formulates the overall sense of the novel very precisely when she comments that "You can't just sashay into the jungle aiming to change it all over to the Christian style, without expecting the jungle to change you right back" (584). Except that she has it the wrong way round; this is the *Heart of Darkness* view, the view that the jungle means the loss of civilization. Rachel quickly disqualifies herself as a social commentator by reflecting on American blacks, "having riots for their civil rights and predominating the sports and popular-music industries" (584). (The Price family comes from pre–civil rights Georgia: Rachel is true to her background.)

For the novelist, in contrast with the character, the jungle changes you for the better, and interracial marriage especially changes you for the better.

Disliking Africa, then, leads to madness or brutal egoism. Set against this, we have first of all Ruth May, who immediately adapts to the Congolese way of life, plays happily with the African children, learns something of the local language, and is constantly curious about African life and African flora and fauna. Having no need to develop any greater love for Africa, Ruth May dies early. The two characters whose development forms the core of the novel are the twins, Leah and Adah.

Leah starts rather strangely. She is a girl of high Christian principle, wholeheartedly in support of her father's activities. Or is she? What exactly is her tone when she comments that "I crave heaven and to be my father's favorite" (76)? Can anyone as intelligent as Leah fail to see the irony? Be that as it may, Leah does change. She falls in love with the handsome and gentlemanly Anatole and comes to share his life in the Congo and his political perspectives, including his hostility to American neo-colonialism. In the later part of the book, Leah is an admirable figure of modesty, responsibility, loyalty, family affection, realism, and disregard for wealth; she is dedicated to "making something right in at least one tiny corner of the vast house of wrongs" (536).

Adah starts interestingly; her disability leads her to a fascination with wordplays and especially with palindromes (most of them pointless, it seems), and more important, to a sense of herself as outsider, feeling, like the true Romantic outsider, that the real earth is elsewhere (37). For her, very convincingly, the crucial moments are the ant invasion, when her mother abandons her in favor of Ruth May, and the exodus from the village, when her mother protects her in preference to Leah; much later she comes to understand (a lesson, like so many in the book, on the biological foundations of human life) that motherhood means caring for one's youngest. Forced into responsibility, Adah overcomes her disability and uses her outstanding intelligence to study the biology of tropical medicine; she can serve Africa without suffering the hardships that Leah undergoes.

These two characters, then, indicate how far this is a conversion story. The sinners Nathan and Rachel refuse conversion and are damned; the really enlightened are those who come to love life as it is, and especially the life of the Congo. In this they are inspired by two models: Anatole and Brother Fowles. Anatole is enlightened, progressive, articulate, uncompromising, confident, self-sacrificing, modest (notably he refuses to accept the teenage Leah's love when she first declares it), and capable of service to others and to the community. He is a paragon who comes dangerously close to proving the *Uncle Tom* lesson that black people deserve equal treatment with whites because they are morally superior.

The other model character is Brother Fowles, Nathan's predecessor in the mission station who has left under a cloud. The reason for this proves to be that he has abandoned Christianity in any strict sense: he has married a Congolese, as Leah will, adopted a pagan attitude to creation, is prepared to ignore considerable parts of the Bible but defeats Nathan in biblical argument, shows respect for the local people, unconverted as they are, bestows presents on the needy Price family, takes a keen interest in Congolese wildlife, and spends his days following the river in a small boat, dispensing spiritual advice, medical assistance, and quinine. And he has charm; Rachel notes that "he had a white beard and twinkly blue eyes, and all in all gave the impression of what Santa Claus would look like if he'd converted to Christian and gone without a good meal since last Christmas" (276). Fowles offers a pagan sanctity, an instance of how the American can be enriched by the experience of Africa. "God doesn't need to punish us," Leah reflects. "He just grants us a long enough life to punish ourselves" (373). Nathan punishes himself with madness, Rachel with the aridity and solitude of her materialistic lifestyle; Leah and Adah aspire to the serenity of Brother Fowles.

The Poisonwood Bible, then, is in many ways a rich and thoughtful novel. It conveys a serious and well-informed view both of the specific issue of the situation of the Congo as an instance of decolonization, and also of the broader issue of humanity's response to the natural world, which Africa is seen to accept as a life-giving environment but which the West seeks to reject as spiritually secondary. It formulates this view, often, through intensely imagined scenes and with an attractive satirical humor. But there are problems, and these relate to the tension between fact and fiction in the work.

The novelist, unlike the historian, can choose a peripheral viewpoint. Kingsolver may well have been inspired by Merriam, whom she cites in the preface and bibliography, who includes in his important book his very revealing impressions from living in a small village in the Congo in the crucial years of 1959–60. But Merriam also includes a colleague's impressions of life in the large town of Stanleyville in the same period, and these impressions form only part of a study that also includes much thorough research on the political movements and events of the time, at the national as well as the local level. The choice of an even smaller village as the location of most of Kingsolver's novel allows a considerable distancing of the worst aspects of independence. "The Independence seemed to have passed over our village," Leah notes in true biblical style, "just as the plague did on that long ago night in Egypt" (300). There is no suppression of the murders and rapes (so the child Ruth May overhears her mother saying that "they went after the white girls up in Stanleyville" [267], and the reader is chilled by what Ruth May doesn't understand), but they appear in the novel only as hearsay; the critical reader may be conscious that a different narrative rhetoric might have foregrounded these things. A crucial point is the presentation of Lumumba; his inaugural speech is seen through the eyes of the teenage Leah, who is enthralled by his powerful presence, his fiery eyes, his revivalist eloquence in which "heaven and anger get mingled together" (208). The teenage sensibility is convincingly caught, and so is the charisma that historians recognize; what historians also recognize but the novel cannot depict is the man's overall ineffectiveness, constituted by his impulsiveness and insecurity as well as by the overwhelming problems faced by an inexperienced leader of an unprepared and divided nation.[7] The novel seeks to compensate for this partial view in the discussion of Lumumba's assassination between Rachel, Leah, and Adah (543–44), a discussion, however, that is short-circuited by Rachel's racism.

The novel, moreover, unlike history, can choose unrepresentative figures (and, at worst, pass them off as typical). The reader may wonder why a missionary society should appoint someone like Nathan, who has no idea of how to survive in the Congo or of how to persuade the Congolese of the value of his faith. The answer proves to be that it has have not appointed him, and that he has therefore received no training. It has only made him a small monthly allowance as an act of generosity (unwisely, one may suspect, since this could easily be interpreted as constituting a contract). This is why, when in reality large numbers of missionaries were being evacuated from Leopoldville and Stanleyville for their own safety, Nathan can refuse to go. The missionary societies, both Protestant and Catholic, were enormously influential and well organized in pre-independence Congo, being responsible, for instance, for much of the educational system. While their value is no doubt debatable, and they certainly became objects of hatred for many Congolese in 1960, their missionaries were not the incompetent eccentrics we see in the novel.

Finally, as we have seen, fiction can present a highly schematized view of moral life. In this novel, people who show love and humility toward the Congo are essentially good; those who seek to impose Western order upon the country are essentially bad and doomed to decline. Another way of putting this is to say that the dialogic quality, regarded as typical of the novel by many modern critics, following Bakhtin, is only superficially present in this work.[8] The voices of Nathan (reported) and of Rachel (in her own narrative) are not genuinely independent utterances but negative reflections of the serious and unselfish voices of Fowles and the twins.[9] The novel as a genre, one may say, is fascinated by subjectivity and by the differences between the subjective views of different people; in *The Poisonwood Bible* the differences are the product of the author's will to demonstrate the rightness of her own understanding. *The Poisonwood Bible* is not so simply didactic a book as the author's *Prodigal Summer*, which consists to a very large extent of characters who are not well informed about ecology receiving instruction from those who are wiser, but it is nevertheless a didactic work, and the events and characters are very largely illustrations of a body of knowledge.

Or such, at least, is the overall tendency of the book. But there are also some real complexities which the author acutely and honestly shows. The dichotomy in the book between admiration for the unchanging life of the village and sympathy for the revolution of independence has already been noted. There are also occasional hints that Rachel might, just a little, be right. Toward the end of the novel Rachel, in search, with her usual superficiality, of a tourist attraction, takes her sisters to the ancient castle of Abomey, which proves to be a monument to human sacrifice, the walls and furnishings including human bones. Rachel points out that before the arrival of the whites wife murdering and slave bones in the walls were part of African life. As usual, she is disqualified from serious argument, because she then goes on to examine her damaged fingernails. But Leah gives the automatic liberal answer: "You can't assume that what's right or wrong for us is the same as what was right or wrong for them" (556), and the argument gives way to mockery as Rachel attempts to assert the commandment that "thou shalt not kill" and her sisters recall Nathan's confusion of the native words for *good* and *poisonwood*, which leads him to assert that the Bible is poisonwood. But before Leah's resolution of the discussion, Adah has said something important and difficult: "A little ritual killing, a little infant mortality, just a few of the many healthy natural processes we don't care to think about" (556). The *Heart of Darkness* is back. Ritual killing really *is* uncivilized; there *are* humane values that are ignored in African culture. Or *is* ritual killing part of the natural order the book celebrates? No answer is given; an anxiety remains that bears witness to the author's real sense of the incommensurability of values.

Conclusion

"AMERICA WAS A HARSH TRIAL TO THE HUMAN SPIRIT," A CHARACTER in Bellow comments.[1] "Spirit" is vague enough. A little more precisely, America is a trial for the freedom and responsibility of the individual; it is a society dominated by power and inertia, originating in slavery, economic exploitation, and a cultural diversity that may be perceived as disparity rather than wealth, an anomic and alienated society characterized by injustice, violence, corruption, and restriction of human rights, a society in which self-confidence is difficult to attain because distinctive personality is not prized, in which lasting relationships are hard to maintain because feeling is paralyzed. Such at least is the vision of many of the novels of the last fifty years. A ballplayer finds fickle spectators and cynical management and lacks the personal preparedness to perfect his art or his life. A European exile, haunted by the evils of the Holocaust but also by the elegance of European culture, finds in New York brutal crime, crude egoism, unrestrained sexuality, and the cult of the dollar. An apparently safe and orderly Midwestern family is not quite as well-established as it seems, and in any case is the victim of rootless punks. And so it goes. America's novelists are insistent on reporting on the condition of their country, and their vision of it is largely dark. They do not assert that America is a prosperous, democratic country, in which free speech is assured and education widely available, a country whose culture, both popular and elevated, shows an intense vitality that might be emulated by many others, and which is still carrying out the long and sometimes painful process of extending to all groups in society the rights that the United States have been foremost in recognizing as pertaining to all human beings. Novelists emphasize rather the price to be paid for these aspirations and achievements — the price of a materialistic self-assertion, both at personal and at national levels, which can easily replace the independence and self-awareness that contribute to the best American traditions — and the extent to which the paying of this price has held the nation back from the full attainment of its ideals. Perhaps novelists, and other artists, *should* be critical. Perhaps art *should* express discontent. An art of complacency would be both boring and morally insidious, and the novels that have been considered here are certainly not that.

The novelist reports on the condition of America, and he judges it too. A judgment is not wholly different from a report; in conversation or journalism, not much verbal skill is required in order to convey an accurate account of events and states of affairs that also implies (or, less discreetly and so less convincingly, that makes explicit) the degree to which the actual world falls short of a world one could consider normal or ideal. But there is a special challenge to the novelist, if only in view of the length and the variety and breadth of content that readers expect from a novel; he or she has to prove competence as judge and reporter and knowledge of the real world and the criteria by which it can be judged. The proof is a kind of rhetoric; it is a language capable of embracing both the concrete reality of a sometimes harsh world and the abstraction that not only provides a framework of possible ideologies by which to judge but also the intellectual context of the characters' motives and strategies. If European readers are impressed by the density and precision of American prose, it is because they recognize (in various authors) the accuracy of detailed observation of contemporary reality, down to the names of shops and the cut of clothes, the readiness to use high abstraction to name ideas and motives, the shifts of rhythm that echo either forceful action or complex thought, the variety of tone that reproduces differences of character, differences of class, gender, education, formality, and purpose in speaking. These novelists are "lifelike"; in Stendhal's image, they are carrying a mirror along a road. All (even the most fantastic) retain an acute sense of typical behavior, of how people respond not only to the large-scale concerns of sexuality, family, and nation and ethnic group, but of how they respond from moment to moment to quarrelsome speech, to uncertainty as to others' judgment of them, to the opportunity to entertain or to impress, to the small tasks of shopping, cooking, and driving. Many, moreover, anchor their work very precisely in specific places: the huge tire in Ford's Detroit, Columbus Circle in Bellow's New York, the rides at Doctorow's Disneyland, the hills above Oates's Hollywood. They anchor them too in specific facts, the facts that have appeared in the newspapers and the history books: trials, wars, elections, and film shows.

This ensures that the reader can recognize a certain set of virtues in the novelist; comparing the text with his or her own knowledge of the way people behave and of the events and places that make up the given pattern of American life, the reader can see that the novelist is well-informed, careful, rational, serious, has a sound sense of what is important and of what is typical, is fascinated by the variety of ways of life and work: in short that the novelist is modest and objective, that he or she respects the real. Put negatively, readers can recognize that the author does not seek to escape from the world he or she shares with them. These virtues are perhaps not the ones people most readily think of when they try to define what makes a good novelist, but they are real virtues (for a novelist as for anyone else) and they are part of what makes readers trust a novelist. Fenimore Cooper takes time off in *The Last of the Mohicans* to deplore the defective moral courage of Montcalm at Fort William Henry; in doing so he imposes himself on his readers as an author who knows his history and can judge it.

There is a kind of novel that, on the face of it, seeks no virtues other than those of accuracy. This is the "nonfiction novel," and the prime example of it is *In Cold Blood*. Capote's modesty is spectacular: he appears only as "a journalist," and he depicts only the external world he has observed. Individual thoughts and feelings appear only as reported to him. The author appears subservient to an alien world. And this world is an unheroic one; divided between stolid conservatism on one hand and brutal, incompetent, and unimaginative adventure on the other, there is little in it that invites the reader to empathize and not much that invites the reader to admire. There is little in the world depicted, but there is much to empathize with and to admire in the stance of the author. This is not really subservience; this is virtuosity. These sordid events become the material for a dazzling display of echoing voices, of moments of stillness, of a growing sense of the ineluctable, of irony and carefully understated pathos, of humor and grotesqueness. The mask of anonymity is a barrier between the author and his world; against a precarious conformist society, one individual displays his dandyish elegance, his harmony of language, his mastery of pace, his discretion of manner, and his sense of the strangeness of the everyday.

The nonfiction novel, it seems, contents itself with reporting. At the opposite pole, the novel of fabulation (in Scholes's term) delights in inventing. *Giles Goat-Boy* reminds its readers plethorically of the world they know, which Giles doesn't know, the world of World War II, of student rebellion and the homogenization of student experience, of multiple and haphazard religions. Against this world, it offers one in which heroism is normal, the world of the classic myth or folktale; if *In Cold Blood* allows little greatness to individual experience, *Giles* presents the given structures of power and control, political and educational, as subject to challenge from innovative magic. This time the virtuosity is conspicuous and is commented on by the author himself, from his prefaces

CONCLUSION 153

to his afterword, as he persistently asserts his own astonishing inventiveness. The given world is rejected, it seems, in favor of the author's fancy. But it isn't quite so simple: for one thing, the author's fancy is itself the product of the academic culture it mocks (and specifically of the anthropology of storytelling); for another, the hero, whose fresh innocence and lust for self-discovery is set against the inert orthodoxies of academe, is an insensitive oaf, his associates are grotesquely caricatured, and the invented events are often gross and shocking. Barth, one may feel, is proudly demonstrating his own failure; setting up the vitality of myth against the bleakness of history, he produces blatant simplification. He knows it; the fascination of the book is in the elaborate tension between its awareness of the real and its irony toward the imagined.

Between these two poles, of reporting and fabulation, lie the books that follow the traditional strategy of the novel. Against the given reality, specific or general, as the reader recognizes it, against what Conrad called "the irremediable life of the earth as it is," the authors set characters who seek some self-fulfillment.[2] It seems to be characteristic of recent American fiction that this self-fulfillment may entail an adjustment to political actuality: a decision to accept or reject the verdict of an American court, or to accept or reject such opportunities as are open to black people after the abolition of slavery, the attainment of a clear judgment on American policy in Africa; on a less directly political level, a old man has to learn how far he can detach himself from a culture of youth and greed, an actress has to distinguish talent from sexual desirability, and a betrayed daughter has to distance herself from male domination and female competition. In these cases, unlike the two polar instances, there is a close liaison between author and distinctive individual. "The novel tells of the adventure of interiority," Lukács says in an early study of the genre;[3] what the novelist invents, what he adds to the real world he reproduces, is a consciousness, a consciousness that feels itself to be in disharmony with its environment and which seeks to change itself or to change the world about it. Sometimes the striving individual is successful: Sethe and Denver come to find love, family, personal growth, and community, and Daniel meets the senile Mindish and realizes that the past is finished. Sometimes the individual is defeated: Roy strikes out, Sammler shamefully contributes to an act of violence, and Marilyn is murdered by an agent of the state. In either case, the concern of the reader is with the sensibility of the central character, with his or her sensitivity, lucidity, purposiveness, integrity, goodwill, or openness to changing experience. By and large these are the qualities of classic liberal humanism; they are the virtues of the authentic individual. If there is a specifically American aspect to them, it may lie in a greater sense of the individual's self-reliance than has been common in Europe: how many of these characters are self-made, without effective parents or structured upbringing?

The author's task is twofold: to present these individual qualities convincingly and with an appropriate level of sympathy (or of implied criticism), and to show that, within the given inhospitable society, these qualities lead plausibly to disaster or to an acceptance of restraint or compromise. Hence the major distinctive features of fiction: the author's control of point of view and access to the thoughts of others, including the possibility of first-person narration, and the ability to invent sequences of incidents that the reader accepts on grounds of verisimilitude (and not of documentary evidence). To illustrate the skill and intelligence with which authors have exploited these possibilities of fiction would be to retrace the analyses of the whole of this book. But a further point remains to be made. Since the sequence of events (with some exceptions) is justified by possibility rather than logical necessity, the reader's response is in part to its appropriateness, to its moral rightness. Roy might not have struck out; Sethe might not have been reminded of the horrors of the past by Bodwin's arrival, or he might not have arrived at the same time as the group of black women. Negatively, readers sometimes feel that there is *contrivance* when a more or less plausible set of events coincides too neatly with their feeling for a desirable pattern of lives. The less plausible the events, the more they feel the contrivance. In *To Kill a Mockingbird*, one man and two children can turn back a lynch mob, because justice must be preserved in fiction, even in pre-civil rights Alabama. The scene is persuasively written and acutely dramatic, but the persuasiveness comes in part from the viewpoint of the child, with her sharp observation but her limited grasp of the situation; readers will know that in reality black people have been lynched, and that mobs are not gentlemanly. It is quite proper to speak of contrivance in such cases, and a reader's annoyance at being manipulated is entirely right; manipulation is a breach of the contract of author and reader, which must assume that both are rational and capable of independent judgment. But, after all, writing fiction *is* contriving. Readers enter upon their reading in the hope—perhaps not a very conscious hope—that the things that happen in a novel will be more orderly than things in real life: that they will illustrate some set of recurring themes, and that there will be some coincidence between plausible events and a significant moral order, whether by bringing about a state of justice or by making manifest the injustice of the world. (One has to add that readers are familiar with more than one significant moral order, which is why the conservative reader can accept, provisionally, for the duration of the reading, a leftist morality.) If this orderliness works out properly, what readers find is that their sense of rightness (or of indisputable wrongness) is the same sense that has informed the author's decisions about the handling of the plot.

This leads to two further comments. First, one should admire the author for skills, as well as for right feeling. The accomplished novelist needs a complex awareness of historical happenings, and situations, and of typical behavior, including the practice of various trades, religions, legal and political activities, sports, and social conventions. The novelist must be able to calculate on the normal operation of chance and the normal effectiveness of social or professional strategies; he or she must be able to predict what the reader will accept as verisimilitude, and he or she must share the reader's sense of what makes a decent life and ideally be able to extend, modify, or enrich that sense. These capacities imply ingenuity, inventiveness, craft, and readiness to innovate: no small gifts, and different in their orientation from the impersonal modesty that was identified above as a merit of the novelist's reproduction of the real.

Second, readers know that this is fiction. They know that it is the product of an author's decisions and that they can never be certain that the way the author presents the intentions and reactions of his characters corresponds to the way people really act and feel. At the very least, they know that they as readers are given a privileged access to the inner life of the characters which affords a degree of confidence and intimacy about their intentions and reactions, but which they could never conceivably have with real people. The special status of the fictional narrator may make his world closer to the world of history, or it may make it closer to the world of imagination. This means in turn that perception of the given world as it appears in fiction may be of two sorts (and readers may not always be sure which sort of perception they are offered at a given moment).

One may be fascinated and perhaps bewildered to find the real events transformed into the matter of fiction. (I sometimes pass Crannog Lake near the Northern Ireland coast, but is it a real place or a location in Jane Urquhart's *Away*?) There is a shock of recognition, to misapply the classic phrase; readers suddenly discover that the things they know do not belong just to them, or to an impersonal public domain, but are part of someone else's imagination.

Or one may see the world of the text as supplanting, after all, the real world; one may ask oneself if the ugliness of Bellow's New York belongs to the real city, or whether it is a product of contrast, a foil to the refinement and gravity of Mr. Sammler. Seeing, philosophers and psychologists have shown, is *seeing as*; perception is not automatic reproduction but interpretation (I am not a camera). Fiction makes us aware of that interpretation, of our ability to see New York as hell or a ballpark as an arena for heroic self-discovery, which means that readers are aware of the author's wish to make them see this way. They become absorbed in a world of endeavor, in which the character's consciousness is both complemented by and opposed to the world they know—though perhaps the world seen at a new angle. The situation of the characters parallels that of the author; the author too has to endeavor to find in the world both what complements and what opposes a sense of people's potential. The author has to yoke together a public world, inert and restrictive and so calling for moral commitment and judgment, with a private world of freedom and individualism, of play, spontaneity, excess, fantasy, desire, and will.

Frank in Malamud's *The Assistant* tells Helen that he prefers true books to fiction such as that of Dostoyevsky. "It is the truth," she replies.[4] Many readers will respond warmly to her claim. There *is* a truth of fiction. But in what sense are Dostoyevsky's works true? Readers are obviously not asked to believe that there was once a man called Myshkin who spent hours of intimate conversation with a murderer called Rogozhin and then relapsed into idiocy. But most readers do not believe either that it is true that the Russian Orthodox church is the central repository of human value, or that liberalism is perverse and unpatriotic, or that the moral life manifests itself most fully in sudden and extreme gesture. And they may find it hard to believe that the behavior of the characters in *The Idiot* is typical of significant human life; it is rare that in conversation with strangers in a railway carriage the heir to a millionaire should recount his quarrels with his family and his relationship with a well-known woman of irregular conduct, to whom on his second meeting with her he has given jewels bought by embezzling thousands of roubles from his father. Dostoyevsky relies not on typicality but on extraordinariness, and this means that the truthfulness of his work is very far from verisimilitude. What readers do recognize is the intense effort of Dostoyevsky in asserting his Christian faith while also reporting on a world that contains brutish self-indulgence, violence, emotional instability, and passionate skepticism. The truth of the novel, in other words, is the energy of the author.

Notes

Introduction

1. Fundamental works are Wayne C. Booth, *The Rhetoric of Fiction*, 2d ed. (Chicago: University of Chicago Press, 1983); Gérard Genette, *Figures III* (Paris: Seuil, 1972; translated as *Narrative Discourse* [Ithaca, N.Y.: Cornell University Press, 1980]); Mieke Bal, *Narratologie* (Paris: Klincksieck, 1977); Seymour Chatman, *Story and Discourse* (Ithaca, N.Y.: Cornell University Press, 1978); Shlomith Rimmon-Kenan, *Narrative Fiction, Contemporary Poetics* (London and New York: Methuen, 1983); a valuable collection of papers is Susana Onega and José Angel Landis, *Narratology* (London: Longman, 1996).
2. Percy Lubbock, *The Craft of Fiction* (London: Cape, 1968).
3. E.g., Peter Lamarque, "Narrative and Invention: The Limits of Fictionality," in *Narrative in Culture*, ed. Cristopher Nash (London: Routledge, 1990), 149; Kendall L. Walton, *Mimesis as Make-Believe* (Cambridge: Harvard University Press,1990), 77.
4. C. G. Prado, *Making Believe* (Westport, Conn.: Greenwood Press, 1984), 134; Barbara Hardy, "Narrative," *Novel* 2 (1968): 2–14. A thoughtful if sometimes debatable account of the importance of narrative as such is Philip John Moore Sturgess, *Narrativity, Theory and Practice* (Oxford: Oxford University Press, 1992), 192.
5. Conversation is subject to a requirement of *quality* (H. Paul Grice, "Logic and Conversation," in *Syntax and Semantics, 3: Speech Acts*, ed. Peter Cole and Jerry L. Morgan [New York: Academic Press, 1975], 41–58) as well as to other restraints, and this extends to storytelling.
6. The outstanding work on such aspects of fiction is Dorrit Cohn, *The Distinction of Fiction* (Baltimore: Johns Hopkins University Press, 1999), in which she argues that the novel is important and distinctive precisely because it allows insight into multiple subjectivities. Her *Transparent Minds* (Princeton: Princeton University Press, 1978) also gives an acute analysis of the way novels present the psychology of the individual character. Other important works relating to these issues are Booth's *Rhetoric of Fiction* and his "Distance and Point of View," in *Essentials of the Theory of Fiction*, 2d ed., ed. Michael J. Hoffmann and Patrick D. Murphy (London: Leicester University Press, 1996), 116–33 (on the unreliable narrator), Käte Hamburger, *Logik der Dichtung*, 2d ed (Stuttgart: E. Klett, 1968), and Ian Watt, *The Rise of the Novel* (Harmondsworth: Penguin, 1957). On free indirect style see Ann Banfield, *Unspeakable Sentences* (London: Routledge, 1982); Roy Pascal, *The Dual Voice* (Manchester: Manchester University Press, 1977).
7. This is one of the ways in which novels can be regarded as constituted by a dialogue of varying voices. This perspective stems from Mikhail Mikhailovich Bakhtin (e.g., *The Dialogic Imagination* [Austin, Tex.: University of Texas Press, 1978]) and has been extremely influential in recent years.

8. William Freedman, "The Literary Motif" in *Essentials of the Theory of Fiction*, 200–12.

9. Cohn, *Distinction of Fiction*, vii and passim, also discusses this issue.

10. Ward Moore, *Bring the Jubilee* (New York: Farrar, Straus & Young, 1953).

11. The term derives from Louise M. Rosenblatt, *The Reader, the Text, the Poem* (Carbondale, Ill.: Southern Illinois University Press, 1978), cited in Donald N. McCloskey, "Story Telling in Economics," in *Narrative in Culture*, ed. Cristopher Nash (London: Routledge, 1990), 16.

12. Thomas G. Pavel, *Fictional Worlds* (Cambridge: Harvard University Press, 1986), 87 ; Walton, *Mimesis as Make-Believe*, 160.

13. Walton, *Mimesis as Make-Believe*, 160.

14. Umberto Eco, *Six Walks in the Fictional Woods* (Cambridge and London: Harvard University Press, 1994), 109.

15. Stanley Cavell. "A Matter of Meaning It," in *Must We Mean What We Say* (Cambridge: Cambridge University Press, 1976), 213–37; Eco, *Six Walks*, 116, Sturgess, *Narrativity*, 62; Gregory Currie, "What Is fiction," *Journal of Aesthetics and Art Criticism* 43 (1985): 385–92.

16. Stephen R. Schiffer, *Meaning* (Oxford: Clarendon Press, 1972).

17. Alan Kennedy, *The Protean Self* (New York: Columbia University Press, 1974), 20. Ricoeur suggestively contrasts the narrative identity we acquire in learning to recount our own lives with the narrative identity of the fictional writer who is the author of the events as well as their narrator: Paul Ricoeur, "Life in Quest of Narrative," in *On Paul Ricoeur*, ed. David Wood (London: Routledge, 1991), 32.

18. Kendall L. Walton, "How Remote Are Fictional Worlds from the Real World?" *Journal of Aesthetics and Art Criticism* 37 (1978–79): 11–23. Erwin Goffmann, *Frame Analysis* (Harmondsworth: Penguin, 1975), 295–69.

19. Ross Chambers, *Story and Situation* (Manchester and Minneapolis: Manchester University Press and University of Minnesota Press, 1984), 9; Michael Bell, "How Primordial Is Narrative," in *Narrative and Culture*, 175. The concept is applied to autobiography in Philippe Lejeune, *Le pacte autobiographique* (Paris: Seuil, 1975). Eco, *Six Walks*, 71 speaks of "fictional agreement." The theatrical conventions discussed by Elizabeth Burns, *Theatricality* (London: Longman, 1992), are a sort of contract: convention means agreement.

20. Samuel R. Levin, "Concerning What Sort of Speech Act a Poem Is," in *Pragmatics of Language and Literature*, ed. Teun A. van Dijk (Amsterdam: North-Holland Publishing Company, 1976), 149.

21. The most important work on this conception is Walton's *Mimesis as Make-Believe*. See also Kendall L. Walton, "How Remote Are Fictional Worlds?"; Gregory Currie, *The Nature of Fiction* (Cambridge: Cambridge University Press, 1990), valuably corrects Walton's perspectives by emphasizing the presence of the author's intention. For criticisms of Walton see Amie Thomasson, *Fiction and Metaphysics* (Cambridge: Cambridge University Press, 1999), 97; Bijoy H. Boruah, *Fiction and Emotion* (Oxford: Clarendon Press, 1988), 64–65; Harold Skulsky, "On Being Moved by Fiction," *Journal of Aesthetics and Art Criticism* 39 (1980–81): 5–14. For a general discussion of philosophical issues concerning fiction, see Christopher New, *Philosophy of Literature: An Introduction* (New York and London: Routledge, 1999).

22. Walton, *Mimesis as Make-Believe*, 37.

23. Cf. Wolfgang Iser, *The Fictive and the Imaginary* (Baltimore: Johns Hopkins University Press, 1993), 16–17.

24. Peter Lamarque and Stein Hauge Olsen, *Truth, Fiction and Literature* (Oxford: Clarendon Press, 1994), 77 and 244. For different kinds of belief in fiction, see Eva Schaper, "Fiction and the Suspension of Disbelief," *British Journal of Aesthetics* 18 (1978): 31–44.

25. See Mark Currie, ed., *Metafiction* (London: Longman, 1995); Patricia Waugh, *Metafiction: Theory and Practice of Self-Conscious Narrative* (London and New York: Methuen, 1984).

26. Pavel, *Fictional Worlds*, 28.

27. Currie, *The Nature of Fiction*, 50.

28. See Lamarque and Olsen, *Truth, Fiction and Literature*, 318; Tzvetan Todorov, *Qu'est-ce que le structuralisme* (Paris: Seuil, Points, 1968), 36–39; Roland Barthes, "L'effet de réel," in *Le bruissement de la langue* (Paris: Seuil, 1984), 167–74 (for an ironic view of realism); Inge Crosman Wimmers, *Poetics of Reading* (Princeton: Princeton University Press, 1988), 24, who stresses the links between verisimilitude and decorum.

29. Lars Ole Sauerberg, *Fact into Fiction* (London: Macmillan, 1991), 3; George Levine, "Realism Reconsidered," in *Essentials of the Theories of Fiction*, 235–45; Peter J. Rabinowitz, *Before Reading* (Ithaca, N.Y.: Cornell University Press, 1987), 94.

30. John Searle, "The Logical Status of Fictional Discourse," *New Literary History* 6 (1975): 319–32, also in *Expression and Meaning* (Cambridge: Cambridge University Press, 1979), 58–75.

31. Cohn, *The Distinction of Fiction*, 20; Currie, *The Nature of Fiction*, 12; Stanley Fish, *Is There a Text in This Class?* (Cambridge: Harvard University Press, 1980), 235; Lamarque and Olsen, *Truth, Fiction and Literature*, 284; Pavel, *Fictional Worlds*, 18; Walton, *Mimesis as Make-Believe*, 82; Wimmers, *Poetics of Reading*, 14.

32. Walter B. Gallie, *Philosophy and the Historical Understanding* (London: Chatto and Windus, 1964).

33. Amongst many others: Colin Radford and Michael Weston, "How Can We Be Moved by the Fate of Anna Karenina?" *Proceedings of the Aristotelian Society*, supplementary volume 49 (1975): 67–93; Schaper, "Fiction and the Suspension of Disbelief"; Skulsky, "On Being Moved by Fiction"; Simo Säätelä, "Fiction, Make-Believe and Quasi Emotions," *British Journal of Aesthetics* 34 (1994): 25–34; Boruah, *Fiction and Emotion*.

34. Joan Rockwell, *Fact in Fiction* (London: Routledge and Kegan Paul, 1974), viii.

35. W. H. Auden, "The Sea and the Mirror," in *Collected Longer Poems* (London: Faber, 1968), 232.

36. E. Goffmann, *Frame Analysis* (Harmondsworth: Penguin, 1975), 295–96. Cf. Oscar Wilde, *The Importance of Being Earnest* Act II: "The good ended happily, and the bad unhappily. That is what Fiction means." in Oscar Wilde, *Selected Writings*, ed. Richard Ellmann (London: Oxford University Press, 1961), 319.

37. Lamarque and Olsen, *Truth, Fiction and Literature*, 261, 286, etc.; Ruth Ronen, *Possible Worlds in Literary Theory* (Cambridge: Cambridge University Press, 1994), 146.

38. This emphasis is especially associated with the important work of Hayden White. An economical formulation is Hayden White, "The Historical Text as Literary Artefact," in *History and Theory: Contemporary Readings*, ed. Brian Fay et al. (Oxford: Blackwell, 1998), 15–33; for a counterargument, see Noel Carroll, "Interpretation, History and Narrative," in ibid., 34–56.

39. Iser, *The Fictive and the Imaginary*, xxvii–xviii, etc.; Walton, *Mimesis as Make-Believe*, 224.

40. Milan Kundera, *The Art of the Novel* (London: Faber, 1988), 134.
41. Pavel, *Fictional Worlds*, 57.
42. The conception goes back to Aristotle's *Poetics*, which argues that poetry is truer than history because it is more general. Cf. Ricoeur, *Time and Narrative*, 41, which interprets Aristotle's claim in terms of the *typicality* of the story. For modern views see Lamarque and Olsen, *Truth, Fiction and Literature*, 122, and Waugh, *Metafiction*, 104 (which *excepts* metafiction). Umberto Eco, in *The Limits of Interpretation* (Bloomington, Ind.: Indiana University Press, 1990), argues that a drunkard exhibited as a work of art would become a sign of the *class* of drunkards.
43. Pavel, *Fictional Worlds*, 25.
44. Ronen, *Possible Worlds in Literary Theory*, 197.
45. Sauerberg, *Fact into Fiction*, 43; D. W. Theobald, "Philosophy and Fiction," *British Journal of Aesthetics* 14 (1974): 17–25.
46. Arthur N. Applebee, *The Child's Conception of Story* (Chicago: University of Chicago Press, 1978), 41; Sauerberg, *Fact into Fiction*, 40; Lilian R. Furst, *All Is True* (Durham, N.C.: Duke University Press, 1995), 162, quotes the Goncourts as saying that "history is a novel that happened, fiction is history that might have happened."
47. Mas'ud Zavarzadeh, *The Mythopoeic Reality* (Urbana, Ill.: University of Illinois Press, 1976).
48. John Bayley, *The Uses of Division* (London: Chatto and Windus, 1976), 17.
49. A perceptive and systematic account of didactic fiction is Susan Rubin Suleiman, *Authoritative Fictions* (New York: Columbia University Press, 1983).
50. Wayne C. Booth, *The Company We Keep* (Berkeley and Los Angeles: University of California Press, 1988), e.g., 136.
51. Peter Lamarque, *Fictional Points of View* (Ithaca, N.Y.: Cornell University Press, 1996), 107; Prado, *Making Believe*, 108; Catherine Wilson, "Literature and Knowledge," *Philosophy* 58 (1983): 489–96; Wayne C. Booth, *The Company We Keep*, 184.

Chapter 1. Malamud

1. Marcus Klein, *After Alienation* (Freeport, N.Y.: Books for Libraries Press, 1970), 263.
2. References in the text are to Bernard Malamud, *The Natural* (London: Eyre and Spottiswood, 1963).
3. Iska Alter, *The Good Man's Dilemma* (New York: AMS Press, 1981), 3, 8.
4. Alter, *The Good Man's Dilemma*, 93, notes Iris's connection with time.
5. Henry James, *Literary Criticism, European Writers and the Prefaces*, ed. Leon Edel (New York: Library of America, 1984), 1095.
6. J. M. Mellard, "Four Versions of Pastoral," in *Modern Critical Views: Bernard Malamud*, ed. Harold Bloom (New York: Chelsea House, 1986), 109.
7. Evelyn G. Avery, *Rebels and Victims* (Port Washington, N.Y.: Kennikat Press, 1978), 3.
8. Max F. Schulz, *Radical Sophistication* (Athens, Ohio: Ohio University Press, 1969), 64.
9. J. Baumbach, "The economy of love," in *Modern Critical Views*, 29.
10. Jeffrey Helterman, *Understanding Bernard Malamud* (Columbia, S.C.: University of South Carolina Press, 1985), 24.

11. Helterman, *Understanding Bernard Malamud*, 107.
12. Frederick Turner, "Myth inside and out," *Novel* 2 (1968): 133–39, rather confusingly discusses "myth" not in the sense of "socially endorsed stories" but in that of "false values."
13. Helterman, *Understanding Bernard Malamud*, 107.
14. Alter, *The Good Man's Dilemma*, 4; Helterman, *Understanding Bernard Malamud*, 23; E. Wasserman, "*The Natural:* Malamud's World Ceres," in *Modern Critical Views*, 47.
15. Klein, *After Alienation*, 256 (referring to an article by Podhoretz).
15. Ibid., 258.
16. Alter, *The Good Man's Dilemma*, 3.
17. Everett W. Knight, *Theory of the Classical Novel* (London: Routledge Kegan Paul, 1970).
18. E.g., Baumbach, "The Economy of Love," in *Modern Critical Views*, 23.
19. Alter, *The Good Man's Dilemma*, 180, notes "the role of the inheritor, so critical a moral function in his work."
20. Schulz, *Radical Sophistication*, 60.
22. Klein, *After Alienation*, 262.

CHAPTER 2. BELLOW

1. A major study of Bellow's historical sense is Judie Newman, *Saul Bellow and History* (Macmillan: London, 1984); she stresses not only Bellow's ongoing meditation on the sense of the past, but also his "extremely precise attention to the specificity of history" (185).
2. Peter Hyland, *Saul Bellow* (Macmillan: London, 1992), 9; for biography of Bellow see also James Atlas, *Bellow* (London: Faber, 2000).
3. Tony Tanner, *Saul Bellow* (Edinburgh: Oliver and Boyd, 1965; New York: Chip's Bookshop, 1978), 14.
4. Hyland, *Saul Bellow*, 69.
5. References in the text, unless otherwise indicated, are to Saul Bellow, *Mr. Sammler's Planet* (Harmondsworth: Penguin, 1971). Other references are to Saul Bellow, *Dangling Man* (Harmondsworth: Penguin, 1966) (*DM*); *The Adventures of Augie March* (Harmondsworth: Penguin, 1966) (*AM*); *Humboldt's Gift* (London: Secker and Warburg, 1975) (*HG*); *The Dean's December* (London: Secker and Warburg, 1982) (*D*); *More Die of Heartbreak* (London: Secker and Warburg, 1987) (*MDH*). *Henderson the Rain King* (Harmondsworth: Penguin, 1966) (*HRK*) *The Victim* (Harmondsworth: Penguin, 1966) (*V*)
6. E.g., Tanner, *Saul Bellow*, 111; Keith M. Opdahl, *The Novels of Saul Bellow* (University Park, Pa.: Pennsylvania State University Press, 1978), 163, refers to "Bellow's ability to evoke an intensely real world."
7. Leslie A. Fiedler, *Olaf Stapledon* (Oxford: Oxford University Press, 1983); Robert Crossley, *Olaf Stapledon: Speaking for the Future* (Liverpool: Liverpool University Press, 1994).
8. Eugen Kogon, *Der SS-Staat* (Munich: Kindler, 1985), 300, confirms the sale of saucepans but gives the date of 1938.
9. Malcolm Bradbury, *Saul Bellow* (London: Methuen, 1982), 79.
10. Ibid., 82, 81.

11. M. Gilbert Porter, *Whence the Power?* (Columbia, Mo.: University of Missouri Press, 1974), 5; cf. also 179.
12. Porter, *Whence the Power*, 178.
13. Cf. Richard A. York, "Bellow's Passionate Speech," *Orbis Litterarum* 57 (2002): 120–33.
14. Opdahl, *The Novels of Saul Bellow*, 20.
15. Malcolm Easton and Michael Holroyd, *The Art of Augustus John* (London: Secker and Warburg, 1974).
16. Hyland, *Saul Bellow*, 73.
17. Albert Corde, according to his friend and opponent Spangler, is "assigned" to reveal the truth about Chicagoan corruption (D 243).
18. Hyland, *Saul Bellow*,. 77.
19. R. F. Kiernan, "The Styles of Saul Bellow," in *Saul Bellow and the Struggle at the Center*, ed. Eugene Hollahan (New York: AMS Press, 1996), 94.

Chapter 3. Capote

1. Mas'ud Zavarzadeh, *The Mythopoeic Reality* (Urbana, Ill.: University of Illinois Press, 1976).
2. For information on the writing of *In Cold Blood*, see Gerald Clarke, *Capote* (London: Hamish Hamilton, 1988); George Plimpton, *Truman Capote* (London: Picador, 1998). One should add that that these sources indicate that the accuracy of certain details of *In Cold Blood* has been challenged by participants.
3. References in the text are to Truman Capote, *In Cold Blood* (Harmondsworth: Penguin, 1966).
4. Dorrit Cohn, *The Distinction of Fiction* (Baltimore: Johns Hopkins University Press, 1999).
5. F. W. Dupee cited in Kenneth T. Reed, *Truman Capote* (Boston: Twayne, 1981), 123. For similar comments on immediacy and omniscience see also John Hollowell, *Fact and Fiction* (Chapel Hill, N.C.: University of North Carolina Press, 1977), 70, 72.
6. Plimpton, *Truman Capote*, 203.
7. Capote shares Flaubert's feeling that "an artist's principal task" is "to tame and shape the raw creative vision" (Truman Capote, *The Dogs Bark* [London: Weidenfeld and Nicolson, 1974], 7). He specifically expresses admiration for Flaubert in an interview: Charles Ruas, *Conversations with American Writers* (London: Quartet, 1984), 42. Linda Hutcheon considers *In Cold Blood* to be "a modern rewriting of the realist novel—universalist in its assumptions and omniscient in its narrative technique"—and so not postmodernist: *A Poetics of Postmodernism* (London: Routledge, 1988), 115.
8. Reed, *Truman Capote*, 107.
9. Ibid., 106.
10. Hollowell, *Fact and Fiction*, 85.
11. Helen S. Garson, *Truman Capote* (N.Y.: Ungar, 1980), 164.
12. Lars Ole Sauerberg, *Fact into Fiction* (London: Macmillan, 1991), 22.
13. Capote, *The Dogs Bark*, 398. Cf. Hollowell's suggestive comparison with the "chosiste" aspects of the French New Novelists, (*Fact and Fiction*, 79).
14. Garson, *Truman Capote*, 164.

Chapter 4. Barth

1. References in the text, unless otherwise indicated, are to John Barth, *Giles Goat-Boy* (Harmondsworth: Penguin, 1967). Other references are to John Barth, *The Friday Book* (Baltimore and London: Johns Hopkins University Press, 1997) (*FB*); *Letters* (New York: Putnam's, 1979) (*L*); *Lost in the Funhouse* (London: Secker and Warburg, 1969) (*LiF*); *Once upon a Time* (London: Sceptre, 1994) (*OT*); *The Sot-Weed Factor* (London: Granada, 1965) (*SWF*).
2. Tony Tanner, *City of Words* (London: Cape, 1971), 230.
3. Tanner, *City of Words*, 248.
4. Cf. Alan Lindsay, *Death in the Funhouse* (New York: Peter Lang, 1995), 52.
5. Joe David Bellamy, *The New Fiction* (Urbana, Ill.: University of Illinois Press, 1974), 8.
6. Cf. Lindsay, *Death in the Funhouse*.
7. Gerhard Joseph, *John Barth* (Minneapolis: University of Minnesota Press, 1970), 6.
8. Frank D. McConnell, *Four Postwar American Novelists* (Chicago: University of Chicago Press, 1977), 146–47. Richard Poirier comments that "the intricacy of the pattern is spoofed by the blatant clarity of most of the allegorical items in it," *The Performing Self* (London: Chatto and Windus, 1971), 20.
9. Tanner, *City of Words*, 247.
10. Heide Ziegler, *John Barth* (London: Methuen, 1987), 40.
11. Robert E. Scholes, *Fabulation and Metafiction* (Urbana, Ill.: University of Illinois Press, 1979), 75, 101.
12. Ziegler, *John Barth*, 13.
13. Joseph, *John Barth*, 33.
14. Bellamy, *The New Fiction*, 13. Tanner, *City of Words*, 253.

Chapter 5. Doctorow

1. References in the text are to E. L. Doctorow, *The Book of Daniel* (London: Picador, 1982).
2. Paul Levine, *E. L. Doctorow* (London: Methuen, 1985), 73; B. Estrin, "Surviving McCarthyism," in *E. L. Doctorow: Essays and Conversations*, ed. Richard Trenner (Princeton: Ontario Review Press, 1983), 197.
3. S. B. Girgus, "In His Own Voice," in *E. L. Doctorow: A Democracy of Perception*, ed. Herwig Friedl and Dieter Schultz (Essen: Die Blaue Eule, 1988), 88.
4. Christopher D. Morris, *Models of Misrepresentation* (Jackson, Miss.: University of Mississippi Press, 1991), 110.
5. On the significance of transitions, cf. Linda Hutcheon, *A Poetics of Postmodernism* (London: Routledge, 1988), 44.
6. E. L. Doctorow, *The Waterworks* (London: Picador, 1995), 111.
7. A. Saltzman, "The Stylistic Energy of E. L. Doctorow," in *E. L. Doctorow*, 86.
8. Trenner, *E. L. Doctorow*, 220, 48.
9. For information on the Rosenberg trial and the historical context, see Alvin H. Goldstein, *The Unquiet Death of Julius and Ethel Rosenberg* (New York: Lawrence Hill, 1975); Ronald Radosh and Joyce Milton, *The Rosenberg File*, 2d ed. (New Haven: Yale

University Press, 1997); David Caute, *The Great Fear* (New York: Simon and Schuster, 1978); Ellen Schrecker, *Many Are the Crimes* (Boston: Little Brown, 1998); Marjorie Garber and Rebecca L. Walkowitz, *Secret Agents* (London: Routledge, 1995). The Rosenberg letters (in an edition available at the time of Doctorow's writing) are in Julius Rosenberg and Ethel Rosenberg, *The Testament of Julius and Ethel Rosenberg* (New York: Cameron and Kahn, 1954).

10. For the concept of "efferent," see p. 18 above.
11. Morris, *Models of Misrepresentation*, 13.
12. Michael Meeropol and Robert Meeropol, *We Are Your Sons* (Boston: Houghton Mifflin, 1975); Robert Meeropol in *Secret Agents*, 235–252.
13. S. Bloom, "The Book of Daniel and the Rosenberg Case", in *E. L. Doctorow*, 180.
14. Levine, *E. L. Doctorow*, 39.
15. Ibid., 14.
16. E. L. Doctorow in *E. L. Doctorow*, 26.
17. Ibid., 25.
18. Leslie A. Fiedler, "Afterthoughts on the Rosenbergs," in *An End to Innocence* (New York: Stein and Day, 1972), 25–45.
19. E. L. Doctorow in *E. L. Doctorow*, 23.

Chapter 6. Morrison

1. See, inter alia, Jan Furman, *Toni Morrison's Fiction* (Columbia, S.C.: University of South Carolina Press, 1996), 68–69.
2. References in the text are to Toni Morrison, *Beloved* (London: Picador, 1987).
3. Furman, *Toni Morrison's Fiction*, 79. For a less sympathetic view of the repression of Beloved by the community, see James Berger, "Ghosts of Liberalism: Morrison's *Beloved* and the Moynihan Report," *PMLA* 111 (1996): 408–20.
4. Gurleen Grewal, *Circles of Sorrow, Lines of Struggle: The Novels of Toni Morrison* (Baton Rouge: Louisiana State University Press, 1998), 116.
5. Rosemary Jackson, *Fantasy: The Literature of Subversion* (London: Methuen, 1981), 83.
6. Linden Peach, *Toni Morrison* (London: Macmillan, 1995), 101.
7. Jill L. Matus, *Toni Morrison* (Manchester: Manchester University Press, 1998), 112.
8. Peach, *Toni Morrison*, 14.
9. Barbara H. Rigney, *The Voices of Toni Morrison* (Columbus, Ohio: Ohio State University Press, 1991), 36, quoting Patricia Waugh.
10. Ibid., 26.
11. Rafael Pérez-Torres, "Knitting and Knotting the Narrative Thread," in *Toni Morrison: Contemporary Critical Essays*, ed. Linden Peach (Basingstoke: Macmillan, 1998), 128–39.
12. Ashraf Rushdy, "Daughters Signifyin(g) History," in *Toni Morrison: Contemporary Critical Essays*, 140–53.
13. James Phelan, *Narrative as Rhetoric* (Columbus, Ohio: Ohio State University Press, 1996), reflects on the stubborn refusal of the character to yield a single sense, and the implicit challenge to the reader to consider the totality of black experience.
14. Peach, *Toni Morrison*, 102.

15. Jean Wyatt, "Giving Body to the Word: The Maternal Symbolic in Toni Morrison's *Beloved*," *PMLA* 108 (1993): 474–88, makes enlightening use of the Lacanian concepts.

16. Toni Morrison, "Nobel Prize Acceptance Speech," http/www.nobel.se/literature/laureates/1995/morrison

17. Grewal, *Circles of Sorrow, Lines of Struggle*, 110–11, works out very systematically the "naturalist" reading. Neil Cornwell, *The Literary Fantastic* (London: Harvester-Wheatsheaf, 1990), 198–208, and Shlomith Rimmon-Kenan, *A Glance beyond Doubt* (Columbus, Ohio: Ohio State University Press, 1996), 104–24, reflect perceptively on the ambiguities of the novel as between an natural and a supernatural reading.

CHAPTER 7. OATES

1. References in the text, unless otherwise indicated, are to Joyce Carol Oates, *Blonde* (London: Fourth Estate, 2000). Other references are to Joyce Carol Oates, *American Appetites* (London: Macmillan, 1989) (*AA*); *Blackwater* (London: Macmillan, 1992); *A Bloodsmoor Romance* (London: Cape, 1983); *The Edge of Impossibility* (London: Gollancz, 1976) (*EI*); *I Lock the Door upon Myself* (Belfast: Blackstaff, 1990) (*L*); *Marya* (London: Cape, 1987).

2. The biographical works cited by Oates are Fred L. Guiles, *Legend: The Life and Death of Marilyn Monroe* (Lanham: Scarborough House, 1991); Norman Mailer, *Marilyn* (London: Hodder and Stoughton, 1973); Graham McCann, *Marilyn Monroe: The Body in the Library* (London: Polity, 1988); Carl E. Rollyson, *Marilyn Monroe: A Life of the Actress* (London: New English Library, 1990); Anthony Summers, *Goddess: The Secret Lives of Marilyn Monroe* (London: Vista, 1985).

3. As far as possible, I try to use "Monroe" for the historical figure and "Marilyn" or "Norma Jeane" for the fictitious character.

4. Laura Miller, review of *Blonde*, by Joyce Carol Oates, *New York Times*, 2 April 2000.

5. Guiles, *Legend*, 376.

6. The temptation is to identify Mr. Z with Darren Zanuck (whose general suspicion of Monroe is reflected in Z's later behavior). Biographers make no mention of any sexual contact between Monroe and Zanuck but suggest that her initial success may perhaps have been due in part to her accepting the less-demanding attentions of Joe Schenck.

7. The anachronisms seem to demand no more than a footnote: "raunchy" in the sense of "sexually explicit," "the media" for reporters, the use of a video camera, all in 1953–54. But the last of these is worrying.

8. Anthony Hilfer, *American Fiction since 1940* (London: Longman, 1992), 196.

9. Cf. Josephine Hendin, *Vulnerable People* (Oxford and New York: Oxford University Press, 1978), 157.

10. Joanne V. Creighton, *Joyce Carol Oates: Novels of the Middle Years* (New York: Twayne, 1992), 9, 57.

11. Joe David Bellamy, *The New Fiction* (Urbana, Ill.: University of Illinois Press, 1974), 25.

Chapter 8. Ford

1. Alice Hoffman, "A Wife Named X, a Poodle Named Elvis," review of *The Sportswriter*, by Richard Ford, *New York Times*, 23 March 1986.
2. References in the text, if not otherwise indicated, are to Richard Ford, *The Sportswriter* (London: Harvill, 1996). Other references are to Richard Ford, *Independence Day* (London: Harvill, 1996) (*ID*); *A Piece of My Heart* (London: Flamingo, 1988) (*PH*); *Rock Springs* (London: Harvill Collins, 1988) (*RS*).

Chapter 9. Smiley

1. References in the text, unless otherwise indicated, are to Jane Smiley, *A Thousand Acres* (London: Harper-Collins Flamingo, 1992). Other references are to Jane Smiley, *At Paradise Gate* (London: Flamingo, 1995) (*PG*); *The All-True Travels and Adventures of Lidie Newton* (London: Harper-Collins Flamingo, 1999) (*LN*).
2. See for instance David Finkelhor, *Child Sexual Abuse* (New York: Free Press, 1984); David Finkelhor et al., *Sourcebook on Child Sexual Abuse* (Beverly Hills, Calif.: Sage, 1986).
3. Frank Kermode, *The Genesis of Secrecy* (Cambridge: Harvard University Press, 1980).
4. Peter Conrad, *To Be Continued* (Oxford: Clarendon Press, 1995), 131, 134.
5. Milan Kundera, *Testaments Betrayed* (London: Faber, 1996), 7.
6. See Carolyn R. S. Lenz et al., *The Woman's Part* (Chicago: University of Illinois Press, 1981); Juliet Dusinberre, *Shakespeare and the Nature of Woman* (London: Macmillan, 1975); Ann Thompson, *King Lear* (London: Macmillan, 1988); Kathleen McLuskie, "The Patriarchal Bard," in *Critical Essays on Shakespeare's "King Lear,"* ed. Jay L. Halio (New York: G. K. Hall, 1996), 139–48; Claire McEachern, "Fathering Herself," *Shakespeare Quarterly* 39 (1988): 269–90; Joyce Carol Oates, *Contraries* (New York: Oxford University Press, 1981), who comments on a "wholesale denunciation and destruction of the female element," 63, and considers that "the ultimate tragedy is the experiencing as 'enemy' of the entire female sex," 61.
7. Neil Nakadate, *Understanding Jane Smiley* (Columbia, S.C.: University of South Carolina Press, 1999), 163.
8. A subtle analysis of this refocusing is David Brauner, "Speak Again: The Politics of Rewriting in *A Thousand Acres*," *Modern Language Review* 96 (2001): 654–66.
9. E.g., McEachern, "Fathering Herself," 280.
10. Germaine Greer, *Shakespeare* (Oxford: Oxford University Press, 1986), 88, rightly points out that *King Lear* is about senility and describes Lear in terms that might well fit Larry: "confused, paranoid, arbitrary" (89).
11. William Shakespeare, *King Lear*, edited by Kenneth Muir (London: Methuen, "Arden Edition," 1961), 1.4.284–87.
12. Nakadate, *Understanding Jane Smiley*, 165.
13. Conrad, *To Be Continued*, 134.
14. Nakadate, *Understanding Jane Smiley*, 159.

Chapter 10. Kingsolver

1. Belgian authorities, who are unlikely to have understated the numbers, report about 20 murders and 291 cases of "ignoble treatment" of women: Alan P. Merriam, *Congo: Background to Conflict* (Evanston, Ill.: Northwestern University Press, 1961), 230.

2. References in the text are to Barbara Kingsolver, *The Poisonwood Bible* (London: Faber, 2000).

3. Jonathan Kwitny, *Endless Enemies* (New York: Penguin, 1986).

4. Patrice Lumumba, independence speech, http://www.digitalcongo.net/actualite/01-06-28-discours2.shtml; Merriam, *Congo*, 353.

5. It may not be chance that a later Kingsolver novel, *Prodigal Summer*, is set in Zebulon County—though this is not the same Zebulon County as in Jane Smiley.

6. Merriam, *Congo*, 183.

7. Merriam comments that "Lumumba failed completely to govern his nation," ibid., 64. M. C. Young balances the charisma against the "fatal flaws" of this "mercurial, passionate and impatient man," "Zaire, Rwanda and Burundi" in *The Cambridge History of Africa*, ed. Michael Crowder (Cambridge: Cambridge University Press, 1984), 8, 720–21. Thomas Kanza, an admirer of Lumumba and a member of his government, has to recognize that he was "terribly lacking in realism," *Conflict in the Congo* (Harmondsworth: Penguin, 1972), 327.

8. Cf. p. 18 above, n. 7.

9. A note on a much greater novel: *The Sound and the Fury* contains two really varying subjectivities, one impersonal narrator and one formulation of Faulkner's dislike of commerce.

Conclusion

1. Saul Bellow, *Humboldt's Gift* (London: Secker and Warburg, 1975), 383.
2. Joseph Conrad, *Under Western Eyes* (Harmondsworth: Penguin, 1996), 76.
3. György Lukács, *Theory of the Novel* (London: Merlin, 1971), 89.
4. Bernard Malamud, *The Assistant* (London: Eyre and Spottiswood, 1965), 91.

Bibliography

WORKS OF AUTHORS STUDIED

Barth, John. *The Friday Book*. Baltimore and London: Johns Hopkins University Press, 1997.
———. *Giles Goat-Boy*. Harmondsworth: Penguin, 1967.
———. *Letters*. New York: Putnam's, 1979.
———. *Lost in the Funhouse*. London: Secker and Warburg, 1969.
———. *Once upon a Time*. London: Sceptre, 1994.
———. *The Sot-Weed Factor*. London: Granada, 1965.
Bellow, Saul. *The Adventures of Augie March*. Harmondsworth: Penguin, 1966.
———. *Dangling Man*. Harmondsworth: Penguin, 1966.
———. *The Dean's December*. London: Secker and Warburg, 1982.
———. *Henderson the Rain King*. Harmondsworth: Penguin, 1966.
———. *Humboldt's Gift*. London: Secker and Warburg, 1975.
———. *More Die of Heartbreak*. London: Secker and Warburg, 1987.
———. *Mr. Sammler's Planet*. Harmondsworth: Penguin, 1971.
———. *The Victim*. Harmondsworth: Penguin, 1966.
Capote, Truman. *The Dogs Bark*. London: Weidenfeld and Nicolson, 1974.
———. *In Cold Blood*. Harmondsworth: Penguin, 1966.
Doctorow, Edgar L. *The Book of Daniel*. London: Picador, 1982.
———. *The Waterworks*. London: Picador, 1995.
Ford, Richard. *Independence Day*. London: Harvill, 1996.
———. *A Piece of My Heart*. London: Flamingo, 1988.
———. *Rock Springs*. London: Harvill Collins, 1988.
———. *The Sportswriter*. London: Harvill, 1996.
Kingsolver, Barbara. *The Poisonwood Bible*. London: Faber, 2000.
Malamud, Bernard. *The Assistant*. London: Eyre and Spottiswood, 1965.
———. *God's Grace*. New York: Farar Straus Giroux, 1982.
———. *The Natural*. London: Eyre and Spottiswood, 1963.
Morrison, Toni. *Beloved*. London: Picador, 1987.
———. "Nobel Prize Acceptance Speech," http//www.nobel.se/literature/laureates/1995/morrison
Oates, Joyce Carol. *American Appetites*. London: Macmillan, 1989.
———. *Blackwater*. London: Macmillan, 1992.

———. *Blonde*. London: Fourth Estate, 2000.
———. *A Bloodsmoor Romance*. London: Cape, 1983.
———. *Contraries*. New York: Oxford University Press, 1981.
———. *The Edge of Impossibility*. London: Gollancz, 1976.
———. *I Lock the Door upon Myself*. Belfast: Blackstaff, 1990.
———. *Marya*. London: Cape, 1987.
Smiley, Jane. *The All-True Travels and Adventures of Lidie Newton*. London: Harper-Collins Flamingo, 1999.
———. *At Paradise Gate*. London: Harper-Collins Flamingo, 1995.
———. *A Thousand Acres*. London: Harper-Collins Flamingo, 1992.

CRITICAL DISCUSSION OF THESE AUTHORS

Alter, Iska. *The Good Man's Dilemma*. New York: AMS Press, 1981.
Atlas, James. *Bellow*. London: Faber, 2000.
Avery, Evelyn G. *Rebels and Victims*. Port Washington, N.Y.: Kennikat Press, 1978.
Baumbach, Jonathan. "The Economy of Love," in *Modern Critical Views: Bernard Malamud*, edited by Harold Bloom, 21–36. New York: Chelsea House, 1986.
Bellamy, Joe David. *The New Fiction*. Urbana, Ill.: University of Illinois Press, 1974.
Berger, James. "Ghosts of Liberalism: Morrison's *Beloved* and the Moynihan Report." *PMLA* 111 (1996): 408–20.
Bloom, Harold, ed. *Modern Critical Views: Bernard Malamud*. New York: Chelsea House, 1986.
Bradbury, Malcolm. *Saul Bellow*. London: Methuen, 1982.
Brauner, David. "Speak Again: The Politics of Rewriting in *A Thousand Acres*." *Modern Language Review* 96 (2001): 654–66.
Clarke, Gerald. *Capote*. London: Hamish Hamilton, 1988.
Conrad, Peter. *To Be Continued*. Oxford: Clarendon Press, 1995.
Cornwell, Neil. *The Literary Fantastic*. London: Harvester-Wheatsheaf, 1990.
Creighton, Joanne V. *Joyce Carol Oates: Novels of the Middle Years*. New York: Twayne, 1992.
Estrin, Barbara L. "Surviving McCarthyism: E. L. Doctorow's *The Book of Daniel*" in *E. L. Doctorow: Essays and Conversations*, edited by Richard Tranner, 196–206. Princeton, N.J.: Ontario Review Press, 1983.
Friedl, Herwig, and Dieter Schultz, eds. *E. L. Doctorow: A Democracy of Perception*. Essen: Die Blaue Eule, 1988.
Furman, Jan. *Toni Morrison's Fiction*. Columbia, S.C.: University of South Carolina Press, 1996.
Garson, Helen S. *Truman Capote*. New York: Ungar, 1980.
Grewal, Gurleen. *Circles of Sorrow, Lines of Struggle: The Novels of Toni Morrison*. Baton Rouge, La.: Louisiana State University Press, 1998.
Helterman, Jeffrey. *Understanding Bernard Malamud*. Columbia, S.C.: University of South Carolina Press, 1985.

Hendin, Josephine. *Vulnerable People*. Oxford and New York: Oxford University Press, 1978.

Hilfer, Anthony. *American Fiction since 1940*. London: Longman, 1992.

Hoffman, Alice. "A Wife Named X, a Poodle Named Elvis." *New York Times*, 23 March 1986.

Hollahan, Eugene, ed. *Saul Bellow and the Struggle at the Center*. New York: AMS Press, 1996.

Hollowell, John. *Fact and Fiction*. Chapel Hill, N.C.: University of North Carolina Press, 1977.

Hutcheon, Linda. *A Poetics of Postmodernism*. London: Routledge, 1988.

Hyland, Peter. *Saul Bellow*. London: Macmillan, 1992.

Jackson, Rosemary. *Fantasy: The Literature of Subversion*. London: Methuen, 1981.

Joseph, Gerhard. *John Barth*. Minneapolis: University of Minnesota Press, 1970.

Kiernan, Robert F. "The Styles of Saul Bellow" in *Saul Bellow and the Struggle at the Center*, edited by Eugene Hollahan, 91–100. Chapel Hill, N.C.: University of North Carolina Press, 1977.

Klein, Marcus. *After Alienation*. Freeport, N.Y.: Books for Libraries Press, 1970.

Levine, Paul. *E. L. Doctorow*. London: Methuen, 1985.

Lindsay, Alan. *Death in the Funhouse*. New York: Peter Lang, 1995.

Matus, Jill L. *Toni Morrison*. Manchester: Manchester University Press, 1998.

McConnell, Frank D. *Four Postwar American Novelists*. Chicago: University of Chicago Press, 1977.

Mellard, James M. "Four versions of pastoral," in *Modern Critical Views: Bernard Malamud*, edited by Harold Bloom, 101–12. New York: Chelsea House, 1986.

Miller, Laura. Review of *Blonde*, by Joyce Carol Oates. *New York Times*, 2 April 2000.

Morris, Christopher D. *Models of Misrepresentation*. Jackson, Miss.: University Press of Mississippi, 1991.

Nakadate, Neil. *Understanding Jane Smiley*. Columbia, S.C.: University of South Carolina Press, 1999.

Newman, Judie. *Saul Bellow and History*. London: Macmillan, 1984.

Opdahl, Keith M. *The Novels of Saul Bellow*. University Park, Pa.: Pennsylvania State University Press, 1978.

Peach, Linden. *Toni Morrison*. London: Macmillan, 1995.

Pérez-Torres, Rafael. "Knitting and Knotting the Narrative Thread." In *Toni Morrison: Contemporary Critical Essays*, edited by Linden Peach, 128–39. Basingstoke: Macmillan, 1998.

Phelan, James. *Narrative as Rhetoric*. Columbus, Ohio: Ohio State University Press, 1996.

Plimpton, George. *Truman Capote*. London: Picador, 1998.

Poirier, Richard. *The Performing Self*. London: Chatto and Windus, 1971.

Porter, M. Gilbert. *Whence the Power?* Columbia, Mo.: University of Missouri Press, 1974.

Reed, Kenneth T. *Truman Capote*. Boston: Twayne, 1981.

Rigney, Barbara H. *The Voices of Toni Morrison.* Columbus, Ohio: Ohio State University Press, 1991.

Rimmon-Kenan, Shlomith. *A Glance beyond Doubt.* Columbus, Ohio: Ohio State University Press, 1996.

Ruas, Charles. *Conversations with American Writers.* London: Quartet, 1984.

Rushdy, Ashraf. "Daughters Signifyin(g) History." In *Toni Morrison: Contemporary Critical Essays*, edited by Linden Peach, 140–53. Basingstoke: Macmillan, 1998.

Saltzman, Arthur. "The Stylistic Energy of E. L. Doctorow." In *E. L. Doctorow: Essays and Conversations*, edited by Richard Trennor, 73–108. Princeton, N.J.: Ontario Review Press, 1983.

Scholes, Robert E. *Fabulation and Metafiction.* Urbana, Ill.: University of Illinois Press, 1979.

Schulz, Max F. *Radical Sophistication.* Athens, Ohio: Ohio University Press, 1969.

Tanner, Tony. *City of Words.* London: Cape, 1971.

———. *Saul Bellow.* Edinburgh: Oliver and Boyd, 1965; New York: Chip's Bookshop, 1978.

Trenner, Richard, ed. *E. L. Doctorow: Essays and Conversations.* Princeton: Ontario Review Press, 1983.

Turner, Frederick. "Myth inside and out." *Novel* 2 (1968): 133–39.

Wyatt, Jean. "Giving Body to the Word: The Maternal Symbolic in Toni Morrison's *Beloved*." *PMLA* 108 (1993): 474–88.

York, Richard A. "Bellow's Passionate Speech." *Orbis Litterarum* 57 (2002): 120–33.

Ziegler, Heide. *John Barth.* London: Methuen, 1987.

THEORY OF FICTION

Applebee, Arthur N. *The Child's Conception of Story.* Chicago: University of Chicago Press, 1978.

Bakhtin, Mikhail Mikhailovich. *The Dialogic Imagination.* Austin, Tex.: University of Texas Press, 1978.

Bal, Mieke. *Narratologie.* Paris: Klincksieck, 1977.

Banfield, Ann. *Unspeakable Sentences.* London: Routledge, 1982.

Barthes, Roland. "L'effet de réel." In *Le bruissement de la langue*, 167–74. Paris: Seuil, 1984.

Bayley, John. *The Uses of Division.* London: Chatto and Windus, 1976.

Bell, Michael. "How Primordial Is Narrative?" In *Narrative in Culture*, edited by Cristopher Nash, 167–98. London: Routledge, 1990.

Booth, Wayne C. *The Company We Keep.* Berkeley and Los Angeles: University of California Press, 1988.

———. "Distance and Point of View." In *Essentials of the Theory of Fiction*, 2d ed., edited by Michael J. Hoffmann and Patrick D. Murphy, 116–33. London: Leicester University Press, 1996.

———. *The Rhetoric of Fiction.* 2d ed. Chicago: Chicago University Press, 1983.

Boruah, Bijoy H. *Fiction and Emotion*. Oxford: Clarendon Press, 1988.
Burns, Elizabeth. *Theatricality*. London: Longman, 1992.
Carroll, Noel. "Interpretation, History and Narrative." In *History and Theory: Contemporary Readings*, edited by Brian Fay, Philip Pomper, and Richard T. Vann, 34–56. Oxford: Blackwell, 1998.
Cavell, Stanley. "A Matter of Meaning It." In *Must We Mean What We Say?* 213–37. Cambridge: Cambridge University Press, 1976.
Chambers, Ross. *Story and Situation*. Manchester and Minneapolis: Manchester University Press and University of Minnesota Press, 1984.
Chatman, Seymour. *Story and Discourse*. Ithaca, N.Y.: Cornell University Press, 1978.
Cohn, Dorrit. *The Distinction of Fiction*. Baltimore: Johns Hopkins University Press, 1999.
— — —. *Transparent Minds*. Princeton: Princeton University Press, 1978.
Currie, Gregory. *The Nature of Fiction*. Cambridge: Cambridge University Press, 1990.
— — —. "What Is fiction." *Journal of Aesthetics and Art Criticism* 43 (1985): 385–92.
Currie, Mark, ed. *Metafiction*. London: Longman, 1995.
Eco, Umberto. *The Limits of Interpretation*. Bloomington, Ind.: Indiana University Press, 1990.
— — —. *Six Walks in the Fictional Woods*. Cambridge: Harvard University Press, 1994.
Fish, Stanley. *Is There a Text in This Class*? Cambridge: Harvard University Press, 1980.
Freedman, William. "The Literary Motif." In *Essentials of the Theory of Fiction*, 2d ed., edited by Michael J. Hoffmann and Patrick D. Murphy, 200–12. London: Leicester University Press, 1996.
Furst, Lilian R. *All Is True*. Durham, N.C.: Duke University Press, 1995.
Gallie, Walter B. *Philosophy and the Historical Understanding*. London: Chatto and Windus, 1964.
Genette, Gérard. *Figures III*. Paris: Seuil, 1972.
— — —. *Narrative Discourse*. Ithaca, N.Y.: Cornell University Press, 1980.
Hamburger, Käte. *Logik der Dichtung*. 2d ed. Stuttgart: E. Klett, 1968.
Hardy, Barbara. "Narrative." *Novel* 2 (1968): 2–14.
Iser, Wolfgang. *The Fictive and the Imaginary*. Baltimore: Johns Hopkins University Press, 1993.
Kundera, Milan. *The Art of the Novel*. London: Faber, 1988.
Lamarque, Peter. *Fictional Points of View*. Ithaca, N.Y.: Cornell University Press, 1996.
— — —. "Narrative and Invention: The Limits of Fictionality." In *Narrative in Culture*, edited by Cristopher Nash, 131–53. London: Routledge, 1990.
Lamarque, Peter, and Stein Hauge Olsen. *Truth, Fiction and Literature*. Oxford: Clarendon Press, 1994.
Lejeune, Philippe. *Le pacte autobiographique*. Paris: Seuil 1975.
Levin, Samuel R. "Concerning What Sort of Speech Act a Poem Is." In *Pragmatics of Language and Literature*, edited by Teun A. van Dijk, 141–60. Amsterdam: North-Holland Publishing Company, 1976.
Levine, George. "Realism reconsidered." In *Essentials of the Theory of Fiction*, 2d ed., ed-

ited by Michael J. Hoffmann and Patrick D. Murphy, 234–45. London: Leicester University Press, 1996.

Lubbock, Percy. *The Craft of Fiction*. London: Cape, 1968.

Lukács, György. *Theory of the Novel*. London: Merlin, 1971.

McCloskey, Donald N. "Story Telling in economics." In *Narrative in Culture*, edited by Cristopher Nash, 5–22. London: Routledge, 1990.

Nash, Cristopher, ed. *Narrative in Culture*. London: Routledge, 1990.

New, Christopher. *Philosophy of Literature: An Introduction*. New York and London: Routledge, 1999.

Onega, Susana, and José Angel Landis. *Narratology*. London: Longman, 1996.

Pascal, Roy. *The Dual Voice*. Manchester: Manchester University Press, 1977.

Pavel, Thomas G. *Fictional Worlds*. Cambridge: Harvard University Press, 1986.

Prado, C. G. *Making Believe*. Westport, Conn.: Greenwood Press, 1984.

Rabinowitz, Peter J. *Before Reading*. Ithaca, N.Y.: Cornell University Press, 1987.

Radford, Colin, and Michael Weston. "How Can We Be Moved by the Fate of Anna Karenina?" *Proceedings of the Aristotelian Society*, supplementary volume 49 (1975): 67–93.

Ricoeur, Paul. "Life in Quest of Narrative." In *On Paul Ricoeur*, edited by David Wood, 20–33. London: Routledge, 1991.

———. *Time and Narrative*. Chicago: University of Chicago Press, 1984.

Rimmon-Kenan, Shlomith. *Narrative Fiction, Contemporary Poetics*. London and New York: Methuen, 1983.

Rockwell, Joan. *Fact in Fiction*. London: Routledge and Kegan Paul, 1974.

Ronen, Ruth. *Possible Worlds in Literary Theory*. Cambridge: Cambridge University Press, 1994.

Rosenblatt, Louise M. *The Reader, the Text, the Poem*. Carbondale, Ill.: Southern Illinois University Press, 1978.

Säätelä, Simo. "Fiction, Make-Believe and Quasi Emotions." *British Journal of Aesthetics* 34 (1994): 25–34.

Sauerberg, Lars Ole. *Fact into Fiction*. London: Macmillan, 1991.

Schaper, Eva. "Fiction and the Suspension of Disbelief." *British Journal of Aesthetics* 18 (1978): 31–44.

Searle, John. "The Logical Status of Fictional Discourse." *New Literary History* 6 (1975): 319–32; also in *Expression and Meaning*, 58–75. Cambridge: Cambridge University Press, 1979.

Skulsky, Harold. "On Being Moved by Fiction." *Journal of Aesthetics and Art Criticism* 39 (1980–81): 5–14.

Sturgess, Philip John Moore. *Narrativity, Theory and Practice*. Oxford: Oxford University Press, 1992.

Suleiman, Susan Rubin. *Authoritative Fictions*. New York: Columbia University Press, 1983.

Theobald, D. W. "Philosophy and Fiction." *British Journal of Aesthetics* 14 (1974): 17–25.

Thomasson, Amie. *Fiction and Metaphysics*. Cambridge: Cambridge University Press, 1999.

Todorov, Tzvetan. *Qu'est-ce que le structuralisme?* Paris: Seuil, Points, 1968.

Walton, Kendall L. "How Remote Are Fictional Worlds from the Real World?" *Journal of Aesthetics and Art Criticism* 37 (1978–79): 11–23.

— — —. *Mimesis as Make-Believe.* Cambridge: Harvard University Press, 1990.

Watt, Ian. *The Rise of the Novel.* Harmondsworth: Penguin, 1957.

Waugh, Patricia. *Metafiction: Theory and Practice of Self-Conscious Narrative.* London and New York: Methuen, 1984.

White, Hayden. "The Historical Text as Literary Artefact." In *History and Theory: Contemporary Readings*, edited by Brian Fay, Philip Pomper, and Richard T. Vann, 15–33. Oxford: Blackwell, 1998.

Wilson, Catherine. "Literature and Knowledge." *Philosophy* 58 (1983): 489–96.

Wimmers, Inge Crosman. *Poetics of Reading.* Princeton: Princeton University Press, 1988.

Zavarzadeh, Mas'ud. *The Mythopoeic Reality.* Urbana, Ill.: University of Illinois Press, 1976.

OTHER WORKS REFERRED TO

Auden, W. H. "The Sea and the Mirror." In *Collected Longer Poems*. London: Faber, 1968.

Caute, David. *The Great Fear.* New York: Simon and Schuster, 1978.

Conrad, Joseph. *Under Western Eyes.* Harmondsworth: Penguin, 1996.

Crossley, Robert. *Olaf Stapledon: Speaking for the Future.* Liverpool: Liverpool University Press, 1994.

Crowder, Michael, ed. *The Cambridge History of Africa.* Vol. 8. Cambridge: Cambridge University Press, 1984.

Dusinberre, Juliet. *Shakespeare and the Nature of Woman.* London: Macmillan, 1975.

Easton, Malcolm, and Michael Holroyd. *The Art of Augustus John.* London: Secker and Warburg, 1974.

Fiedler, Leslie A. "Afterthoughts on the Rosenbergs." In *An End to Innocence*, 25–45. New York: Stein and Day, 1972.

— — —. *Olaf Stapledon.* Oxford: Oxford University Press, 1983.

Finkelhor, David. *Child Sexual Abuse.* New York: Free Press, 1984.

Finkelhor, David, with Sharon Araji. *Sourcebook on Child Sexual Abuse.* Beverly Hills, Calif.: Sage, 1986.

Garber, Marjorie, and Rebecca L. Walkowitz. *Secret Agents.* London: Routledge, 1995.

Goffmann, Erwin. *Frame Analysis.* Harmondsworth: Penguin, 1975.

Goldstein, Alvin H. *The Unquiet Death of Julius and Ethel Rosenberg.* New York: Lawrence Hill, 1975.

Greer, Germaine. *Shakespeare.* Oxford: Oxford University Press, 1986.

Grice, H. Paul. "Logic and conversation." In *Syntax and Semantics, 3: Speech Acts*, edited by Peter Cole and Jerry L. Morgan, 41–58. New York: Academic Press, 1975.

Guiles, Fred L. *Legend: The Life and Death of Marilyn Monroe*. Lanham: Scarborough House, 1991.

James, Henry. *Literary Criticism, European Writers and the Prefaces*. Edited by Leon Edel. New York: Library of America, 1984.

Kanza, Thomas. *Conflict in the Congo*. Harmondsworth: Penguin, 1972.

Kennedy, Alan. *The Protean Self*. New York: Columbia University Press, 1974.

Kermode, Frank. *The Genesis of Secrecy*. Cambridge: Harvard University Press, 1980.

Knight, Everett W. *Theory of the Classical Novel*. London: Routledge and Kegan Paul, 1970.

Kogon, Eugen. *Der SS-Staat*. Munich: Kindler, 1985.

Kundera, Milan. *Testaments Betrayed*. London: Faber, 1996.

Kwitny, Jonathan. *Endless Enemies*. New York: Penguin, 1986.

Lenz, Carolyn R. S. et al. *The Woman's Part*. Chicago: University of Illinois Press, 1981.

Lumumba, Patrice. Independence speech, http://www.digitalcongo.net/actualite/01-06-28-discours2.shtml

Mailer, Norman. *Marilyn*. London: Hodder and Stoughton, 1973.

McCann, Graham. *Marilyn Monroe: The Body in the Library*. London: Polity, 1988.

McEachern, Claire. "Fathering Herself." *Shakespeare Quarterly* 39 (1988): 269–90.

McLuskie, Kathleen. "The Patriarchal Bard." In *Critical Essays on Shakespeare's "King Lear,"* edited by Jay L. Halio, 139–48. New York: G. K. Hall, 1996.

Meeropol, Michael, and Robert Meeropol. *We Are Your Sons*. Boston: Houghton Mifflin, 1975.

Meeropol, Robert. "Rosenberg Realities" in *Secret Agents*, edited by Marjorie Garber and Rebecca L. Walkowitz, 235–252. New York: Routledge, 1995.

Merriam, Alan P. *Congo: Background to Conflict*. Evanston, Ill.: Northwestern University Press, 1961.

Moore, Ward. *Bring the Jubilee*. New York, Farar, Straus & Young, 1953.

Radosh, Ronald, and Joyce Milton. *The Rosenberg File*. 2d ed. New Haven: Yale University Press, 1997.

Rosenberg, Julius, and Ethel Rosenberg. *The Testament of Julius and Ethel Rosenberg*. New York: Cameron and Kahn, 1954.

Rollyson, Carl E. *Marilyn Monroe: A Life of the Actress*. London: New English Library, 1990.

Schiffer, Stephen R. *Meaning*. Oxford: Clarendon Press, 1972.

Schrecker, Ellen. *Many Are the Crimes*. Boston: Little Brown, 1998.

Shakespeare, William. *King Lear*, edited by Kenneth Muir. London: Methuen (Arden edition), 1961.

Summers, Anthony. *Goddess: The Secret Lives of Marilyn Monroe*. London: Vista, 1985.

Thompson, Ann. *King Lear*. London: Macmillan, 1988.

Wilde, Oscar. *Selected Writings*, edited by Richard Ellmann. London: Oxford University Press (World's Classics), 1961.

Young, M. Crawford. "Zaire, Rwanda and Burundi." In *The Cambridge History of Africa*, edited by Michael Crowder, 8, 698–754. Cambridge: Cambridge University Press, 1984.

Index

Achebe, Chinua, 142
Addams, Jane, 40
Anticipation, 35
Antinovel, 21
Arendt, Hannah, 42
Auden, W. H., 22
Author, 50, 54, 64, 67, 152; implied, 15; intention, 19; voice, 27

Bakhtin, Mikhail, 71, 149
Barth, John, 63–75; "Anonymiad," 75; *The Floating Opera*, 71; *Giles Goat-Boy*, 63–75, 76, 152, 153; *Letters*, 68; "The Literature of Exhaustion," 71; *Once Upon a Time*, 68; *Sabbatical*, 74; *The Sot-Weed Factor*, 63, 66, 71
Baudrillard, Jean, 105
Bellow, Saul, 24, 38–49, 150, 151; *More Die of Heartbreak*, 49; *Mr. Sammler's Planet*, 24, 38–49, 64, 150, 153, 156; *Ravelstein*, 39
Bezukhov, Pierre, 21, 42
Bloom, S., 86
Booth, Wayne, 15
Bradbury, Malcolm, 42
Browder, Earl, 87
Buchenwald, 41
Bukharin, Nikolay, 77, 87

Campbell, Joseph, 68
Camus, Albert, 118
Capote, Truman, 50–62; *Breakfast at Tiffany's*, 56; *In Cold Blood*, 50–62, 150, 152
Carson, Rachel: *Silent Spring*, 136
Chaplin, Charles, 105
Charles, Ray, 115
Chronology (*see also* time-frames), 50, 59
Clift, Montgomery, 105
Cohn, Dorrit, 16, 53

Cohn, Roy, 87
Coincidence, 46
Comedy, 48, 70, 73, 124
Conrad, Joseph, 72, 139, 153; *Heart of Darkness*, 138, 145, 149
Conrad, Peter, 132, 136
Contract, 20
Cooper, James Fenimore: *The Last of the Mohicans*, 152
Creighton, Joanne, 110

Dante (Alighieri), 69
Defoe, Daniel: *Robinson Crusoe*, 84
Dialogue, 20
Doctorow, E. L., 76–88, 151; *Billy Bathgate*, 87; *The Book of Daniel*, 51, 76–88, 153; *City of God*, 88
Dostoyevsky, Fyodor, 14, 156; *The Idiot*, 156; *Notes from the Underground*, 71

Efferent, 18, 85
Eisenhower, Dwight, 72, 88
Eliot, George, 115, 116
Eliot, T. S., 34

Fantasy, 21, 89, 92, 97, 99, 102, 112, 156
Faulkner, William, 18, 94
Fiedler, Leslie, 40, 87
Flashback, 93
Flaubert, Gustave, 14, 55
Focalization (*see also* point of view), 18, 27, 39, 41, 50, 58, 59, 77, 82, 139
Followability, 22
Ford, Richard, 114–25, 151; *Independence Day*, 114, 125; *The Sportswriter*, 114–25, 126
Free indirect discourse (free indirect style), 18, 50, 53, 83

176

Freud, Sigmund, 72
Furman, Jan, 91

Gardner, Ava, 105
Garner, Margaret, 89
Garson, Helen, 60
Genette, Gerard, 15
Girgus, S. B., 79, 80
Gold, Harry, 87
Grass, Günter: *The Flounder*, 136
Grewal, Gurleen, 91
Guiles, Fred, 108

Heard, Gerald, 40
Hilfer, Anthony, 106
History: process, 78, 88, 102, 112, 140; record, 77, 89, 155; writing (historians), 16, 23, 50–53, 95, 148
Hobbes, Thomas, 122
Hoffman, Alice, 114, 124
Hollowell, John, 60
Holocaust, 24, 38, 42, 64
Hyland, Peter, 48

Immigrant characters, 21
Intertextuality, 35

Jackson, Rosemary, 92
James, Henry, 14, 31; *What Maisie Knew*, 53
Javits, Jacob, 40
John, Augustus, 47
Joyce, James, 33, 117

Kennedy, Jackie, 67
Kermode, Frank, 132
Kiernan, Robert, 49
Kingsolver, Barbara, 138–49; *The Poisonwood Bible*, 138–49; *Prodigal Summer*, 149
Kissinger, Henry, 13
Koestler, Arthur: *Darkness at Noon*, 87
Kundera, Milan, 23, 134
Kwitny, Jonathan, 139

Lacan, Jacques, 98, 99
Lee, Harper: *To Kill a Mockingbird*, 154
Levine, Paul, 86
Lodz, 41
Lubbock, Percy, 14, 15

Lubitsch, Ernst, 40
Lukács, Georg, 153
Lumumba, Patrice, 138, 139, 140, 143, 148

Mailer, Norman, 55, 102
Make-believe, 16, 20
Malamud, Bernard, 25, 26–37; *The Assistant*, 30, 156; *Dubin's Lives*, 26; "The First Seven Years," 30; *The Fixer*, 30; *God's Grace*, 26, 33; *The Natural*, 26–37, 69, 150, 153, 154; *Pictures of Fidelman*, 29
Marx, Karl, 66
Marxism, 78, 104
Matus, Jill, 93
Mauriac, François, 53
McCarthy, Joseph, 76, 80, 97, 88, 105, 107
McConnell, Frank, 69
McEachern, Claire, 134
Merriam, Alan, 147
Metafiction, 21
Miller, Arthur, 112
Monroe, Marilyn, 101–13
Morris, Christopher, 85
Morrison, Toni, 89–100; *Beloved*, 89–100, 153, 154; *Jazz*, 91
Myth, 26, 32, 34, 42, 68, 73, 87, 101, 122, 152, 153

Naipaul, V. S.: *A Bend in the River*, 138
Nakadate, Neil, 135, 136
Napoleon, 21, 42, 140
Narration: first-person, 77, 130; third-person, 77, 82, 83, 107, 111
Narrative, 61
Narratology, 14–16, 115
Narrator, 15, 17, 31, 51, 64, 114, 155; impersonal, 82, 94; omniscient, 17, 50; unreliable, 15, 17, 71, 115
Nietzsche, Friedrich, 72
Nonfiction novel, 24, 50, 152

Oates, Joyce Carol, 101–13, 134, 151; *Blackwater*, 104; *Blonde*, 101–13, 153; *A Bloodsmoor Romance*, 108; *I Lock the Door upon Myself*, 110; *Marya*, 104
Opdahl, Keith, 47

Parody, 72
Peach, Linden, 99
Perceval, 33
Perez-Torres, Rafael, 97
Perspective, 14, 49, 50, 77, 92, 94, 96, 98, 107, 109, 141
Plausibility (*see also* verisimilitude), 21, 40, 52, 126, 139, 143, 145
Poe, Edgar Allan, 79
Point of view (*see also* focalization), 14, 20, 101, 111, 154
Porter, M. Gilbert, 42, 45
Postmodernism, 117, 137
Psychoanalysis, 95, 98

Rabelais, François, 37, 71
Raglan, Lord, 68
Reader, 51, 55, 64, 67, 68, 75, 92, 94, 148, 151, 152, 154; implied, 20
Reed, Kenneth, 60
Repetition, 35, 47, 72, 93, 105
Rhetoric, 16, 42, 43, 102, 111, 151
Rigney, Barbara, 95, 96
Rimbaud, Arthur, 122
Robbe-Grillet, Alain, 21
Robeson, Paul, 77, 105
Roethke, Theodore, 119
Rogers, Roy, 108
Rosenberg, Ethel and Julius, 51, 76, 79, 84–87

Sartre, Jean-Paul, 53, 118, 132
Scholes, Robert, 73, 152
Shakespeare, William: *King Lear*, 131–37
Sinatra, Frank, 108
Smiley, Jane, 126–37; *Barn Blind*, 126; *Duplicate Keys*, 126; *Lidie Newton*, 127; *Ordinary Love*, 127; *A Thousand Acres*, 126–37, 141
Some Like it Hot, 103

Speech-acts, 22
Stapledon, Olaf, 40
Stendhal, 151
Sterne, Laurence: *Tristram Shandy*, 67
Stowe, Harriet Beecher: *Uncle Tom's Cabin*, 147
Strasberg, Paula, 105
Symbolism, 36, 41, 81, 99, 102, 103, 105, 106, 136

Tanner, Tony, 22, 38, 68, 70, 75
Thematic structure (themes), 22, 39, 46, 102, 117, 132, 154
Thompson, Ann, 134
Time frames (*see also* chronology), 102, 111
Tolstoy, Lev, 14, 21, 115, 116; *War and Peace*, 42
Transitions, 80
Trotsky, Lev, 40
Twain, Mark: *Huckleberry Finn*, 65

Urquhart, Jane: *Away*, 155

Verisimilitude (*see also* plausibility), 21, 41, 85, 129, 132, 139, 154, 155
Vietnam War, 78

Wagner, Richard: *Parsifal*, 33
Walton, Kendall, 16
Wells, H. G, 38, 40, 42, 44–46; "The Country of the Blind," 49
White, Hayden, 16
Whitehead, A. N., 40
Widmark, Richard, 108
Wilde, Oscar, 43
Woolf, Virginia, 94
Wordsworth, William, 72

Zavarzadeh, Mas'ud, 50
Ziegler, Heide, 72